Scholastic Canada

Visual
Dictionary

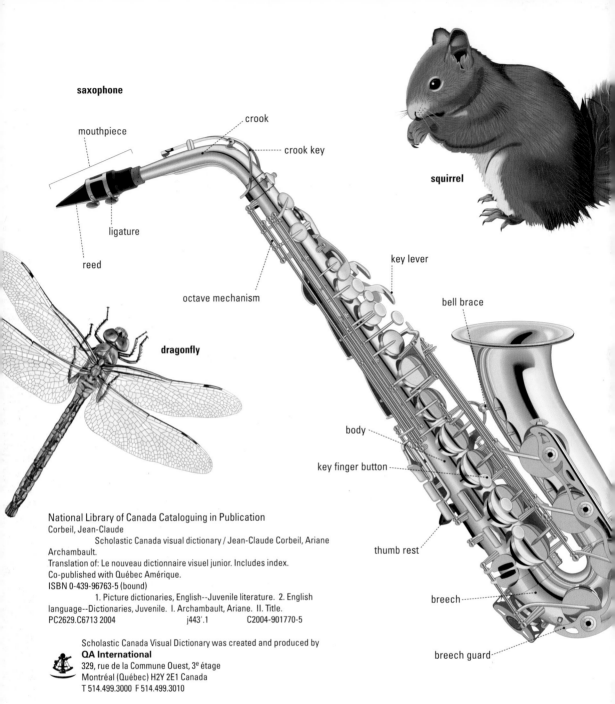

saxophone

crook

mouthpiece

crook key

squirrel

ligature

key lever

reed

bell brace

octave mechanism

dragonfly

body

key finger button

thumb rest

breech

breech guard

National Library of Canada Cataloguing in Publication
Corbeil, Jean-Claude
       Scholastic Canada visual dictionary / Jean-Claude Corbeil, Ariane
Archambault.
Translation of: Le nouveau dictionnaire visuel junior. Includes index.
Co-published with Québec Amérique.
ISBN 0-439-96763-5 (bound)
       1. Picture dictionaries, English--Juvenile literature. 2. English
language--Dictionaries, Juvenile. I. Archambault, Ariane. II. Title.
PC2629.C6713 2004   j443'.1   C2004-901770-5

Scholastic Canada Visual Dictionary was created and produced by
QA International
329, rue de la Commune Ouest, 3e étage
Montréal (Québec) H2Y 2E1 Canada
T 514.499.3000 F 514.499.3010

Published by Scholastic Canada Ltd.
175 Hillmount Road
Markham, Ontario L6C 1Z7

6 5 4 3 2 1   Printed in Singapore   04 05 06 07 08

Scholastic Canada

Visual Dictionary

Jean-Claude Corbeil • Ariane Archambault

EDITORIAL STAFF
Publisher: Jacques Fortin
Editorial Director: François Fortin
Editorial Director, Junior Edition: Caroline Fortin
Editor-in-Chief: Serge D'Amico
Editor-in-Chief, Junior Edition: Martine Podesto
Associate Editor, Junior Edition: Johanne Champagne
Graphic Designer: Josée Noiseux
Scholastic Canada Ltd. Editor: Jennifer MacKinnon

TERMINOLOGY
Jean Beaumont
Catherine Briand
Nathalie Guillo

ILLUSTRATIONS
Art Director: Jocelyn Gardner
Art Director, Junior Edition: Anouk Noël
Jean-Yves Ahern
Rielle Lévesque
Alain Lemire
Mélanie Boivin
Yan Bohler
Claude Thivierge
Pascal Bilodeau
Michel Rouleau
Carl Pelletier

LAY-OUT
Jean-François Nault
Jean-Philippe Bouchard
Nathalie Gignac
Kien Tang

DOCUMENTATION
Gilles Vézina
Kathleen Wynd
Stéphane Batigne
Sylvain Robichaud
Jessie Daigle

DATA MANAGEMENT
Programmer: Daniel Beaulieu

PROOFREADING
Veronica Schami Editorial Services

PRODUCTION
Guylaine Houle

PREPRESS
Sophie Pellerin
Tony O'Riley

CONTRIBUTORS
Jean-Louis Martin, Marc Lalumière, Jacques Perrault, Stéphane Roy,
Alice Comtois, Michel Blais, Christiane Beauregard, Mamadou Togola,
Annie Maurice, Charles Campeau, Mivil Deschênes, Jonathan Jacques,
Martin Lortie, Raymond Martin, Frédérick Simard, Yan Tremblay,
Mathieu Blouin, Sébastien Dallaire, Hoang Khanh Le, Martin Desrosiers,
Nicolas Oroc, François Escalmel, Danièle Lemay, Pierre Savoie, Benoît
Bourdeau, Marie-Andrée Lemieux, Caroline Soucy, Yves Chabot,
Anne-Marie Ouellette, Anne-Marie Villeneuve, Anne-Marie Brault,
Nancy Lepage, Daniel Provost, François Vézina.

Scholastic Canada Ltd.

THEMES AND SUBJECTS

SOLAR SYSTEM

The solar system is our own little corner of the universe. It consists of a single star, the Sun, and all the astral bodies that orbit it: nine planets, more than one hundred natural satellites, thousands of asteroids, and millions of comets. Completing the procession circling around our star are billions of pebbles, dust particles, and gases.

PLANETS AND MOONS

Deimos
Phobos
Moon
Venus
Mercury
Earth
Mars
Callisto
Ganymede
Europa
Io
Jupiter

ORBITS OF THE PLANETS

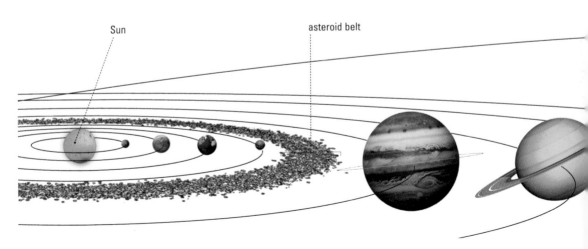

Sun
asteroid belt

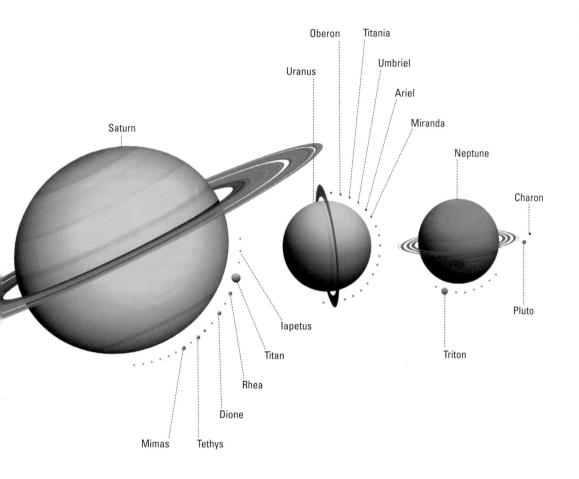

Oberon · Titania · Umbriel · Ariel · Miranda · Uranus · Saturn · Neptune · Charon · Iapetus · Titan · Rhea · Dione · Tethys · Mimas · Triton · Pluto

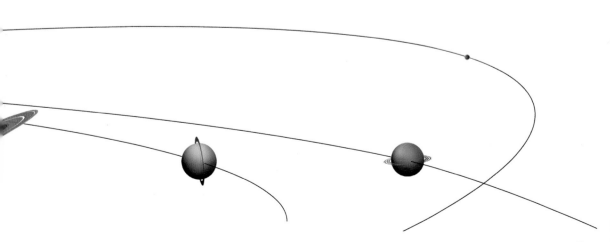

SUN

structure of the Sun

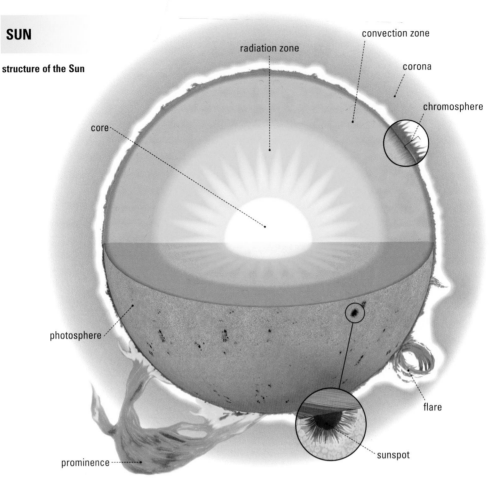

radiation zone

convection zone

corona

chromosphere

core

photosphere

flare

prominence

sunspot

solar eclipse

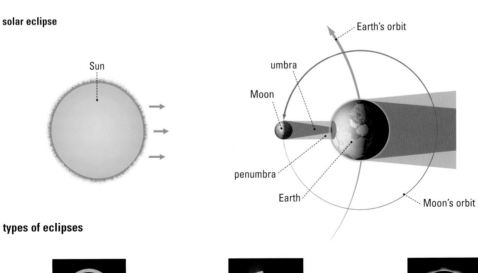

Sun

Earth's orbit

umbra

Moon

penumbra

Earth

Moon's orbit

types of eclipses

annular eclipse   **partial eclipse**   **total eclipse**

MOON

lunar features

cliff

bay

crater

lake

ocean

cirque

wall

highland

sea

mountain range

lunar eclipse

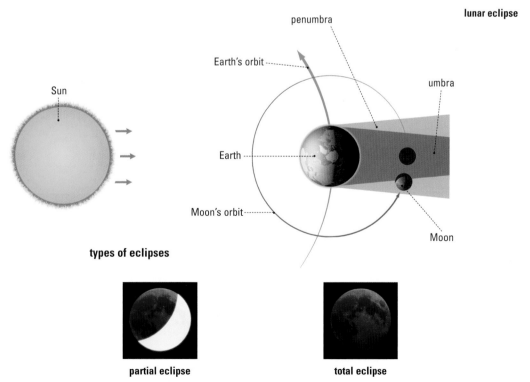

penumbra

Earth's orbit

umbra

Sun

Earth

Moon's orbit

Moon

types of eclipses

partial eclipse

total eclipse

phases of the Moon

new moon

new crescent

first quarter

waxing gibbous

full moon

waning gibbous

last quarter

old crescent

COMET

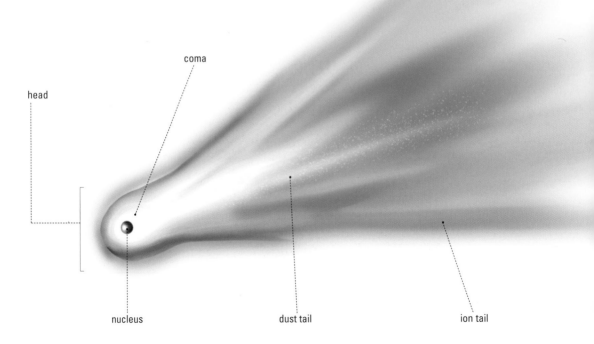

coma

head

nucleus

dust tail

ion tail

The universe contains approximately 100 billion galaxies, each one made up of several billion stars, gases, and dust particles. Our solar system is located at the edge of a galaxy called the Milky Way. Seen from Earth, the Milky Way looks like a bright ribbon spread across the night sky. The whitish trail comes from the light of its 200 to 300 billion stars.

Milky Way (seen from above)

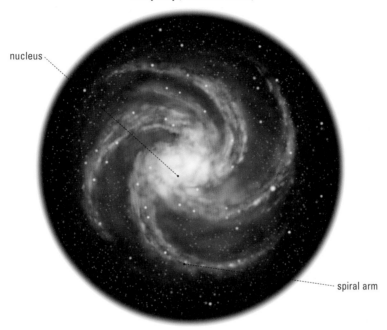

nucleus

spiral arm

Milky Way (side view)

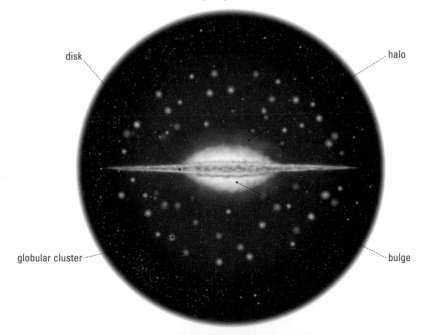

disk

halo

globular cluster

bulge

ASTRONOMICAL OBSERVATION

The invention of the refracting telescope and the reflecting telescope has truly revolutionized our vision of the universe. By collecting the light coming from a celestial object and using lenses or mirrors to concentrate it, these instruments have given us the first enlarged and detailed images of stars and planets ever seen. Specialists today are developing increasingly advanced models of telescopes.

REFRACTING TELESCOPE

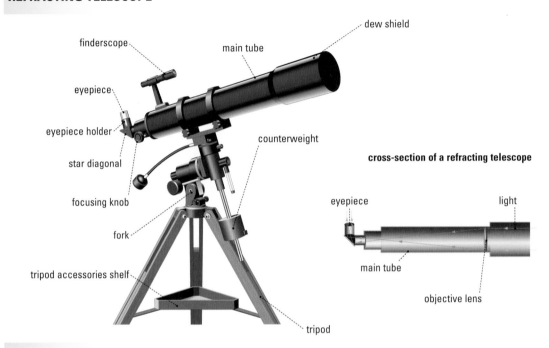

finderscope

main tube

dew shield

eyepiece

eyepiece holder

star diagonal

focusing knob

fork

tripod accessories shelf

counterweight

tripod

cross-section of a refracting telescope

eyepiece

light

main tube

objective lens

REFLECTING TELESCOPE

cross-section of a reflecting telescope

eyepiece

secondary mirror

light

main tube

concave primary mirror

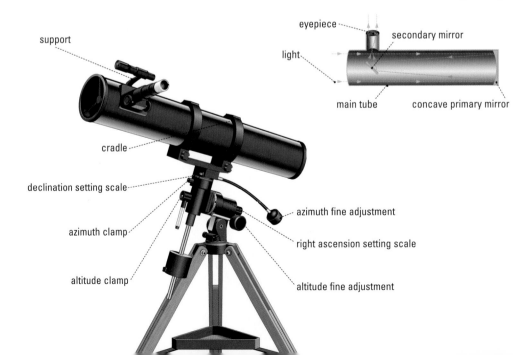

support

cradle

declination setting scale

azimuth clamp

altitude clamp

azimuth fine adjustment

right ascension setting scale

altitude fine adjustment

Space probes explore planets and areas in space where no human being can go. Sent up by the space shuttle or by a space launcher, these ingenious robots are modern-day explorers. Unlike rockets, which can only be used once, the space shuttle is a reuseable vehicle. Among its many missions is the transportation of modules for the international space station.

SPACE PROBES

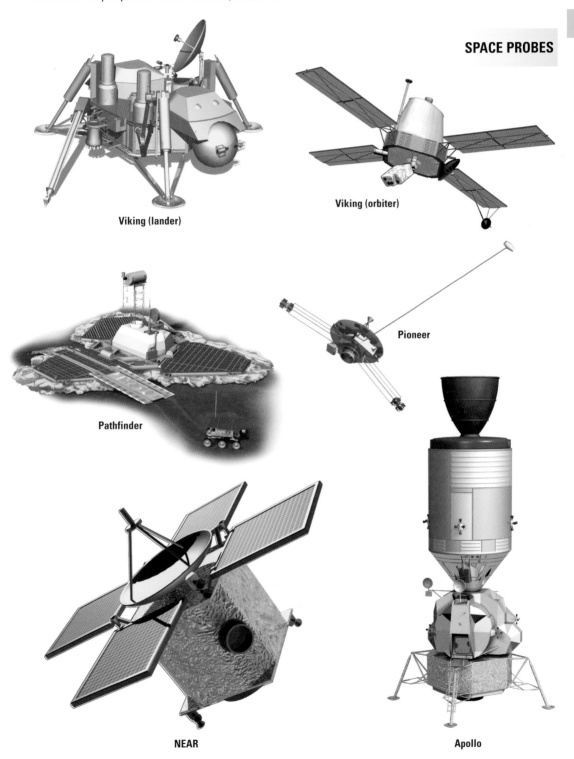

Viking (lander)

Viking (orbiter)

Pioneer

Pathfinder

NEAR

Apollo

ASTRONOMY

INTERNATIONAL SPACE STATION

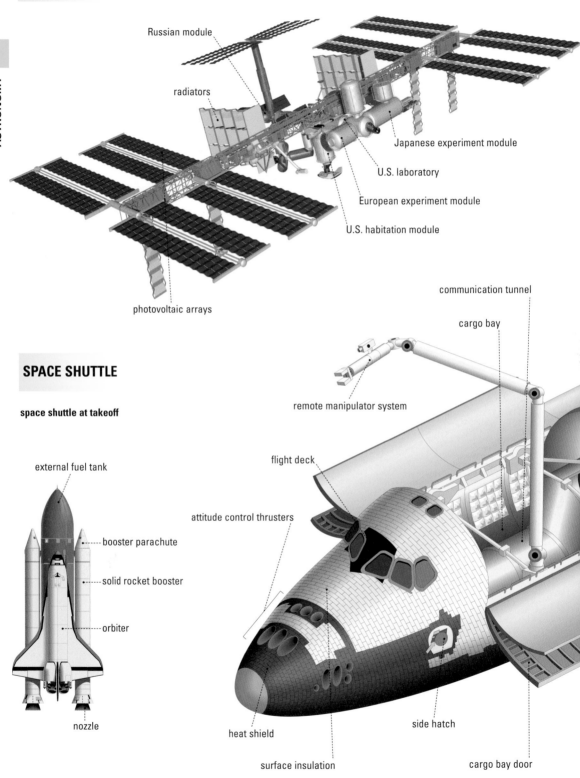

Russian module

radiators

Japanese experiment module

U.S. laboratory

European experiment module

U.S. habitation module

photovoltaic arrays

communication tunnel

cargo bay

SPACE SHUTTLE

space shuttle at takeoff

remote manipulator system

flight deck

external fuel tank

attitude control thrusters

booster parachute

solid rocket booster

orbiter

nozzle

heat shield

surface insulation

side hatch

cargo bay door

orbiter

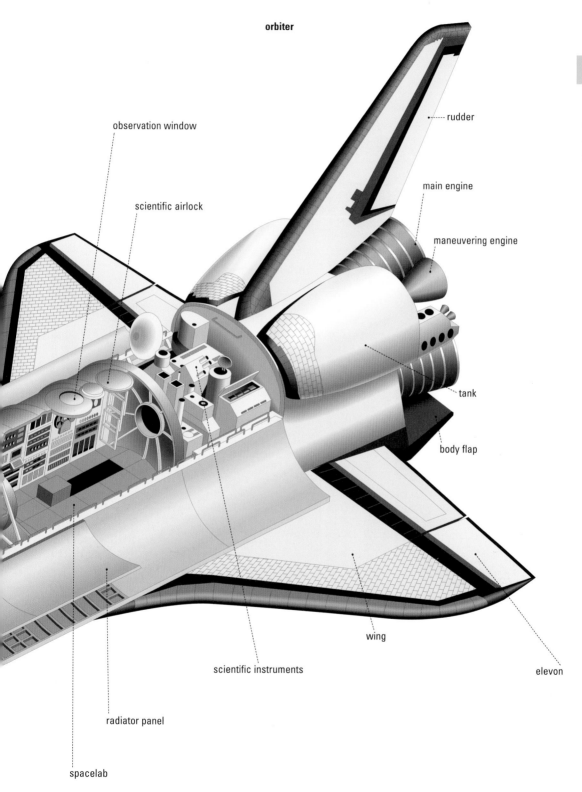

observation window

scientific airlock

rudder

main engine

maneuvering engine

tank

body flap

spacelab

radiator panel

scientific instruments

wing

elevon

SPACE LAUNCHER

cross-section of a space launcher (Ariane V)

examples of space launchers

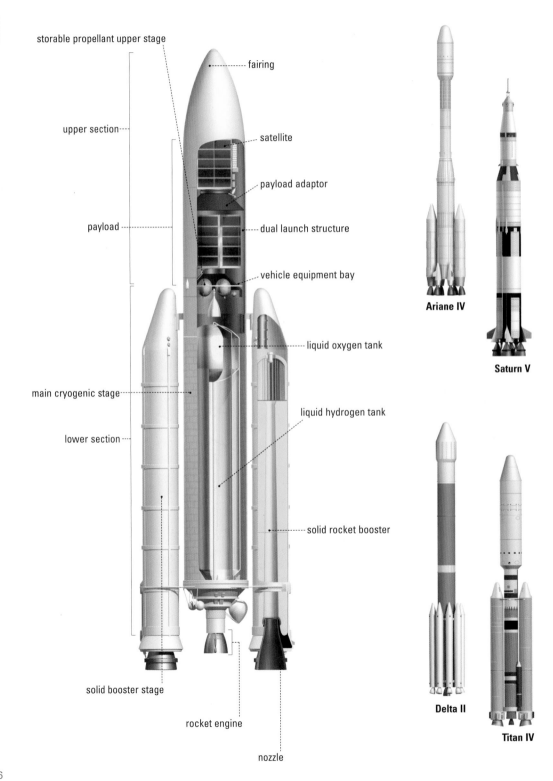

storable propellant upper stage

fairing

upper section

satellite

payload adaptor

payload

dual launch structure

vehicle equipment bay

liquid oxygen tank

main cryogenic stage

liquid hydrogen tank

lower section

solid rocket booster

solid booster stage

rocket engine

nozzle

Ariane IV

Saturn V

Delta II

Titan IV

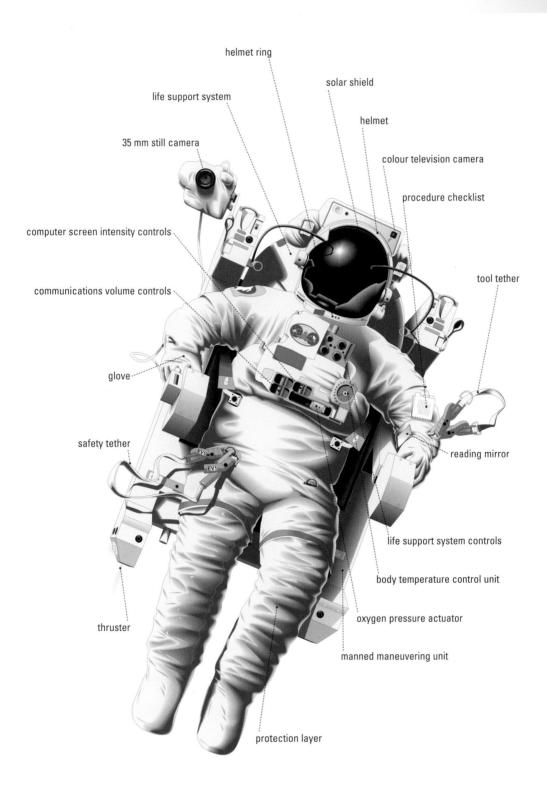

helmet ring

solar shield

life support system

helmet

35 mm still camera

colour television camera

procedure checklist

computer screen intensity controls

tool tether

communications volume controls

glove

reading mirror

safety tether

EV1

EV1

life support system controls

body temperature control unit

thruster

oxygen pressure actuator

manned maneuvering unit

protection layer

CONFIGURATION OF THE CONTINENTS

Our world is divided into seven vast areas of land surrounded by water, called continents. Eurasia is the body of land formed by Europe and Asia together. Even though the two territories are not separated by water, they are considered two distinct continents for historical reasons. Together, the seven continents cover approximately one-third of the surface of the globe. With the exception of Antarctica, they are all inhabited.

MAP OF CONTINENTS

Arctic

Arctic Ocean

North America

Atlantic Ocean

Pacific Ocean

Central America

Caribbean Sea

South America

Eurasia

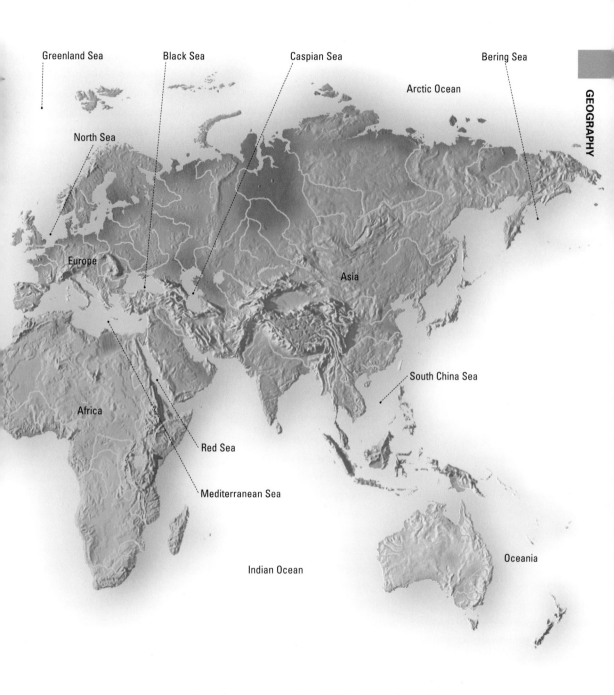

Greenland Sea

Black Sea

Caspian Sea

Bering Sea

Arctic Ocean

North Sea

Europe

Asia

Africa

South China Sea

Red Sea

Mediterranean Sea

Oceania

Indian Ocean

Antarctica

CARTOGRAPHY

To represent the Earth's surface, cartographers draw geographical maps that show, in detail, the different features of a given region. Creating the maps requires much research and gathering of information.

Cartographers also have to select a system of projection that will allow three-dimensional reality to be shown as a flat, two-dimensional map.

EARTH'S COORDINATES AND GRID SYSTEMS

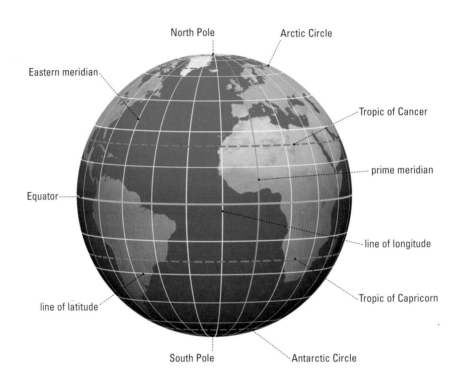

North Pole
Arctic Circle
Eastern meridian
Tropic of Cancer
prime meridian
Equator
line of longitude
Tropic of Capricorn
line of latitude
South Pole
Antarctic Circle

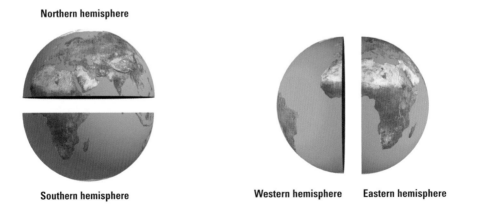

Northern hemisphere

Southern hemisphere

Western hemisphere

Eastern hemisphere

MAP PROJECTIONS

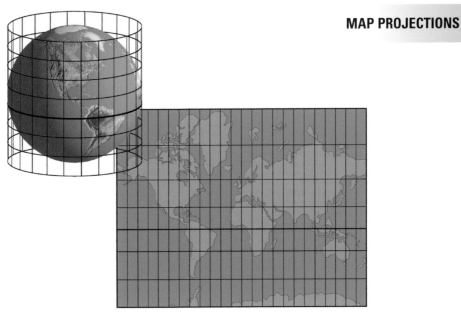

cylindrical projection

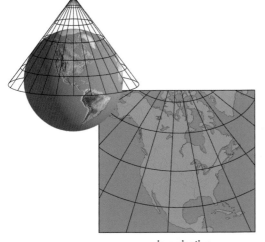

conic projection

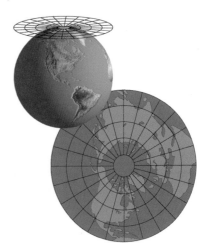

plane projection

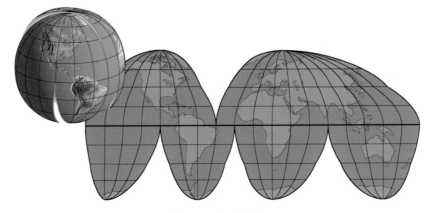

interrupted projection

MAPS

physical map

sea

strait

bay

river estuary

island

lake

prairie

peninsula

archipelago

mountain range

ocean

mountain mass

river

plateau

gulf

cape

plain

river

isthmus

political map

province

internal boundary

CANADA

Edmonton

Vancouver

Calgary

Winnipeg

Seattle

Montréal

Ottawa

Toronto

Detroit

New York

city

Washington

international boundary

San Francisco

Chicago

Denver

UNITED STATES

Los Angeles

San Diego

Atlanta

capital

Dallas

country

Houston

Miami

state

Monterrey

MEXICO

Guadalajara

Ciudad de México

GEOGRAPHY

road map

highway number

highway

rest area

service area

belt highway

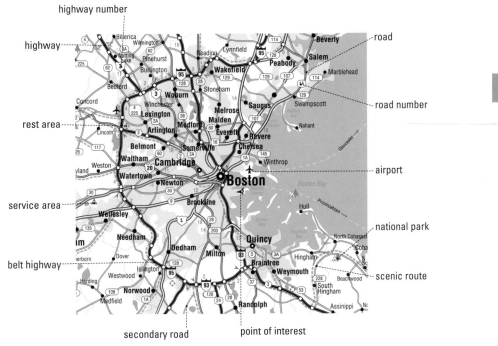

road

road number

airport

national park

scenic route

secondary road

point of interest

COMPASS ROSE

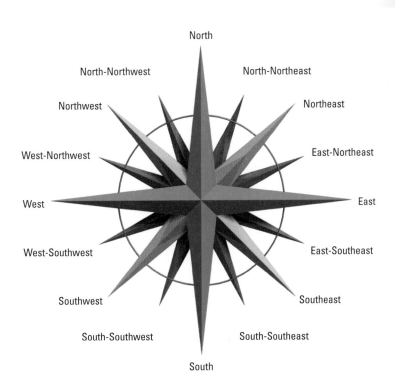

North

North-Northwest

North-Northeast

Northwest

Northeast

West-Northwest

East-Northeast

West

East

West-Southwest

East-Southeast

Southwest

Southeast

South-Southwest

South-Southeast

South

STRUCTURE OF THE EARTH

GEOLOGY

Even if it is impossible to explore Earth's interior, geologists have been able to figure out what the planet is made of by studying the way seismic waves spread underground. Seismic waves are the vibrations that accompany earthquakes. Because these waves move differently according to the rocks and materials that they encounter, geologists have determined that Earth is made up of three principal layers: the crust, the mantle, and the core.

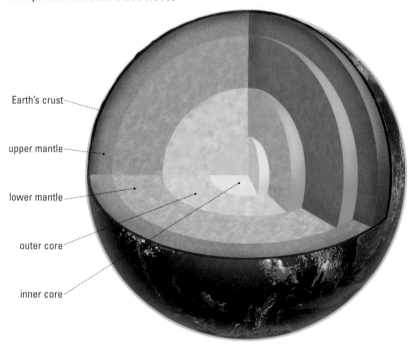

Earth's crust

upper mantle

lower mantle

outer core

inner core

cross-section of the Earth's crust

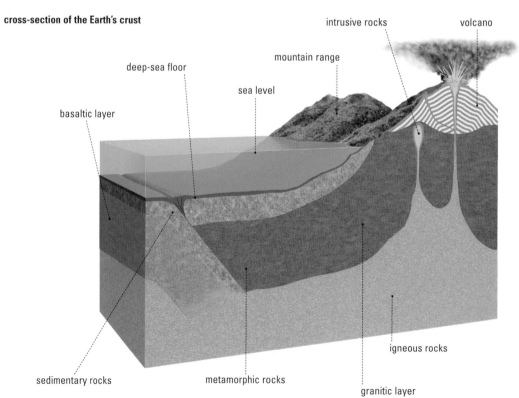

intrusive rocks

volcano

deep-sea floor

mountain range

sea level

basaltic layer

igneous rocks

sedimentary rocks

metamorphic rocks

granitic layer

The Earth's crust is made up of rocks of various origins. All rocks are composed of different kinds of minerals. Granite, for example, is a very hard rock containing several minerals including quartz. There are about 3,500 different minerals that can be distinguished, among other ways, by their colour and their hardness. Many minerals, such as gold and diamond, are sought after for their value.

minerals

quartz

silver

gold

diamond

graphite

mica

malachite

rocks

rock salt

sandstone

chalk

coal

limestone

marble

slate

basalt

granite

GEOLOGICAL PHENOMENA

Volcanoes and earthquakes are spectacular geological phenomena that demonstrate Earth's continuous activity. Similar to a jigsaw puzzle, Earth's crust is made up of about a dozen pieces called tectonic plates. Earthquakes occur regularly at the meeting point of two plates that are in movement. Most of the volcanoes likely to cause violent eruptions are found at the edges of the plates.

EARTHQUAKE

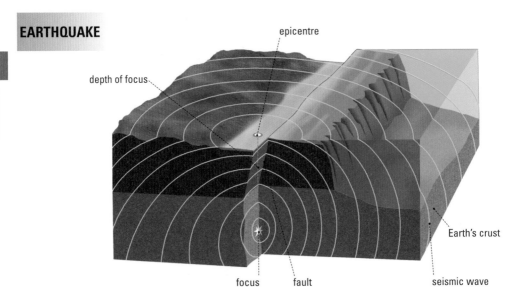

seismographs

vertical seismograph

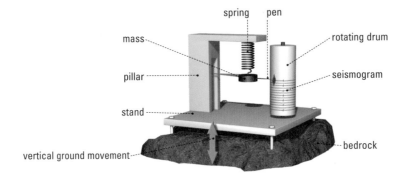

horizontal seismograph

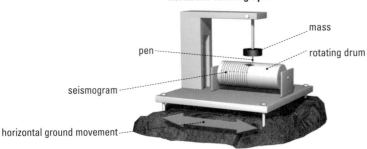

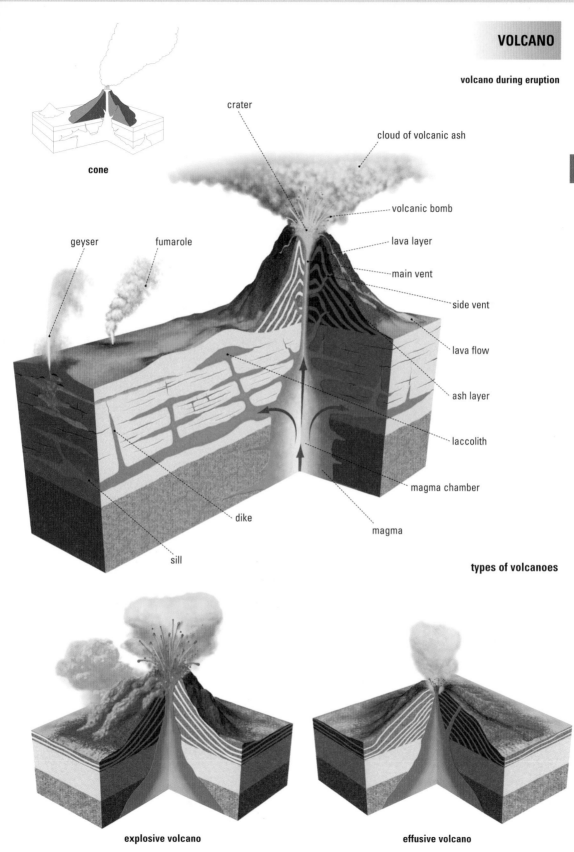

VOLCANO

volcano during eruption

cone

crater

cloud of volcanic ash

volcanic bomb

lava layer

geyser

fumarole

main vent

side vent

lava flow

ash layer

laccolith

magma chamber

dike

magma

sill

types of volcanoes

explosive volcano

effusive volcano

EARTH'S FEATURES

Since the birth of our planet, some oceans have formed while others have disappeared. Chains of mountains have risen from Earth's surface, and have eventually flattened out. Although the landscape around us seems unchanging, it is constantly evolving. The transformation may be radical, as in a seismic event, or slow, as in seawater gradually altering the shape of a country's coastline.

MOUNTAIN

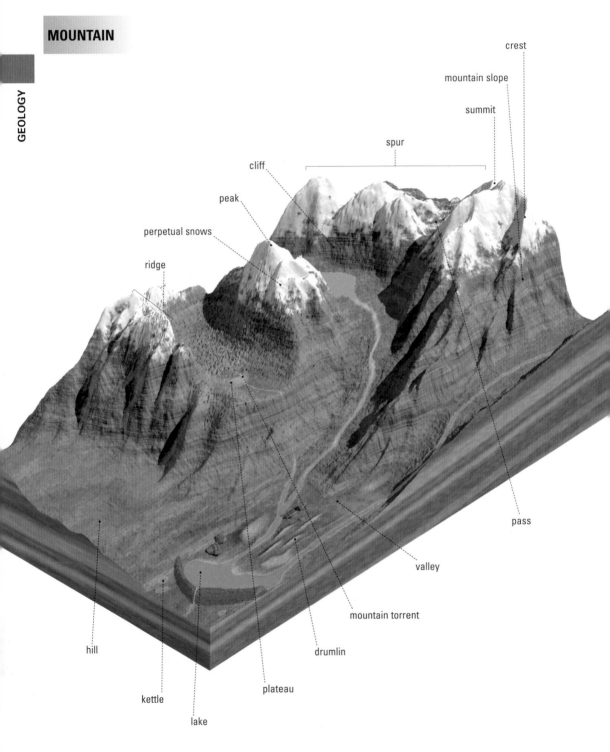

crest

mountain slope

summit

spur

cliff

peak

perpetual snows

ridge

pass

valley

mountain torrent

hill

drumlin

kettle

plateau

lake

GLACIER

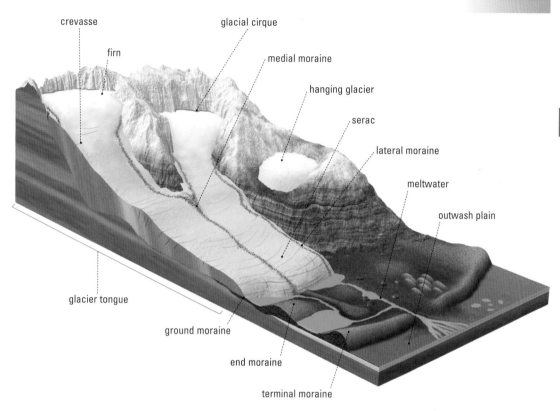

crevasse

firn

glacial cirque

medial moraine

hanging glacier

serac

lateral moraine

meltwater

outwash plain

glacier tongue

ground moraine

end moraine

terminal moraine

DESERT

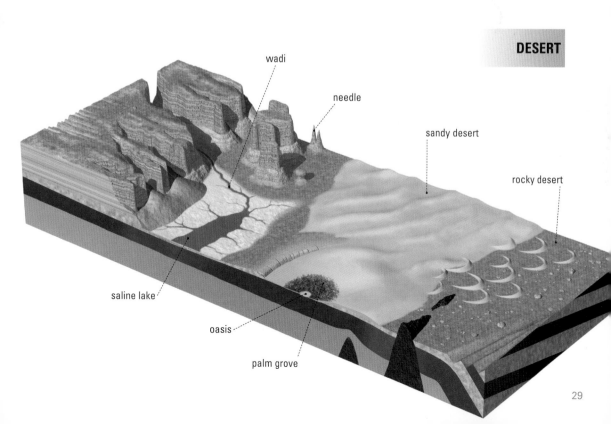

wadi

needle

sandy desert

rocky desert

saline lake

oasis

palm grove

GEOLOGY

WATERCOURSE

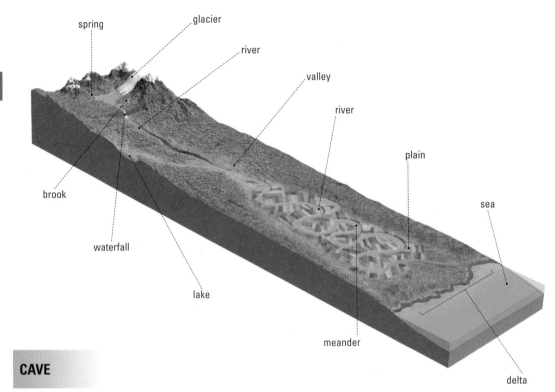

spring
glacier
river
valley
river
plain
brook
sea
waterfall
lake
meander
delta

CAVE

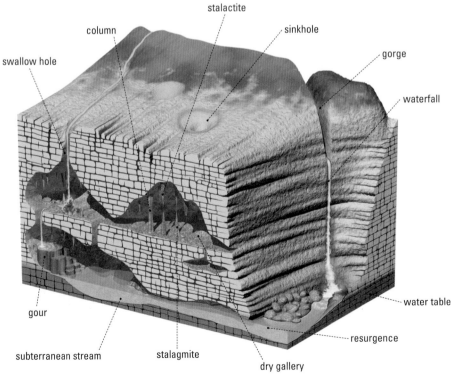

stalactite
column
sinkhole
swallow hole
gorge
waterfall
gour
water table
subterranean stream
stalagmite
dry gallery
resurgence

COMMON COASTAL FEATURES

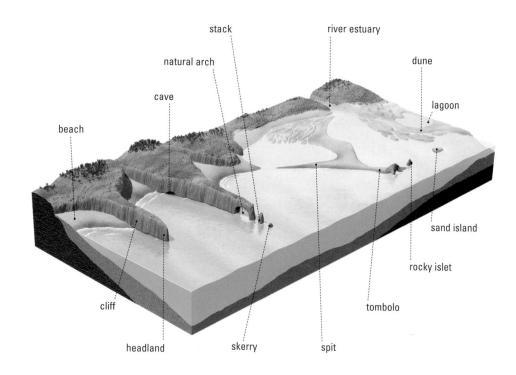

stack

river estuary

natural arch

dune

cave

lagoon

beach

sand island

rocky islet

cliff

tombolo

headland   skerry   spit

examples of shorelines

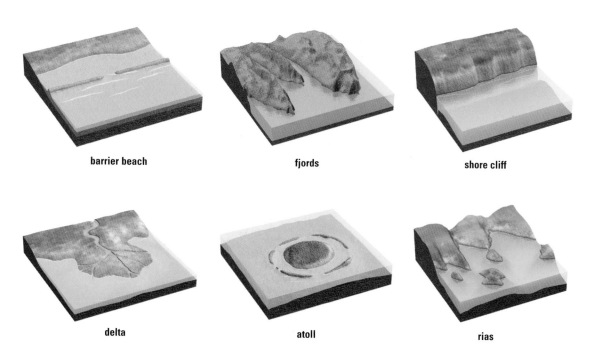

barrier beach

fjords

shore cliff

delta

atoll

rias

ATMOSPHERE

Earth's atmosphere is the envelope of gases that surround the planet. The atmosphere is made up of a successive series of layers, each of which play a role in maintaining life on our planet. The layer closest to the ground, for example, the troposphere, contains the air we breathe. It is also in this layer that most meteorological phenomena, such as winds and tornadoes, are produced.

PROFILE OF EARTH'S ATMOSPHERE

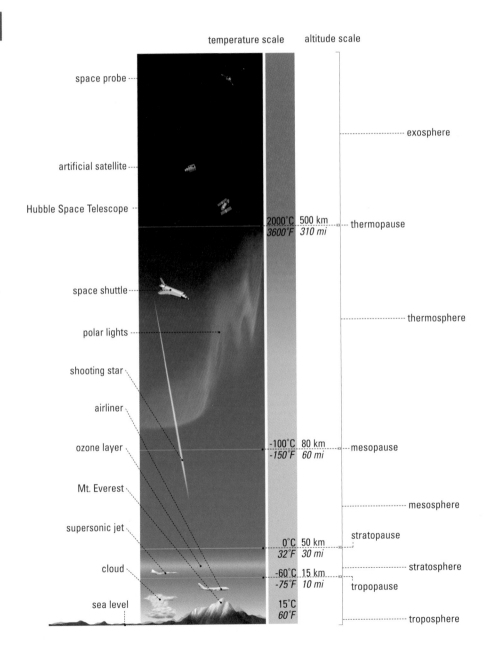

temperature scale   altitude scale

space probe

artificial satellite

Hubble Space Telescope

space shuttle

polar lights

shooting star

airliner

ozone layer

Mt. Everest

supersonic jet

cloud

sea level

2000°C 500 km
3600°F 310 mi — thermopause

-100°C 80 km
-150°F 60 mi — mesopause

0°C 50 km
32°F 30 mi

-60°C 15 km
-75°F 10 mi

15°C
60°F

exosphere

thermosphere

mesosphere

stratopause

stratosphere

tropopause

troposphere

Climate is the set of meteorological conditions that are common to a given region. The amount of solar energy that a part of the world receives is mostly responsible for its climate. Because Earth travels around the Sun in a slightly tilted position, either its northern or its southern half is heated more intensely, depending on the time of year. This phenomenon creates Earth's seasons, which are opposite in the Northern hemisphere from the Southern hemisphere.

SEASONS OF THE YEAR

METEOROLOGY

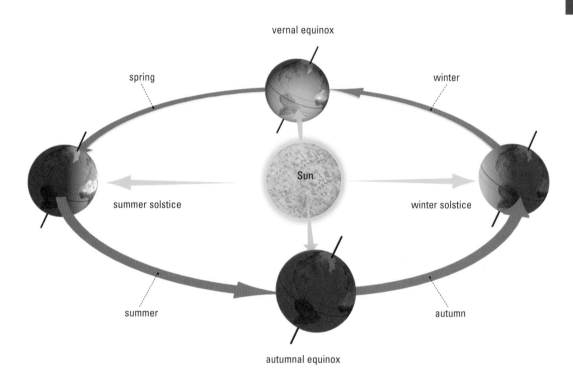

seasons in the cold temperate climates

spring   summer   autumn   winter

CLIMATES OF THE WORLD

cold temperate climates

humid continental - hot summer

humid continental - warm summer

subarctic

tropical climates

tropical rain forest

tropical wet-and-dry (savanna)

dry climates

steppe

desert

warm temperate climates

humid subtropical

Mediterranean subtropical

marine

polar climates

polar tundra

polar ice cap

highland climates

highland

Whether it is liquid like rain or solid like snow, precipitation often accompanies storms. Some atmospheric disturbances, like cyclones and tornadoes, are distinguished by violent winds and can cause considerable damage. Unfortunately, the most devastating of these storms, tornadoes, are difficult to predict because little is known about the mechanisms that drive them.

CLOUDS

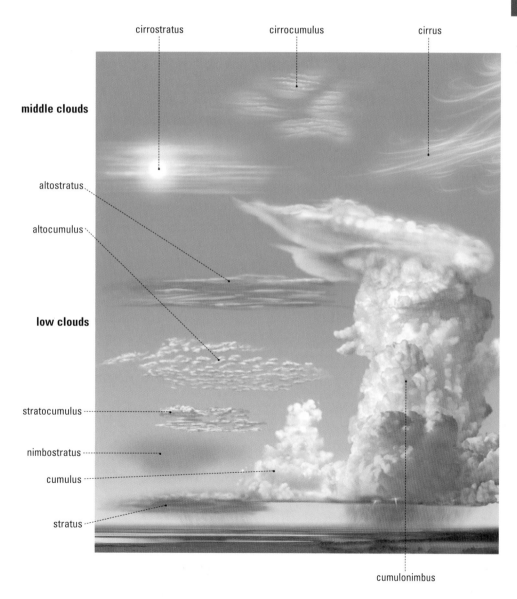

high clouds

cirrostratus

cirrocumulus

cirrus

middle clouds

altostratus

altocumulus

low clouds

stratocumulus

nimbostratus

cumulus

stratus

cumulonimbus

clouds of vertical development

METEOROLOGY

PRECIPITATIONS

drizzle

rain

heavy rain

dew

sleet

snow

freezing rain

mist

fog

THUNDERSTORM

lightning

cloud

rain

rainbow

TROPICAL CYCLONE

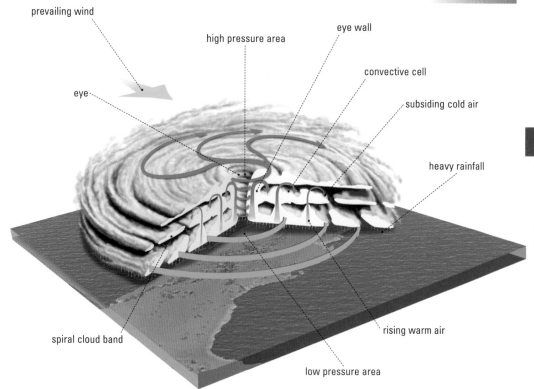

prevailing wind

high pressure area

eye wall

eye

convective cell

subsiding cold air

heavy rainfall

spiral cloud band

rising warm air

low pressure area

TORNADO

debris

funnel cloud

wall cloud

METEOROLOGICAL FORECAST

There are approximately 12,000 weather stations around the world. They are equipped with instruments that take many measurements on a daily basis and record wind speed and direction, temperature, and rainfall. All the observations are then sent to the World Meteorological Organization. With the help of these data, which are fed into computer models, meteorologists can fairly accurately predict the weather.

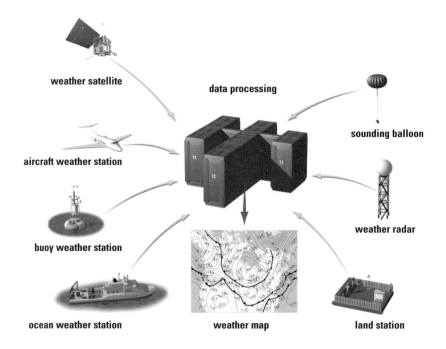

weather satellite

data processing

sounding balloon

aircraft weather station

buoy weather station

weather radar

ocean weather station

weather map

land station

METEOROLOGICAL STATION

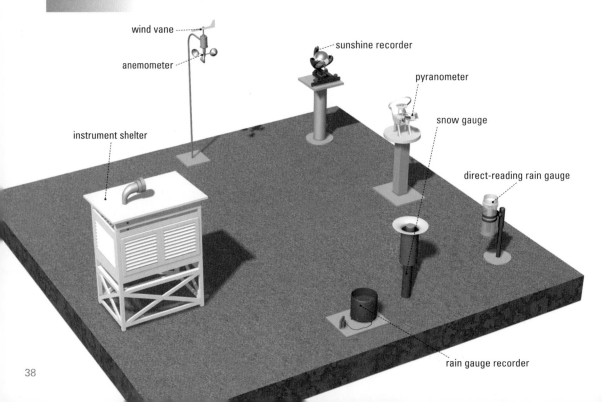

wind vane

anemometer

sunshine recorder

pyranometer

snow gauge

instrument shelter

direct-reading rain gauge

rain gauge recorder

METEOROLOGICAL MEASURING INSTRUMENTS

measure of rainfall

rain gauge recorder

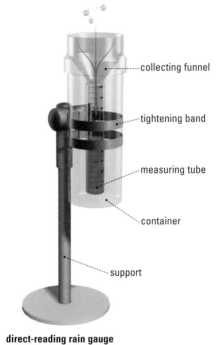

- collecting funnel
- tightening band
- measuring tube
- container
- support

direct-reading rain gauge

measure of air pressure

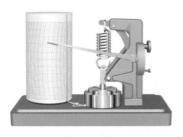

barograph

measure of temperature

maximum thermometer

minimum thermometer

measure of wind direction

wind vane

measure of wind strength

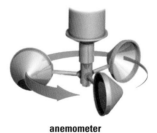

anemometer

measure of humidity

hygrograph

BIOSPHERE

Living organisms inhabit many different kinds of environments on Earth. However, no life forms are found outside the very thin layer of earth, air, and water we call the biosphere. This habitable part of our planet is a complex world where all species live in very close relationship to their environment. All living things draw the energy they need to survive from their food. The feeding pattern can be looked at as a series of links that form a chain.

VEGETATION AND BIOSPHERE

vegetation regions

elevation zones and vegetation

- tropical rain forest
- temperate forest
- boreal forest
- tundra
- savanna
- desert
- grassland
- maquis

- glacier
- tundra
- coniferous forest
- mixed forest
- deciduous forest
- tropical forest

structure of the biosphere

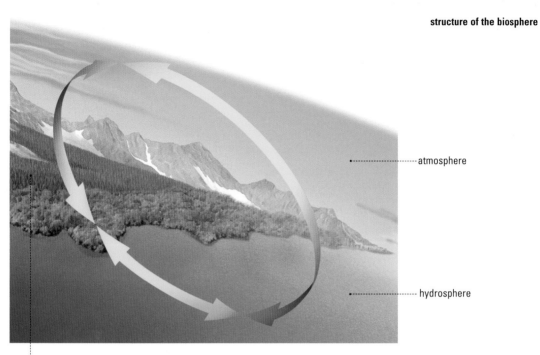

atmosphere

hydrosphere

lithosphere

FOOD CHAIN

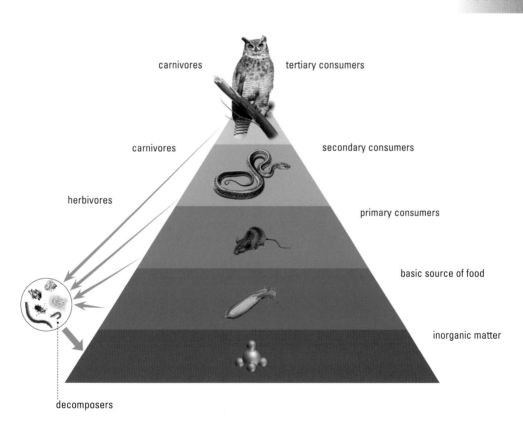

carnivores — tertiary consumers

carnivores — secondary consumers

herbivores — primary consumers

basic source of food

inorganic matter

decomposers

WATER CYCLE

The Sun's heat creates a constant exchange between the ocean and the atmosphere. Water vapour, condensed in the clouds, falls toward Earth as rain or snow. When it lands on a continent, the water penetrates the ground, runs into lakes and rivers, and eventually returns to the ocean. Some of the water evaporates over the ocean and rises once again into the atmosphere. This process is called the water cycle.

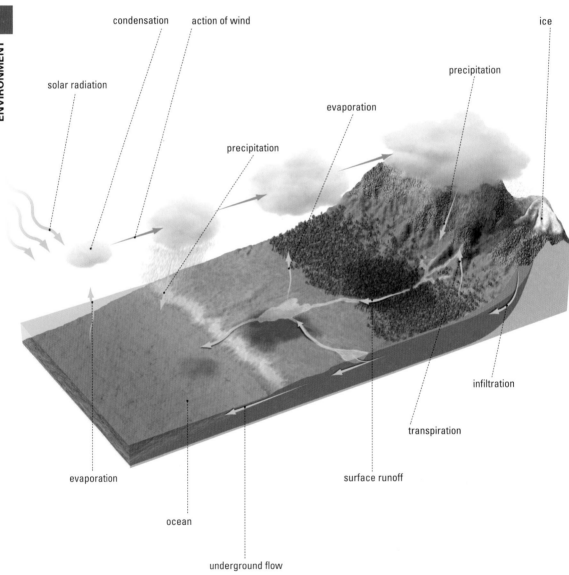

condensation

action of wind

ice

solar radiation

precipitation

evaporation

precipitation

evaporation

infiltration

transpiration

surface runoff

evaporation

ocean

underground flow

Some of the Sun's rays are absorbed by the ground and thrown back into the atmosphere in the form of heat. Certain gases in the atmosphere have the ability to trap this heat. Because of this natural phenomenon called the "greenhouse effect," temperatures on Earth are suitable for supporting life. For over 150 years, however, human activity has increased the amount of greenhouse gases released into the atmosphere, contributing to global warming.

ENVIRONMENT

natural greenhouse effect

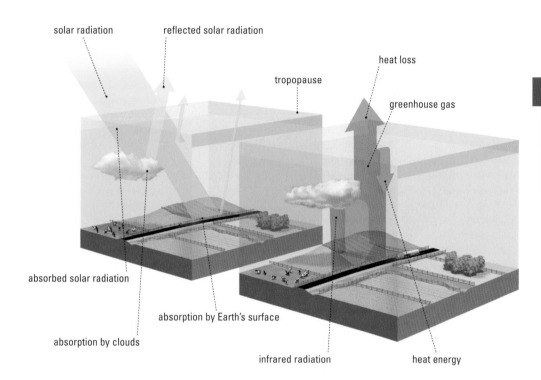

solar radiation

reflected solar radiation

heat loss

tropopause

greenhouse gas

absorbed solar radiation

absorption by Earth's surface

absorption by clouds

infrared radiation

heat energy

enhanced greenhouse effect

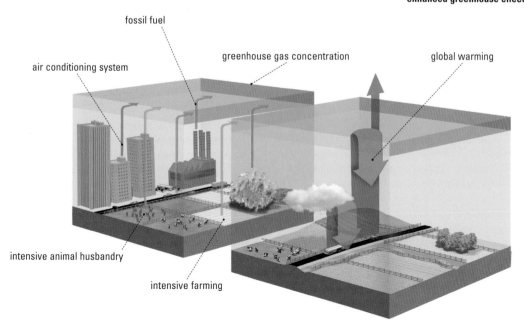

fossil fuel

greenhouse gas concentration

global warming

air conditioning system

intensive animal husbandry

intensive farming

POLLUTION

Industries release large quantities of chemical waste into the environment. Some of it is extremely toxic. Thermal power stations and motorized vehicles also do their share of polluting. Fortunately, more and more people are beginning to realize that natural resources are not inexhaustible and that we cannot continue to pollute the air, earth, and water without affecting the future of our planet.

LAND POLLUTION

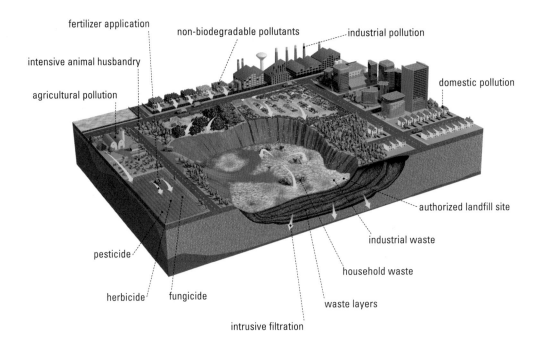

fertilizer application

non-biodegradable pollutants

industrial pollution

intensive animal husbandry

domestic pollution

agricultural pollution

authorized landfill site

industrial waste

household waste

pesticide

waste layers

herbicide

fungicide

intrusive filtration

AIR POLLUTION

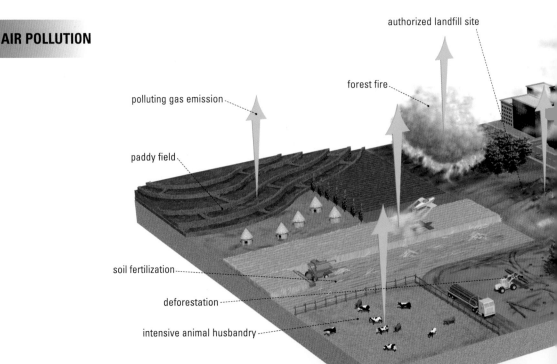

authorized landfill site

forest fire

polluting gas emission

paddy field

soil fertilization

deforestation

intensive animal husbandry

WATER POLLUTION

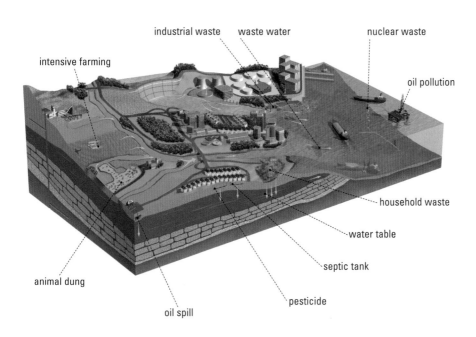

industrial waste   waste water

nuclear waste

intensive farming

oil pollution

household waste

water table

septic tank

animal dung

pesticide

oil spill

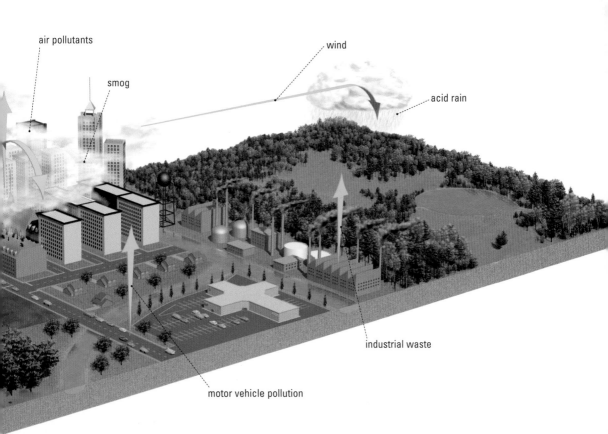

air pollutants

wind

smog

acid rain

industrial waste

motor vehicle pollution

SELECTIVE SORTING OF WASTE

A large portion of the household waste produced in industrialized countries can be recycled. More and more cities have a system for the selective sorting of waste. Garbage is brought to sorting plants where workers and machines separate recyclable materials like glass, metal, plastic, and paper. These materials then go through a number of cleaning and transformation operations.

sorting plant

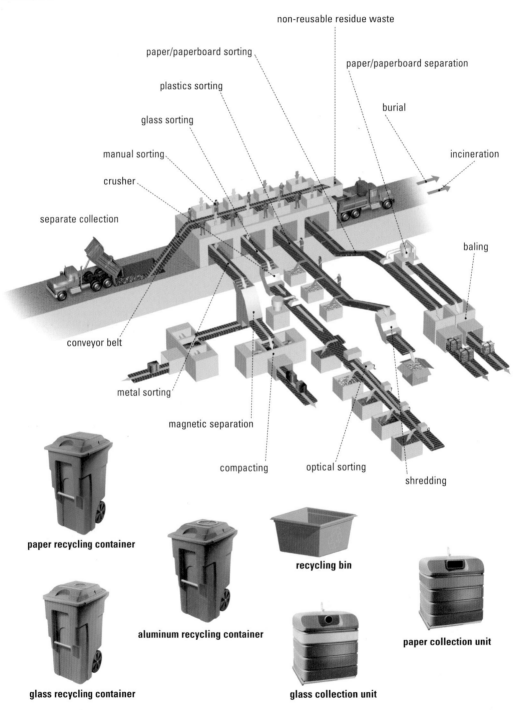

non-reusable residue waste

paper/paperboard sorting

paper/paperboard separation

plastics sorting

burial

glass sorting

incineration

manual sorting

crusher

separate collection

baling

conveyor belt

metal sorting

magnetic separation

compacting

optical sorting

shredding

paper recycling container

aluminum recycling container

recycling bin

glass recycling container

glass collection unit

paper collection unit

Although all vegetables are made up of plant cells, they do not all have the same structure. The simplest vegetables, such as algae, lichen, mosses, ferns, and mushrooms, have no leaves, flowers, or seeds.

Mushrooms do not even have chlorophyll, the pigment that gives plants their green colour. This is why biologists classify mushrooms in a separate kingdom.

structure of a mushroom

MUSHROOM

deadly poisonous mushroom

destroying angel

poisonous mushroom

fly agaric

ALGA, LICHEN, MOSS, AND FERN

structure of a fern

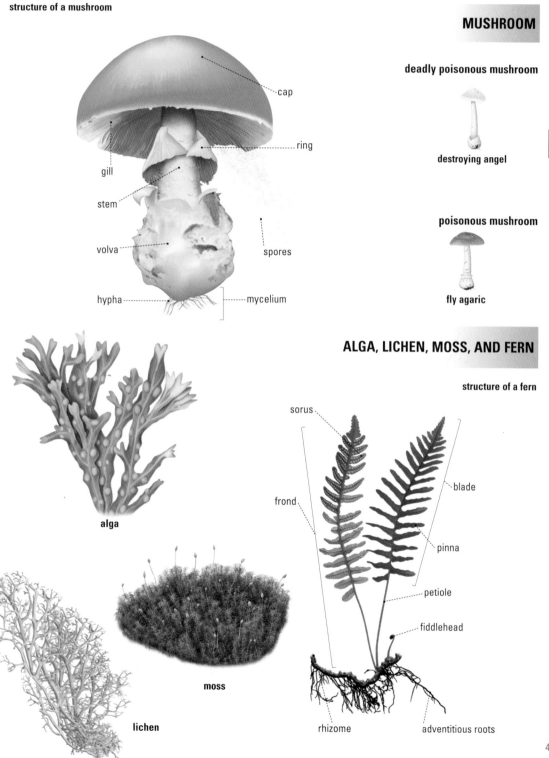

cap

ring

gill

stem

volva

spores

hypha

mycelium

alga

moss

lichen

sorus

frond

blade

pinna

petiole

fiddlehead

rhizome

adventitious roots

VEGETABLE KINGDOM

FLOWERING PLANTS

Reproduction in flowering plants is ensured, in part, by the seed that protects a tiny plant embryo. During germination, the embryo develops by taking in nutritive substances contained in the seed and quickly becomes a new, independent plant. The majority of plants familiar to us belong to this very diversified group that includes more than 235,000 species.

STRUCTURE OF A PLANT AND GERMINATION

structure of a plant

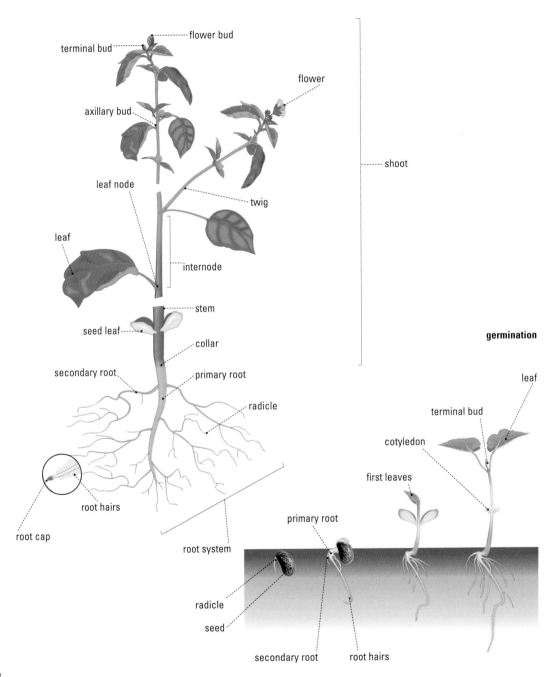

flower bud

terminal bud

flower

axillary bud

shoot

leaf node

twig

leaf

internode

stem

seed leaf

collar

germination

secondary root

primary root

radicle

leaf

terminal bud

cotyledon

first leaves

root hairs

primary root

root cap

root system

radicle

seed

secondary root   root hairs

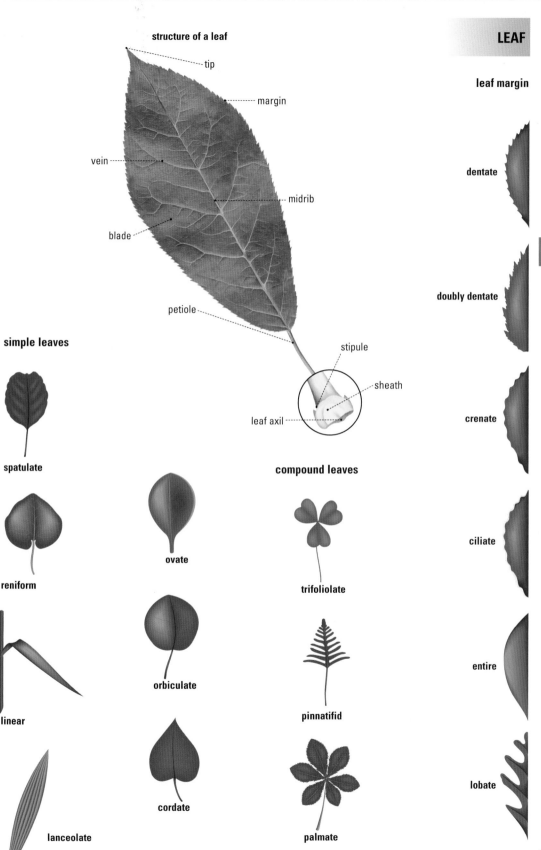

structure of a leaf

tip

margin

vein

midrib

blade

petiole

stipule

sheath

leaf axil

LEAF

leaf margin

dentate

doubly dentate

crenate

ciliate

entire

lobate

simple leaves

spatulate

reniform

linear

lanceolate

ovate

orbiculate

cordate

compound leaves

trifoliolate

pinnatifid

palmate

VEGETABLE KINGDOM

FLOWER

structure of a flower

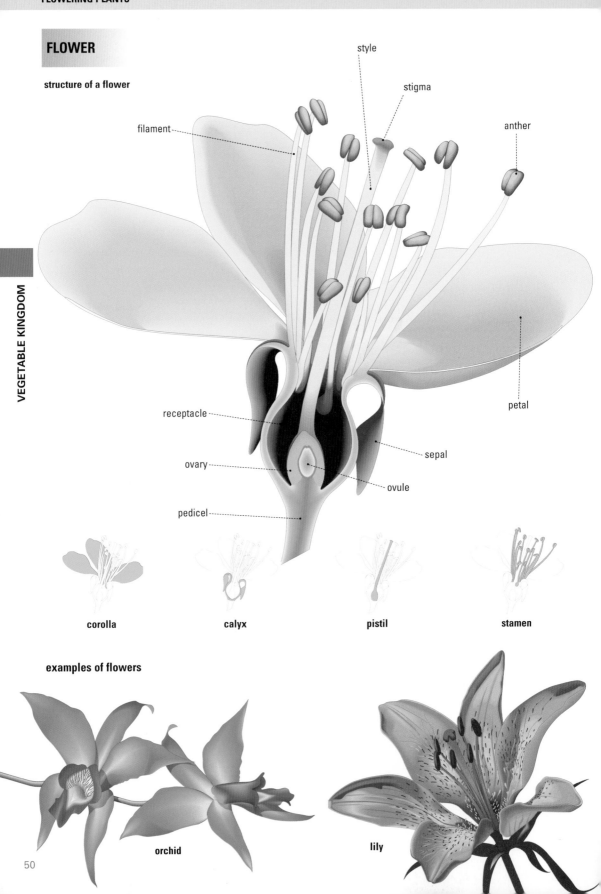

style

stigma

anther

filament

petal

receptacle

sepal

ovary

ovule

pedicel

corolla

calyx

pistil

stamen

examples of flowers

orchid

lily

daffodil

tulip

primrose

begonia

daisy

buttercup

violet

thistle

lily of the valley

poppy

carnation

dandelion

sunflower

crocus

rose

TREE

Trees are plants that can reach considerable dimensions. There are two principal categories: broad-leaved trees, which grow fairly large leaves, and conifers, which have narrow leaves in the form of needles or scales. Conifers are said to be evergreen because, with just a few exceptions, they retain their leaves throughout the year. Broad-leaved trees are called deciduous, which means "falling off" in Latin, because their leaves generally fall before winter.

STRUCTURE OF A TREE

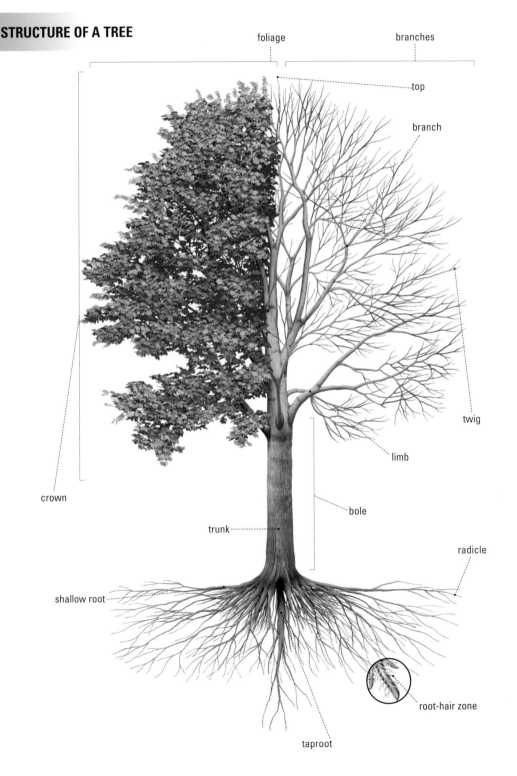

foliage

branches

top

branch

twig

limb

crown

bole

trunk

radicle

shallow root

root-hair zone

taproot

stump

cross-section of a trunk

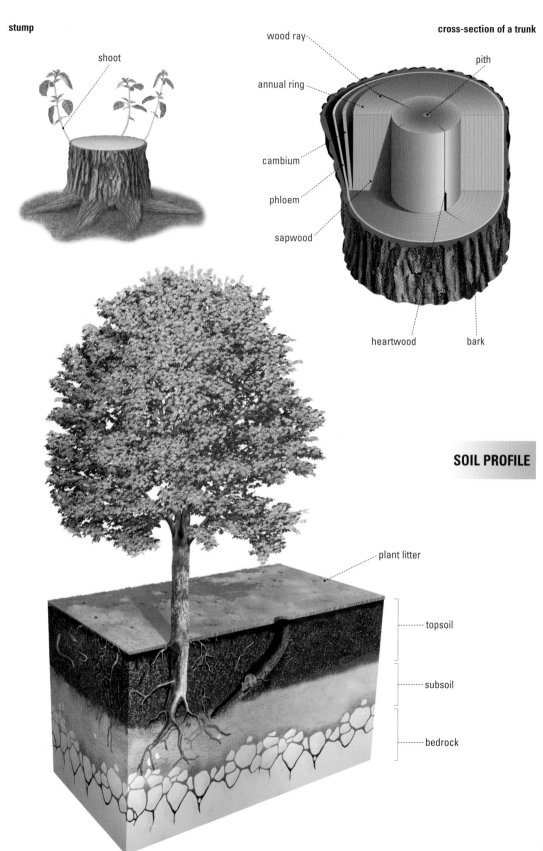

shoot

wood ray

pith

annual ring

cambium

phloem

sapwood

heartwood

bark

SOIL PROFILE

plant litter

topsoil

subsoil

bedrock

EXAMPLES OF BROAD-LEAVED TREES

maple

willow

oak

palm tree

walnut

poplar

beech

birch

branch

pine seeds

EXAMPLES OF CONIFERS

cone

cedar of Lebanon

larch

spruce

fir

pine

Whether they consist of a single cell, like the amoeba or the paramecium, or billions of cells, like the blue whale, all animals are made of animal cells. Excluding unicellulars, now classified in a separate kingdom, there are two principal groups: the vertebrates, which have a vertebral column, and the invertebrates, which do not. If sponges are the most primitive of invertebrates, echinoderms are among the most highly evolved.

ANIMAL CELL

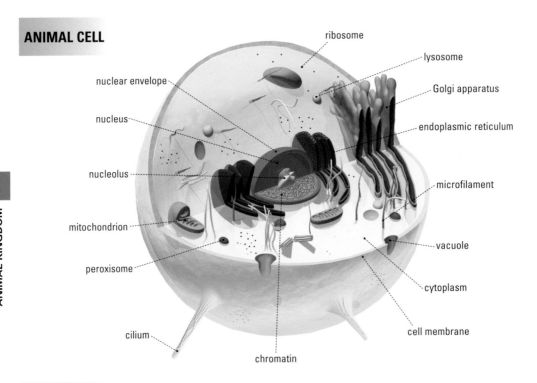

ribosome

lysosome

nuclear envelope

Golgi apparatus

nucleus

endoplasmic reticulum

nucleolus

microfilament

mitochondrion

vacuole

peroxisome

cytoplasm

cilium

cell membrane

chromatin

UNICELLULARS, SPONGE, AND ECHINODERMS

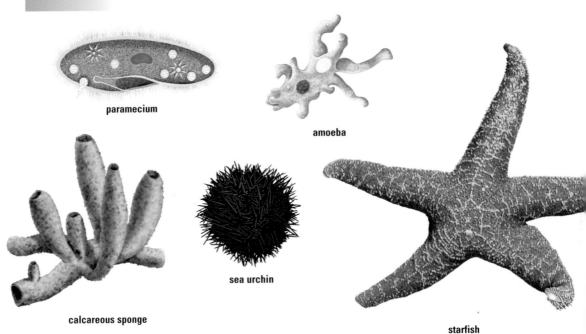

paramecium

amoeba

calcareous sponge

sea urchin

starfish

Molluscs are named after the Latin *molluscus*, which means "soft." These soft-bodied animals have no skeleton but they usually have a shell. The majority of the 100,000 species are aquatic and breathe with the help of gills. Land molluscs, like the snail or the slug, breathe using lungs. Some of these invertebrates are both male and female at the same time. They are called hermaphrodites.

SNAIL

morphology of a snail

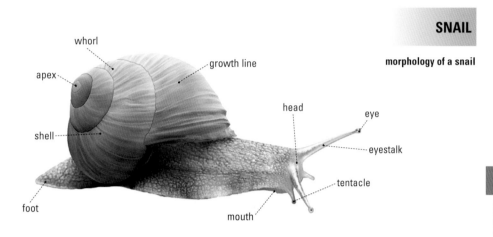

whorl

growth line

apex

head

eye

shell

eyestalk

tentacle

foot

mouth

EXAMPLES OF MOLLUSCS

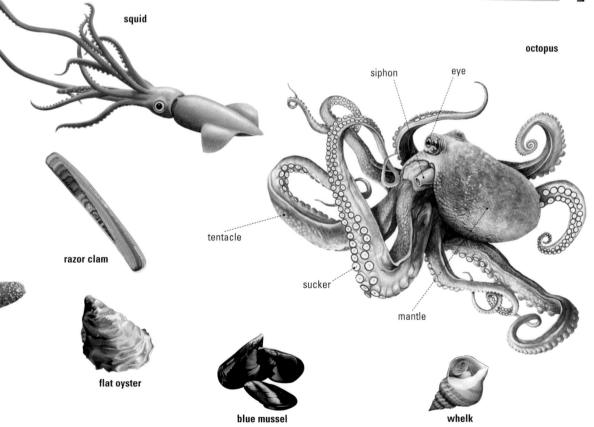

squid

octopus

siphon

eye

tentacle

razor clam

sucker

mantle

flat oyster

blue mussel

whelk

CRUSTACEANS

Like insects and spiders, crustaceans belong to the arthropods, a group of invertebrates characterized by the presence of jointed legs. In front of the legs, which are used for walking or swimming, are pincers that help crustaceans pick up food. The 30,000 species of crustaceans are distinguished by, among other things, two pairs of antennae, ten legs, and a body covered by a protective carapace.

LOBSTER

morphology of a lobster

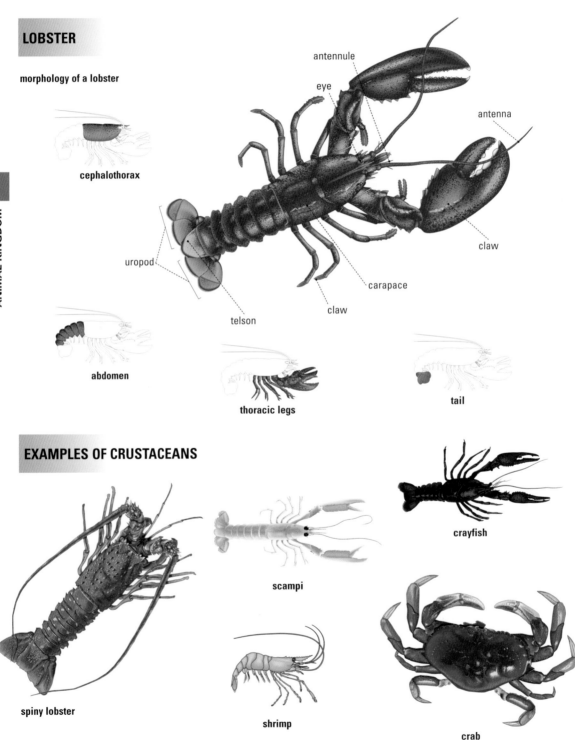

cephalothorax

antennule

eye

antenna

claw

uropod

telson

claw

carapace

abdomen

thoracic legs

tail

EXAMPLES OF CRUSTACEANS

crayfish

scampi

spiny lobster

shrimp

crab

Spiders are the best known of the arachnids, a principal group of invertebrates that include more than 50,000 species. All the representatives of this group have, in front of the mouth, a pair of pincers in which they hold their prey. Contrary to insects and crustaceans, arachnids do not have antennae. They are also distinguished by their eight legs.

morphology of a spider

SPIDER

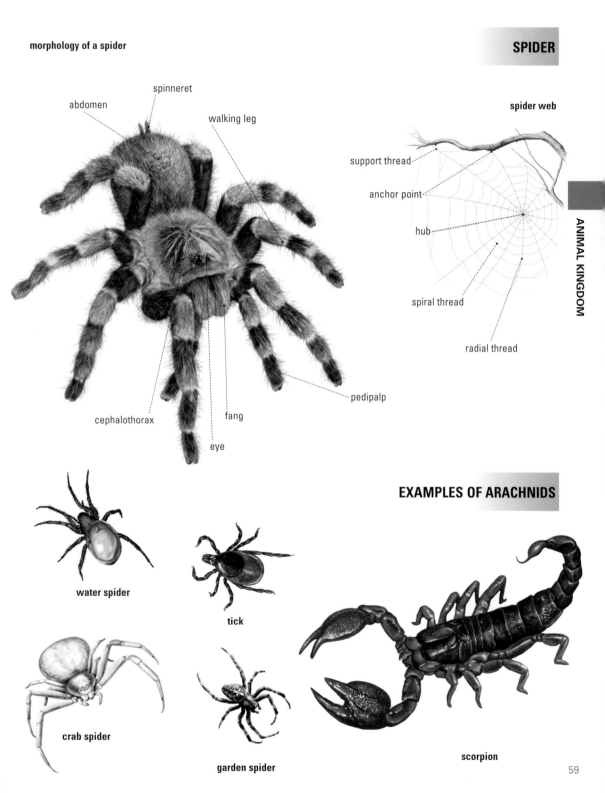

spinneret

abdomen

walking leg

spider web

support thread

anchor point

hub

spiral thread

radial thread

pedipalp

cephalothorax

fang

eye

EXAMPLES OF ARACHNIDS

water spider

tick

crab spider

garden spider

scorpion

Insects are the most numerous as well as the most diversified group of land animals. Today, there are more than one million species, which abound in every environment. Insects are distinguished from other arthropods by their six legs and, in most cases, by the presence of wings. They are the only invertebrates capable of flying.

ANIMAL KINGDOM

HONEYBEE

morphology of a honeybee (worker)

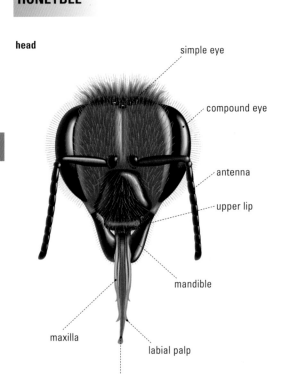

head

simple eye

compound eye

antenna

upper lip

mandible

maxilla

labial palp

tongue

thorax

antenna

mouthparts

foreleg

middle leg

castes

queen

worker

drone

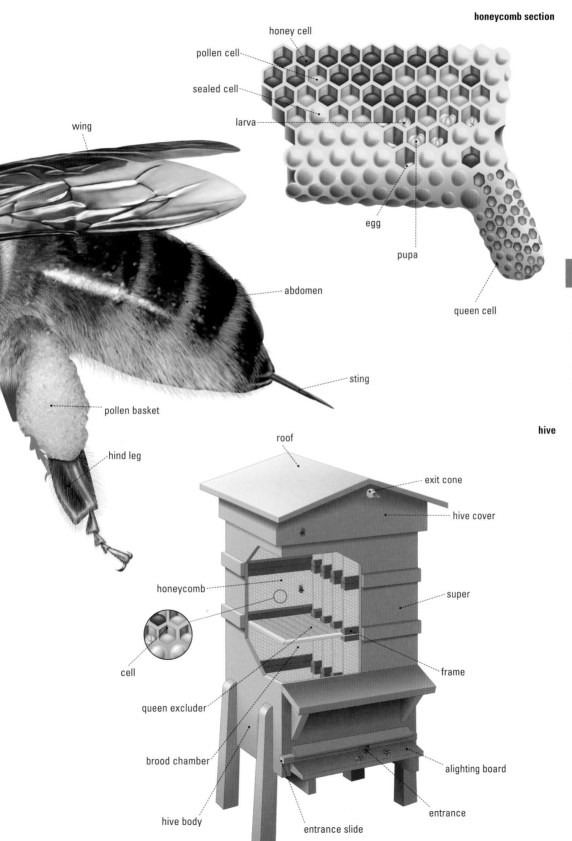

honeycomb section

honey cell

pollen cell

sealed cell

larva

egg

pupa

queen cell

wing

abdomen

sting

pollen basket

hind leg

hive

roof

exit cone

hive cover

honeycomb

super

cell

frame

queen excluder

brood chamber

hive body

entrance slide

entrance

alighting board

ANIMAL KINGDOM

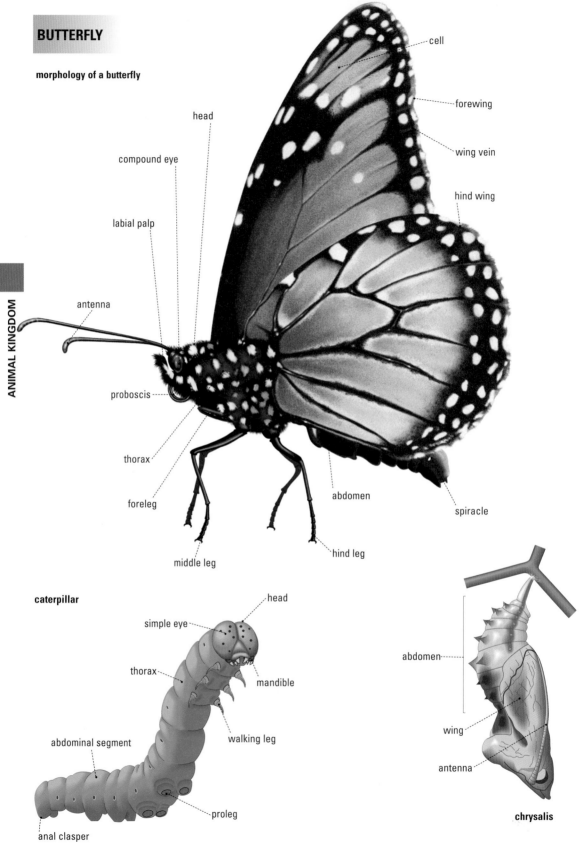

BUTTERFLY

morphology of a butterfly

cell

forewing

wing vein

hind wing

head

compound eye

labial palp

antenna

proboscis

thorax

foreleg

middle leg

hind leg

abdomen

spiracle

ANIMAL KINGDOM

caterpillar

head

simple eye

thorax

mandible

walking leg

abdominal segment

proleg

anal clasper

abdomen

wing

antenna

chrysalis

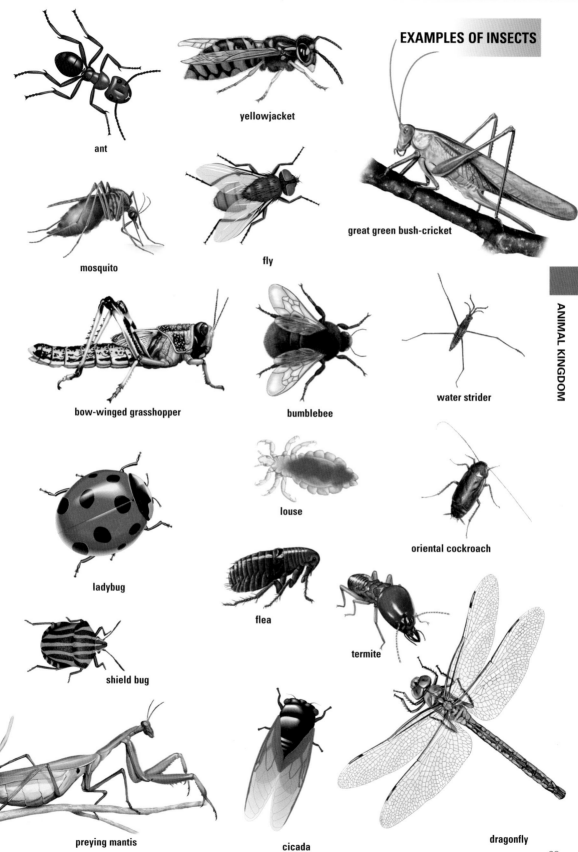

EXAMPLES OF INSECTS

yellowjacket

ant

great green bush-cricket

mosquito

fly

bow-winged grasshopper

bumblebee

water strider

ladybug

louse

oriental cockroach

flea

shield bug

termite

preying mantis

cicada

dragonfly

CARTILAGINOUS FISH

Fish are the oldest vertebrate animals. The majority of modern species are divided into two groups: bony fish and cartilaginous fish. This second group, which is distinguished by the presence of a skeleton made of cartilage, is mainly represented by rays and sharks. All fish, whether cartilaginous or bony, are perfectly adapted to aquatic life, and have tapering bodies, fins, and gills.

SHARK

morphology of a shark

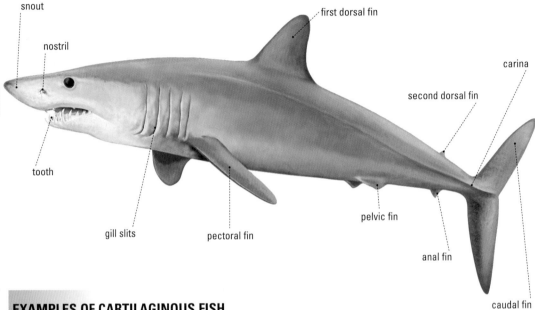

snout

nostril

first dorsal fin

carina

second dorsal fin

tooth

gill slits

pectoral fin

pelvic fin

anal fin

caudal fin

EXAMPLES OF CARTILAGINOUS FISH

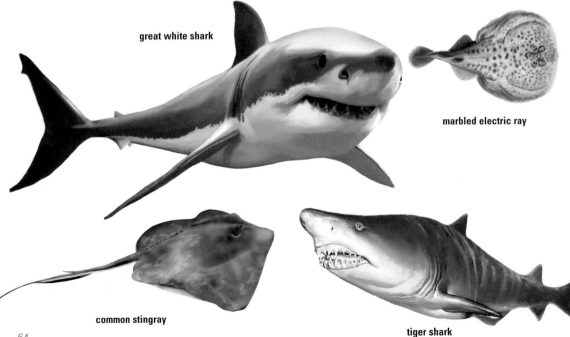

great white shark

marbled electric ray

common stingray

tiger shark

As their name suggests, bony fish possess a skeleton made entirely or partially of bone. Appearing on Earth 150 million years after the cartilaginous fish, the more highly evolved bony fish are represented today by more than 20,000 species as varied as the eel, the seahorse, the tiny sardine, and the spiny-finned perch. Bony fish are found in most aquatic environments on the planet.

morphology of a perch

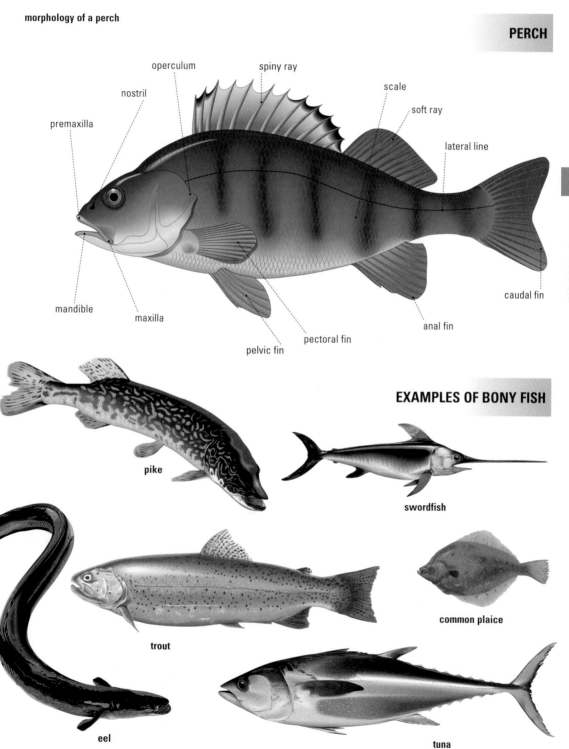

PERCH

- operculum
- spiny ray
- nostril
- scale
- soft ray
- premaxilla
- lateral line
- mandible
- maxilla
- pectoral fin
- pelvic fin
- anal fin
- caudal fin

EXAMPLES OF BONY FISH

pike

swordfish

trout

common plaice

eel

tuna

AMPHIBIANS

Amphibians are characterized by their ability to live as much in water as on land. Without losing their swimming skills, they were the first vertebrates to leave their aquatic environment and gain solid ground thanks to their legs and their lungs. The great majority of the 3,000 known species live in humid land environments or in fresh water.

FROG

morphology of a frog

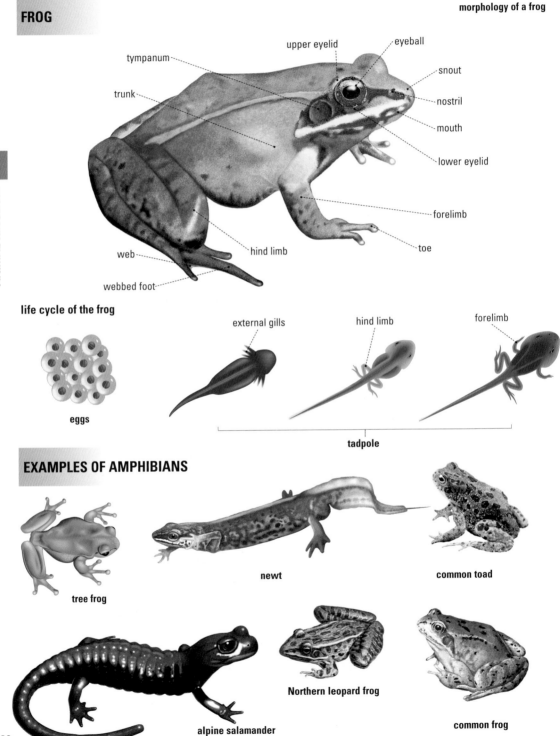

upper eyelid

eyeball

tympanum

snout

trunk

nostril

mouth

lower eyelid

forelimb

web

hind limb

toe

webbed foot

life cycle of the frog

external gills

hind limb

forelimb

eggs

tadpole

EXAMPLES OF AMPHIBIANS

newt

common toad

tree frog

Northern leopard frog

alpine salamander

common frog

Thanks to a shell or scaly skin that prevents them from losing water, and to well-developed lungs, reptiles were the first vertebrates completely adapted to living on land. These cold-blooded animals owe their popularity to certain families that have long been extinct: the dinosaurs. Today there are some 6,500 known species of reptiles, living mainly in tropical regions.

morphology of a turtle

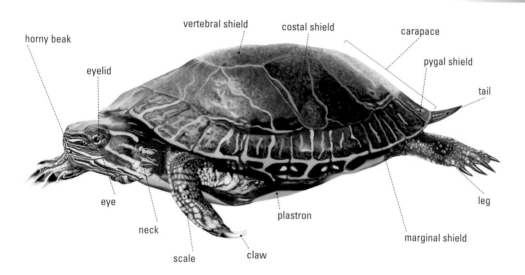

horny beak
vertebral shield
costal shield
carapace
pygal shield
eyelid
tail
eye
leg
neck
plastron
marginal shield
scale
claw

morphology of a venomous snake (head)

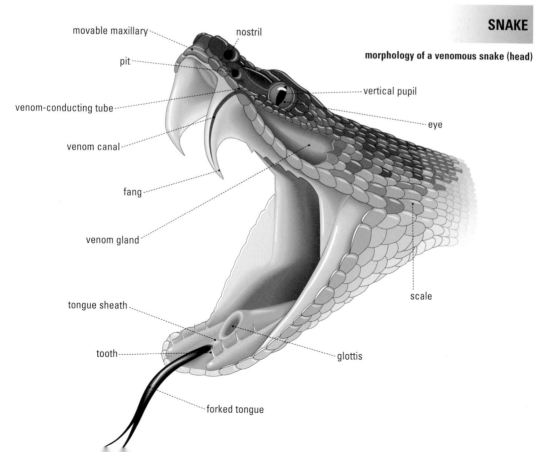

movable maxillary
nostril
pit
vertical pupil
venom-conducting tube
venom canal
eye
fang
venom gland
scale
tongue sheath
tooth
glottis
forked tongue

EXAMPLES OF REPTILES

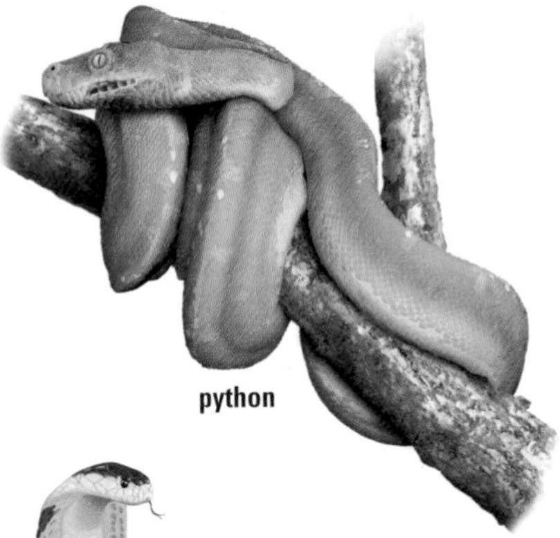

python

leatherback turtle

garter snake

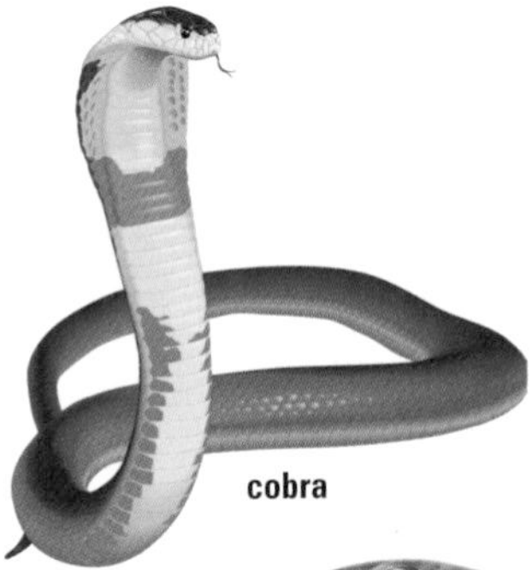

cobra

coral snake

rattlesnake

boa

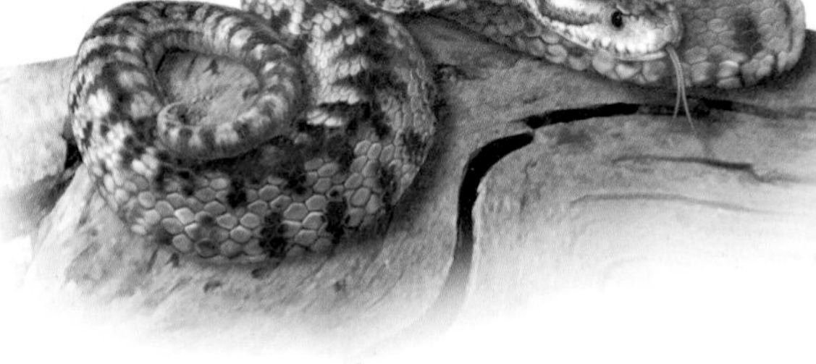

viper

monitor lizard

chameleon

lizard

iguana

alligator

caiman

crocodile

DINOSAURS

stegosaurus

spinosaurus

allosaurus

parasauroloph

hadrosaurus

diplodocus

tyrannosaurus

pachycephalosaurus

ankylosaurus

deinonychus

triceratops

brachiosaurus

BIRDS

With the exception of the bat, birds are the only verte-brates capable of flying. Their light skeleton and feather-covered wings make them the best aviators in the animal kingdom. The scientific classification of birds is based on characteristics that can be difficult to recognize, such as the structure of their feathers. This is why the 10,000 known species are often presented simply by distinguishing aquatic and shorebirds from terrestrial birds.

BIRD

morphology of a bird

bird feeder

birdhouse

nest

nostril

bill

chin

throat

wing covert

breast

abdomen

nape

wing

inner toe

claw

middle toe

outer toe

egg

blastodisc

air space

yolk

shell

albumen

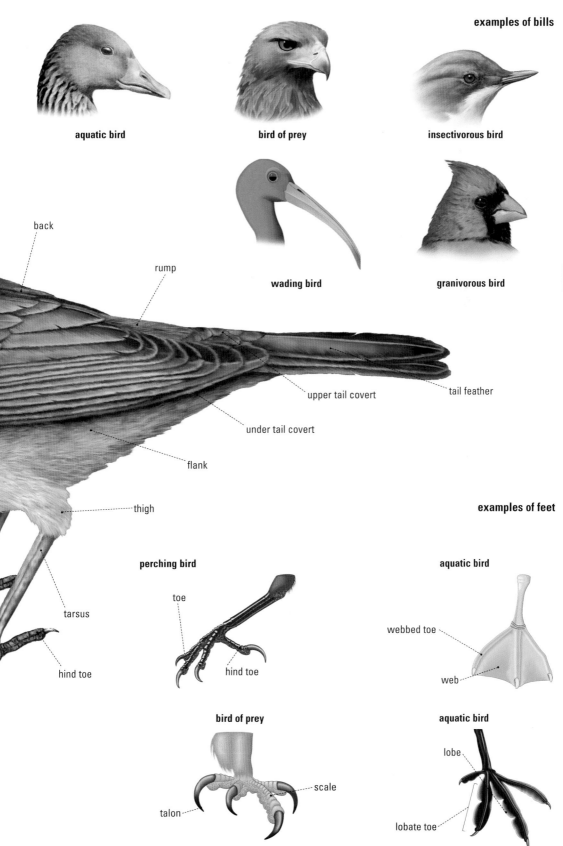

examples of bills

aquatic bird

bird of prey

insectivorous bird

wading bird

granivorous bird

back

rump

upper tail covert

tail feather

under tail covert

flank

thigh

examples of feet

tarsus

hind toe

perching bird

toe

hind toe

aquatic bird

webbed toe

web

bird of prey

scale

talon

aquatic bird

lobe

lobate toe

EXAMPLES OF TERRESTRIAL BIRDS

cardinal

jay

goldfinch

hummingbird

swallow

finch

raven

sparrow

starling

great horned owl

pigeon

partridge

toucan

eagle

macaw

falcon

peacock

rooster

chick

hen

turkey

goose

ostrich

EXAMPLES OF AQUATIC AND SHOREBIRDS

flamingo

penguin

oystercatcher

stork

duck

kingfisher

tern

pelican

MAMMALS

The 4,600 species of mammals are recognized at first glance by their hair-covered skin. All females feed their young with milk produced by their mammary glands, that is where the name "mammal" comes from. They are the most highly evolved vertebrates. Along with birds, they are the only animals able to maintain a constant internal body temperature.

MARSUPIAL MAMMALS

morphology of a kangaroo

examples of marsupials

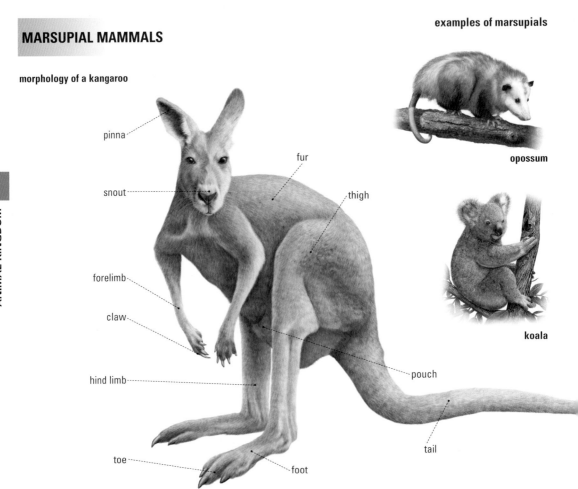

pinna

snout

fur

thigh

forelimb

claw

hind limb

pouch

toe

foot

tail

opossum

koala

EXAMPLES OF INSECTIVOROUS MAMMALS

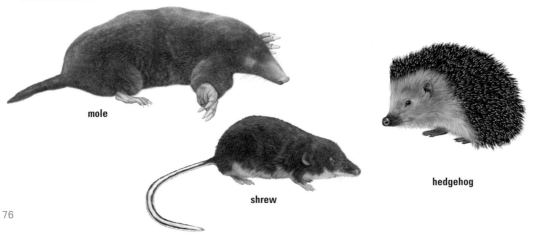

mole

shrew

hedgehog

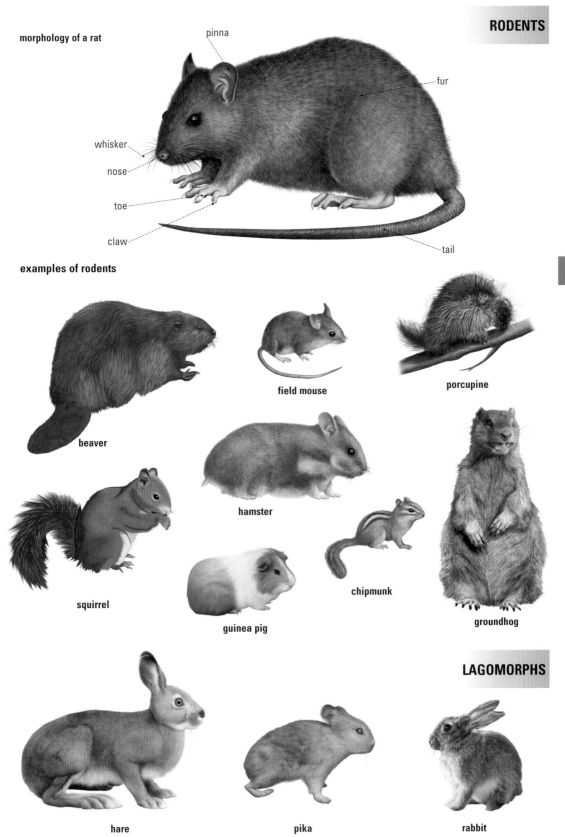

RODENTS

morphology of a rat

pinna

fur

whisker

nose

toe

claw

tail

examples of rodents

field mouse

porcupine

beaver

hamster

squirrel

guinea pig

chipmunk

groundhog

LAGOMORPHS

hare

pika

rabbit

ANIMAL KINGDOM

CARNIVOROUS MAMMALS (DOG)

ANIMAL KINGDOM

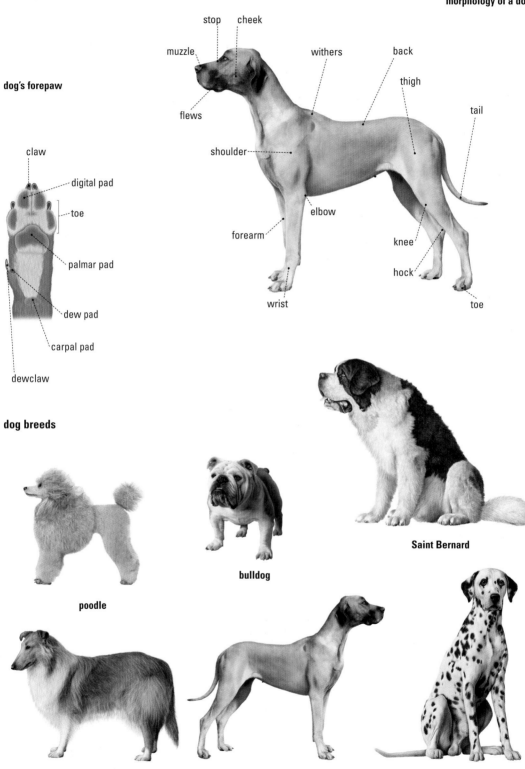

morphology of a dog

stop
cheek
muzzle
withers
back
thigh
tail
flews
shoulder
elbow
forearm
knee
hock
wrist
toe

dog's forepaw

claw
digital pad
toe
palmar pad
dew pad
carpal pad
dewclaw

dog breeds

poodle

bulldog

Saint Bernard

collie

Great Dane

Dalmatian

CARNIVOROUS MAMMALS (CAT)

morphology of a cat

head

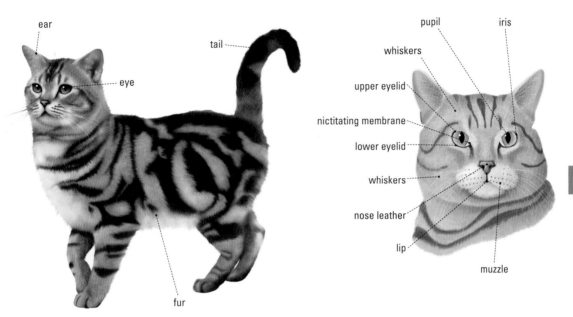

ear

tail

eye

fur

pupil

iris

whiskers

upper eyelid

nictitating membrane

lower eyelid

whiskers

nose leather

lip

muzzle

cat breeds

Abyssinian

Manx

Maine coon

Persian

American shorthair

Siamese

EXAMPLES OF CARNIVOROUS MAMMALS

badger

river otter

weasel

mongoose

mink

hyena

fennec

raccoon

wolf

fox

skunk

black bear

polar bear

jaguar

lynx

leopard

lion

tiger

cheetah

FLYING MAMMALS

morphology of a bat

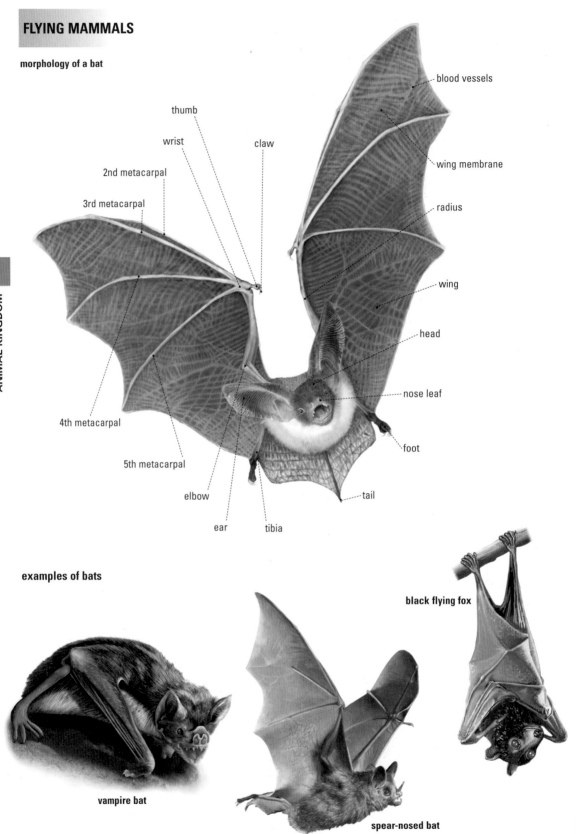

blood vessels

thumb

wrist

claw

wing membrane

2nd metacarpal

radius

3rd metacarpal

wing

head

nose leaf

4th metacarpal

foot

5th metacarpal

elbow

tail

ear

tibia

examples of bats

black flying fox

vampire bat

spear-nosed bat

PRIMATE MAMMALS

morphology of a gorilla

face

fur

arm

hand

prehensile digit

leg

foot

opposable thumb

examples of primates

lemur

orangutan

gibbon

baboon

macaque

chimpanzee

UNGULATE MAMMALS

morphology of a horse

horse's hoof

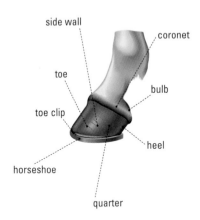

side wall

coronet

toe

bulb

toe clip

heel

horseshoe

quarter

horseshoe

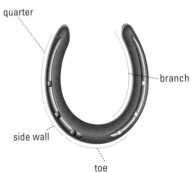

quarter

branch

side wall

toe

flank

loin

back

croup

tail

thigh

stifle

gaskin

belly

hock

fetlock

cannon

fetlock joint

pastern

coronet

hoof

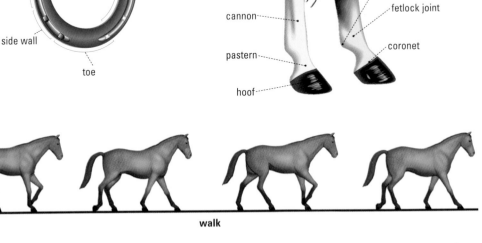

gaits

walk

trot

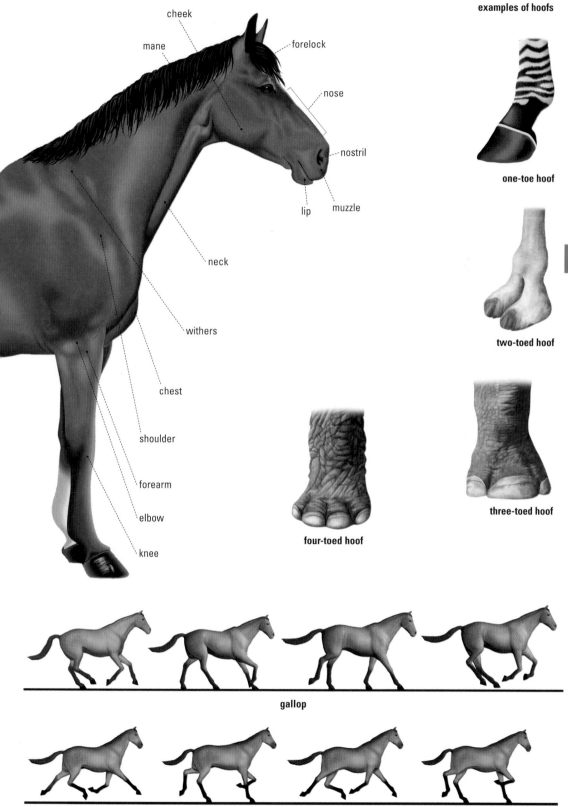

cheek

mane

forelock

nose

nostril

lip   muzzle

neck

withers

chest

shoulder

forearm

elbow

knee

examples of hoofs

one-toe hoof

two-toed hoof

three-toed hoof

four-toed hoof

gallop

pace

examples of ungulate mammals

pig

cow

yak

bison

white-tailed deer

mouflon

goat

sheep

rhinoceros

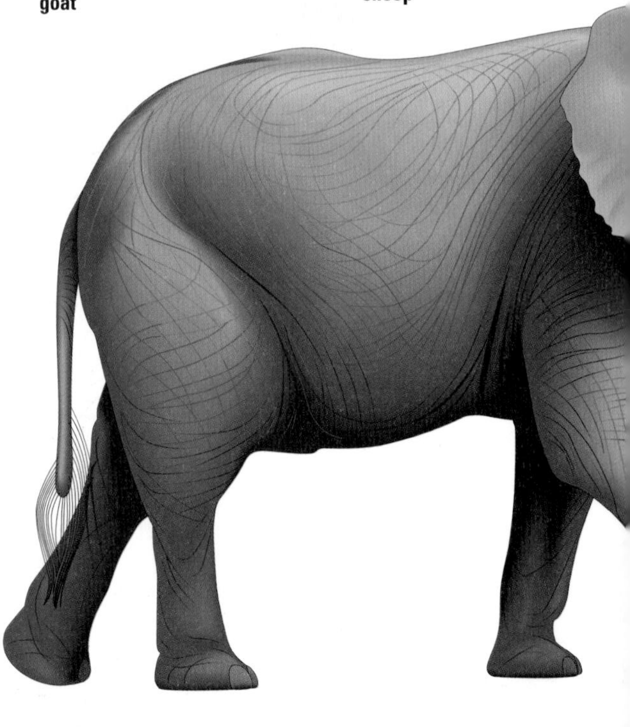

dromedary camel

bactrian camel

donkey

zebra

llama

hippopotamus

giraffe

elephant

okapi

87

MARINE MAMMALS

morphology of a dolphin

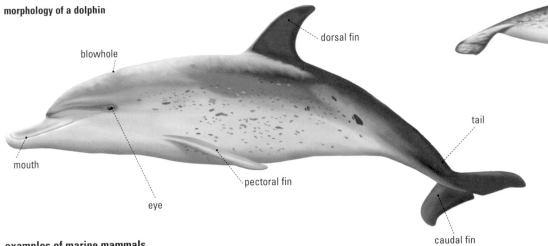

- dorsal fin
- blowhole
- tail
- mouth
- pectoral fin
- eye
- caudal fin

examples of marine mammals

seal

sea lion

walrus

northern right whale

narwhal

dolphin

porpoise

humpback whale

beluga whale

killer whale

sperm whale

Like the body of most animals, that of humans presents a bilateral symmetry. This means that most parts are duplicated on both the left and the right sides of the body. Even if they are based on the same model, every body is unique. The shape, height, and proportions of the human body vary greatly from one individual to another.

body (anterior view)

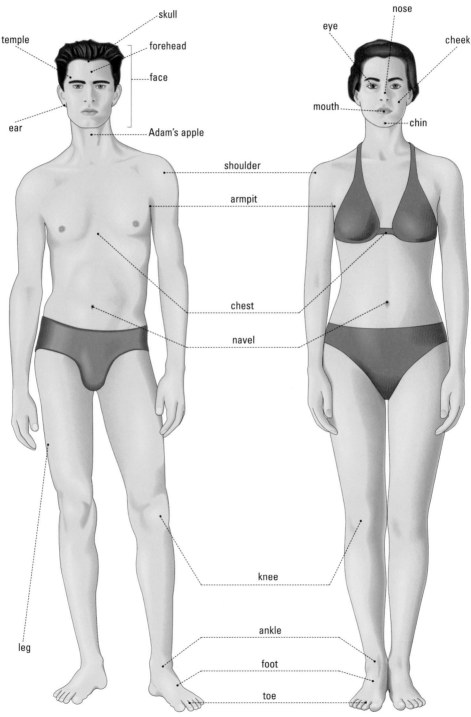

skull

temple

forehead

face

ear

Adam's apple

nose

eye

cheek

mouth

chin

shoulder

armpit

chest

navel

knee

ankle

leg

foot

toe

body (posterior view)

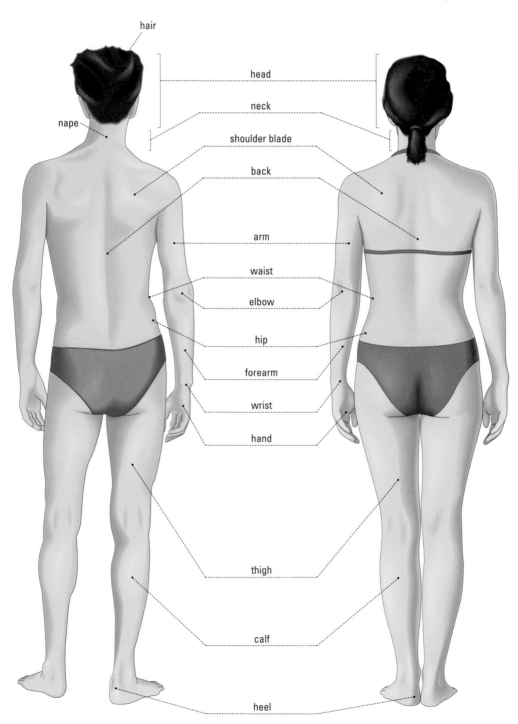

hair

head

neck

nape

shoulder blade

back

arm

waist

elbow

hip

forearm

wrist

hand

thigh

calf

heel

SKELETON

The skeleton is the framework of the body. Its 206 bones support and protect the organs. The bones of the skull, for example, protect the brain. The skeleton has three types of bones, categorized according to their form: short, long, and flat. Most bones are linked together by joints. With the help of the muscles that put them into action, bones allow the body to remain standing and to move about.

principal bones

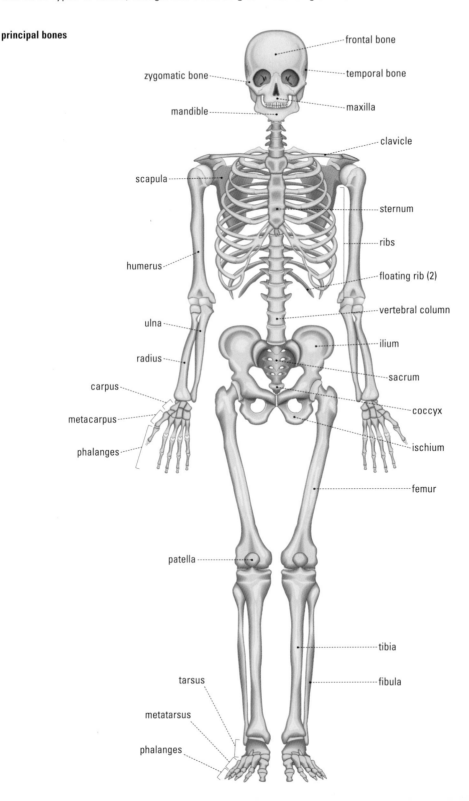

- frontal bone
- temporal bone
- zygomatic bone
- maxilla
- mandible
- clavicle
- scapula
- sternum
- ribs
- floating rib (2)
- humerus
- vertebral column
- ulna
- ilium
- radius
- sacrum
- carpus
- coccyx
- metacarpus
- ischium
- phalanges
- femur
- patella
- tibia
- tarsus
- fibula
- metatarsus
- phalanges

adult's skull

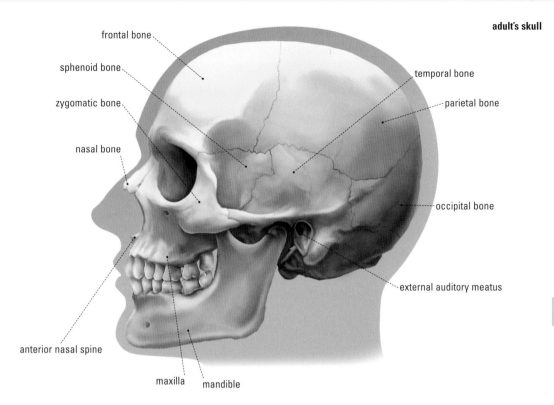

frontal bone

sphenoid bone

zygomatic bone

nasal bone

temporal bone

parietal bone

occipital bone

external auditory meatus

anterior nasal spine

maxilla   mandible

child's skull

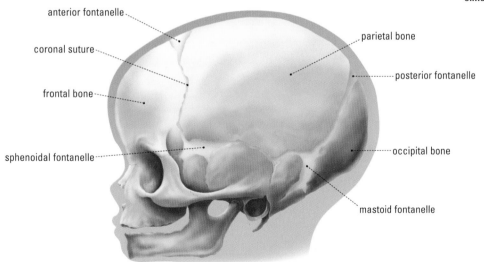

anterior fontanelle

coronal suture

frontal bone

sphenoidal fontanelle

parietal bone

posterior fontanelle

occipital bone

mastoid fontanelle

types of bones

short bone

long bone

flat bone

TEETH

Solidly inserted in the bones of the jaw, teeth play a vital role in chewing, the first step in the process of digestion. Each type of tooth participates in the transformation of food into small pieces that are easy to swallow. The cutting incisors, located at the front of the mouth, slice the food, the pointed canines tear it up, and the large premolars and molars grind it up.

human dentition

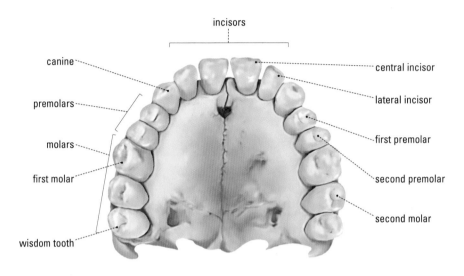

- incisors
- canine
- central incisor
- lateral incisor
- premolars
- molars
- first premolar
- first molar
- second premolar
- second molar
- wisdom tooth

cross-section of a molar

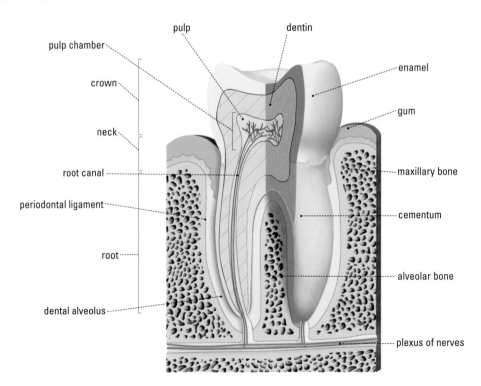

- pulp
- dentin
- pulp chamber
- crown
- enamel
- neck
- gum
- root canal
- maxillary bone
- periodontal ligament
- cementum
- root
- alveolar bone
- dental alveolus
- plexus of nerves

Without muscles, the body would be nothing more than an immobile mass of bones and organs. All the body's movements are produced by skeletal muscles. Under orders from the brain, these muscles contract and lift the bones, thus allowing the body to move. Some muscles, like the 15 or so that go into action when one smiles, do not act on the bones but on the skin.

principal muscles

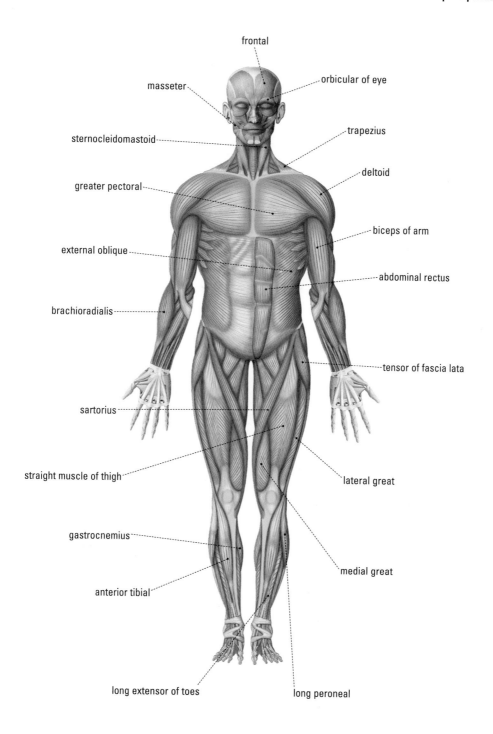

frontal

orbicular of eye

masseter

trapezius

sternocleidomastoid

deltoid

greater pectoral

biceps of arm

external oblique

abdominal rectus

brachioradialis

tensor of fascia lata

sartorius

straight muscle of thigh

lateral great

gastrocnemius

medial great

anterior tibial

long extensor of toes

long peroneal

HUMAN BEING

The human body possesses 11 different systems made up of organs. Although each organ system plays a particular role, they all work together to ensure the body functions correctly. The lungs, one of the organs in the respiratory system, fill the body with oxygen. It is the vessels in the circulatory system, however, that distribute the oxygen to every cell in the body.

DIGESTIVE SYSTEM

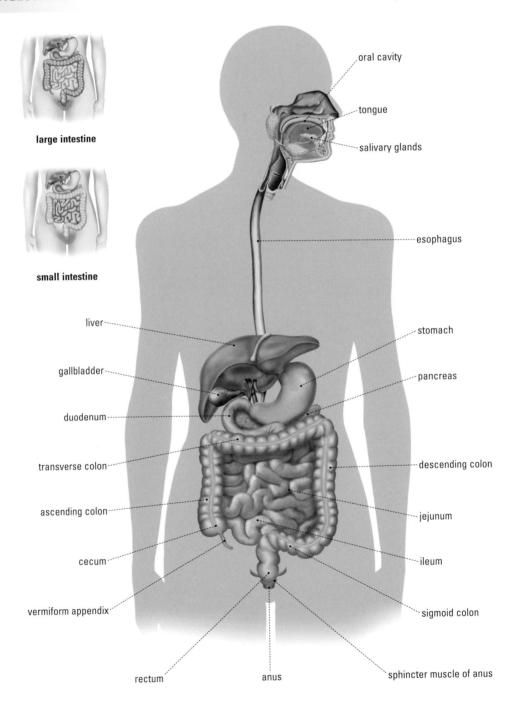

large intestine

small intestine

oral cavity

tongue

salivary glands

esophagus

liver

stomach

gallbladder

pancreas

duodenum

transverse colon

descending colon

ascending colon

jejunum

cecum

ileum

vermiform appendix

sigmoid colon

rectum

anus

sphincter muscle of anus

RESPIRATORY SYSTEM

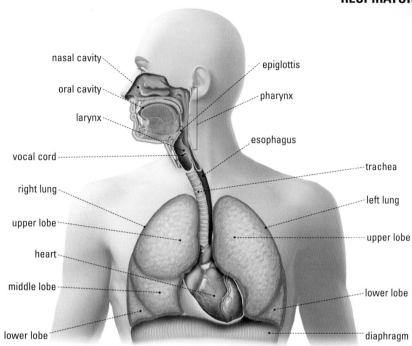

nasal cavity

oral cavity

larynx

vocal cord

right lung

upper lobe

heart

middle lobe

lower lobe

epiglottis

pharynx

esophagus

trachea

left lung

upper lobe

lower lobe

diaphragm

NERVOUS SYSTEM

central nervous system

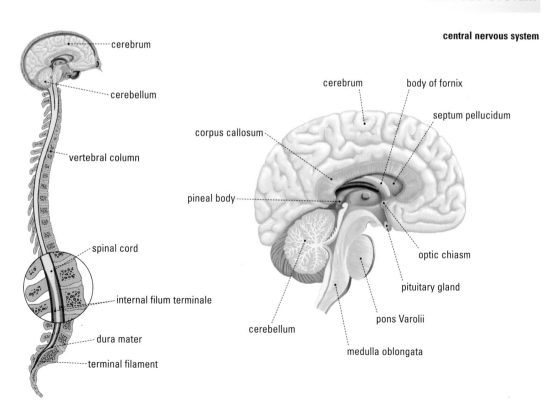

cerebrum

cerebellum

vertebral column

spinal cord

internal filum terminale

dura mater

terminal filament

cerebrum

corpus callosum

pineal body

cerebellum

body of fornix

septum pellucidum

optic chiasm

pituitary gland

pons Varolii

medulla oblongata

CIRCULATORY SYSTEM

heart

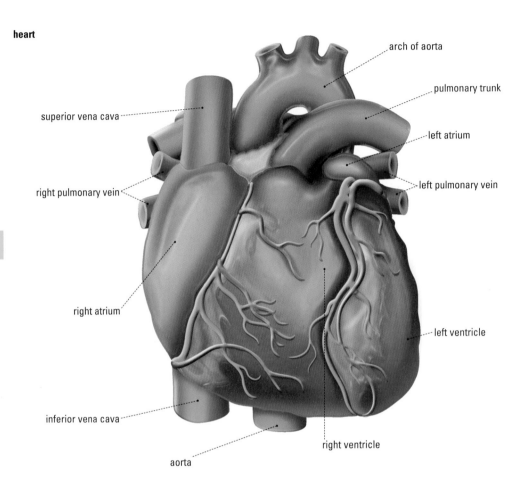

- arch of aorta
- pulmonary trunk
- superior vena cava
- left atrium
- left pulmonary vein
- right pulmonary vein
- right atrium
- left ventricle
- inferior vena cava
- right ventricle
- aorta

composition of blood

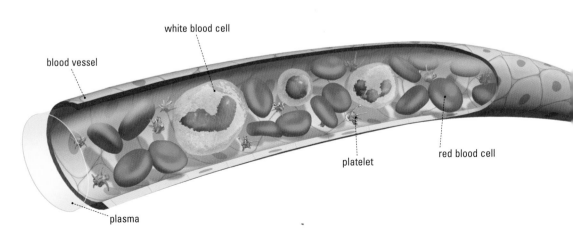

- white blood cell
- blood vessel
- platelet
- red blood cell
- plasma

principal veins and arteries

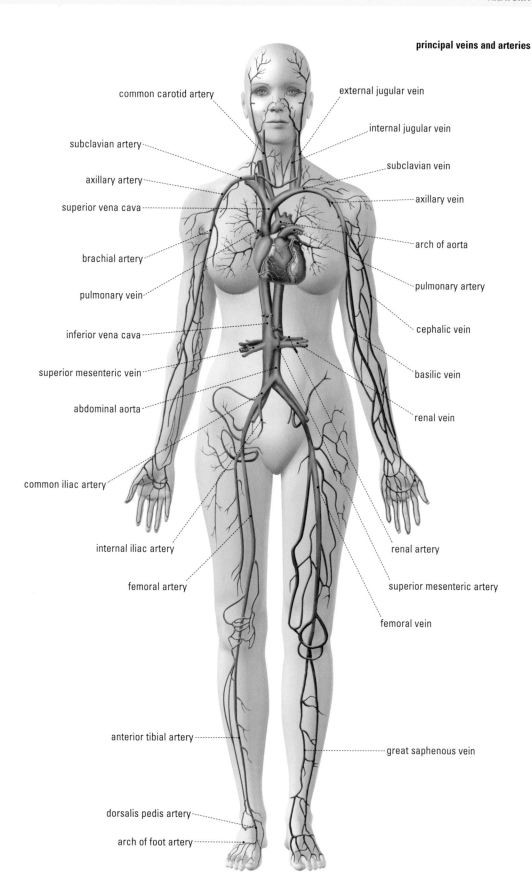

common carotid artery

external jugular vein

internal jugular vein

subclavian artery

subclavian vein

axillary artery

axillary vein

superior vena cava

brachial artery

arch of aorta

pulmonary vein

pulmonary artery

inferior vena cava

cephalic vein

superior mesenteric vein

basilic vein

abdominal aorta

renal vein

common iliac artery

internal iliac artery

renal artery

femoral artery

superior mesenteric artery

femoral vein

anterior tibial artery

great saphenous vein

dorsalis pedis artery

arch of foot artery

SENSE ORGANS

The five senses inform a human being of what is going on around him or her. The sense organs are equipped with special cells called sensory receptors. These cells collect information and transmit it to the nerves, which then send the information to the brain. In translating these signals into sensations like sound, images, or odours, the brain permits the body to react to the world surrounding it.

HEARING

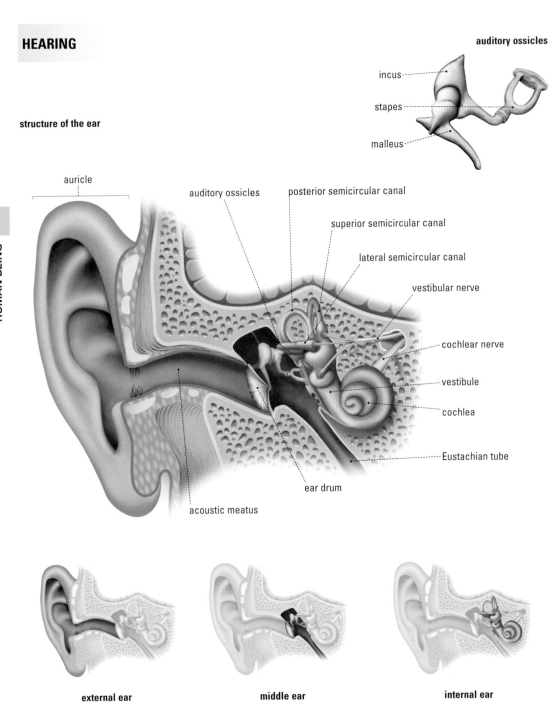

auditory ossicles

incus

stapes

malleus

structure of the ear

auricle

auditory ossicles

posterior semicircular canal

superior semicircular canal

lateral semicircular canal

vestibular nerve

cochlear nerve

vestibule

cochlea

Eustachian tube

ear drum

acoustic meatus

external ear

middle ear

internal ear

TOUCH

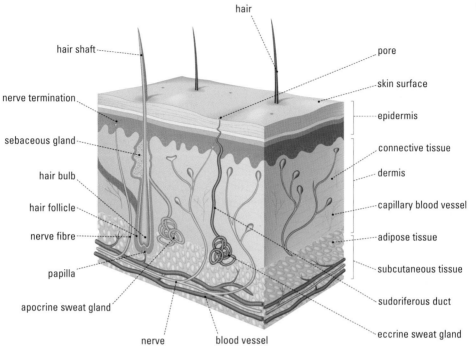

skin

hair

hair shaft

nerve termination

sebaceous gland

hair bulb

hair follicle

nerve fibre

papilla

apocrine sweat gland

nerve   blood vessel

pore

skin surface

epidermis

connective tissue

dermis

capillary blood vessel

adipose tissue

subcutaneous tissue

sudoriferous duct

eccrine sweat gland

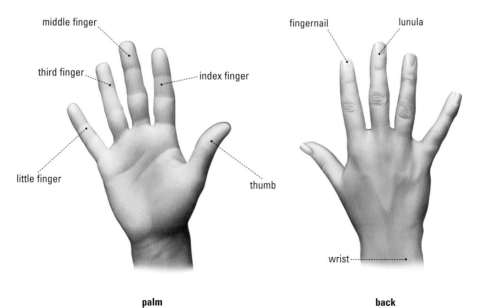

hand

middle finger

third finger

index finger

little finger

thumb

fingernail

lunula

wrist

palm

back

SIGHT

eye

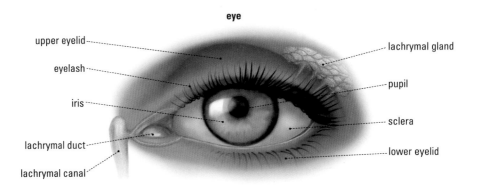

upper eyelid

eyelash

iris

lachrymal duct

lachrymal canal

lachrymal gland

pupil

sclera

lower eyelid

SMELL AND TASTE

external nose

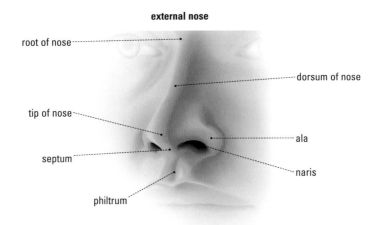

root of nose

tip of nose

septum

philtrum

dorsum of nose

ala

naris

mouth

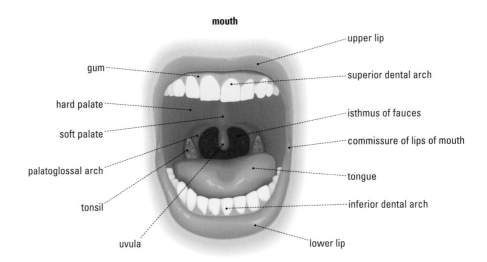

gum

hard palate

soft palate

palatoglossal arch

tonsil

uvula

upper lip

superior dental arch

isthmus of fauces

commissure of lips of mouth

tongue

inferior dental arch

lower lip

Vegetables belong to the group of edible plants included in the human diet. They are classified according to the part of the plant that is eaten. The pepper is considered a fruit vegetable, spinach a leaf vegetable, and asparagus a stalk vegetable. Whether eaten as an accompaniment or as a main dish, vegetables are part of people's diets almost everywhere in the world.

BULB VEGETABLES

cross-section of a bulb

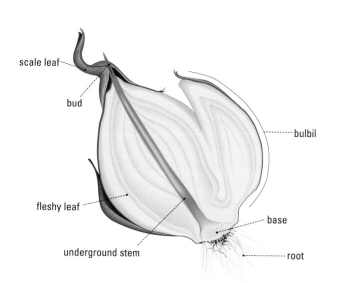

scale leaf

bud

bulbil

fleshy leaf

base

underground stem

root

FOOD

EXAMPLES OF BULB VEGETABLES

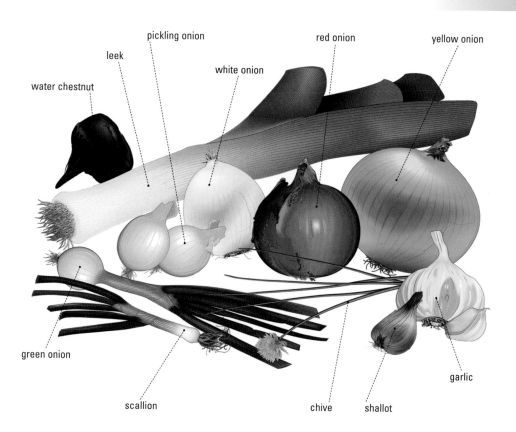

pickling onion

red onion

yellow onion

leek

white onion

water chestnut

green onion

scallion

chive

shallot

garlic

TUBER VEGETABLES

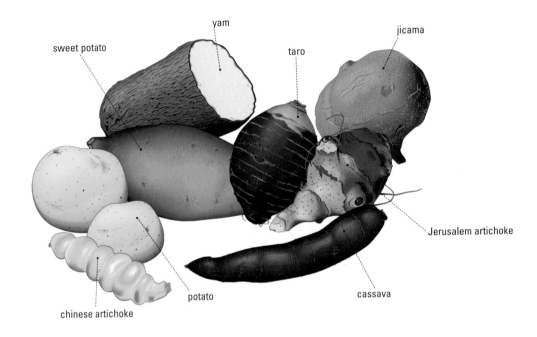

yam

sweet potato

taro

jicama

Jerusalem artichoke

potato

cassava

chinese artichoke

ROOT VEGETABLES

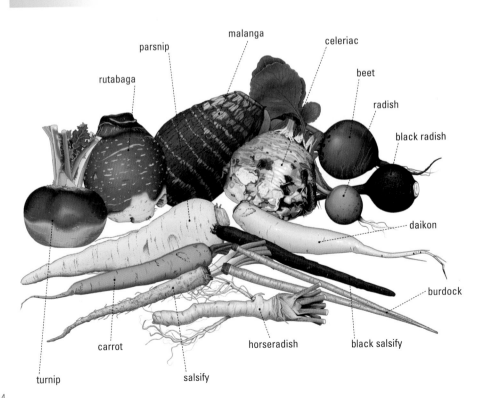

malanga

parsnip

celeriac

rutabaga

beet

radish

black radish

daikon

burdock

carrot

horseradish

black salsify

turnip

salsify

STALK VEGETABLES

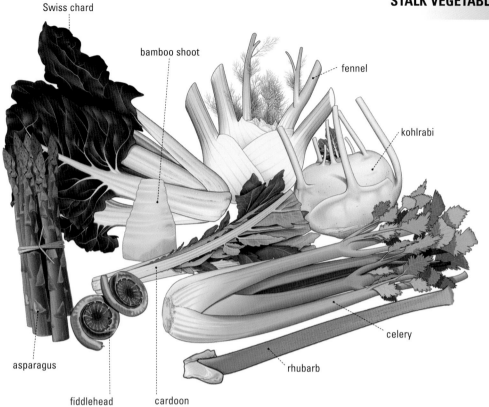

Swiss chard

bamboo shoot

fennel

kohlrabi

asparagus

fiddlehead

cardoon

celery

rhubarb

INFLORESCENT VEGETABLES

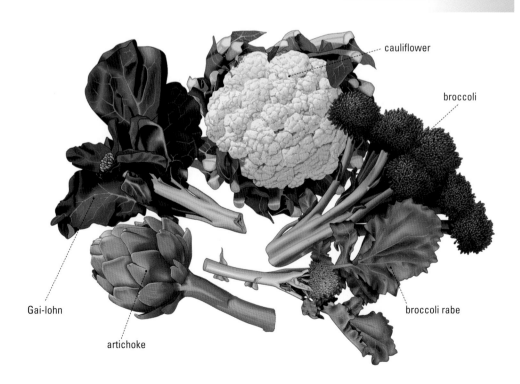

cauliflower

broccoli

Gai-lohn

artichoke

broccoli rabe

LEAF VEGETABLES

red cabbage

green cabbage

savoy cabbage

white cabbage

Belgian endive

pe-tsai

romaine lettuce

bok choy

collards

sea kale

curled kale

curled endive

escarole

radicchio

ornamental kale

iceberg lettuce

leaf lettuce

celtuce

grape leaf

garden cress

Brussels sprouts

garden sorrel

butterhead lettuce

purslane

nettle

watercress

dandelion

spinach

arugula

corn salad

FRUIT VEGETABLES

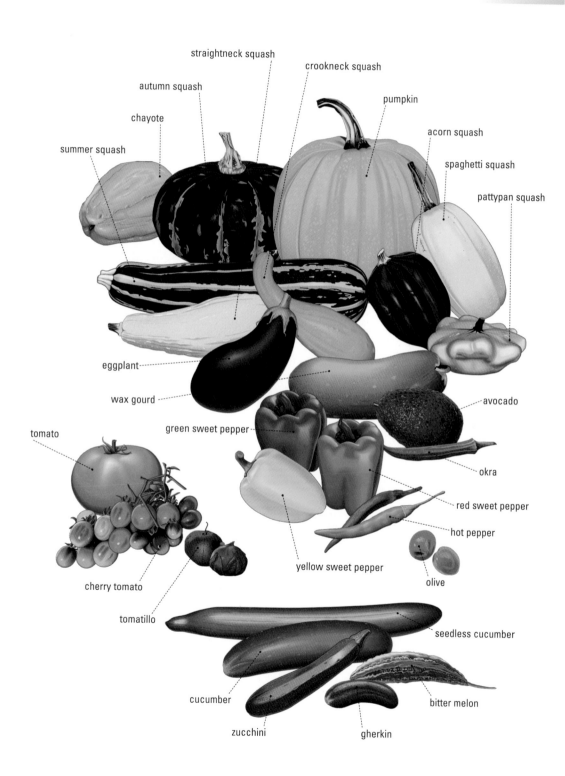

straightneck squash

crookneck squash

autumn squash

pumpkin

chayote

acorn squash

summer squash

spaghetti squash

pattypan squash

eggplant

avocado

wax gourd

green sweet pepper

okra

tomato

red sweet pepper

hot pepper

yellow sweet pepper

olive

cherry tomato

tomatillo

seedless cucumber

cucumber

bitter melon

zucchini

gherkin

FOOD

Approximately 13,000 plant species make up the large family of legumes. These vegetables are distinguished by their pod-shaped fruits, which contain many highly nutritious seeds. Lentils, beans, and peanuts are a few examples of legumes. In many South American countries legumes have long been considered a staple food.

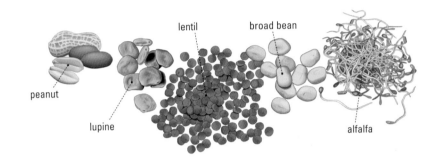

lentil

broad bean

peanut

lupine

alfalfa

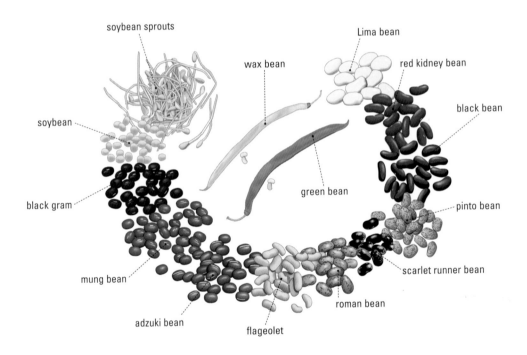

soybean sprouts

Lima bean

wax bean

red kidney bean

soybean

black bean

black gram

green bean

pinto bean

mung bean

scarlet runner bean

adzuki bean

roman bean

flageolet

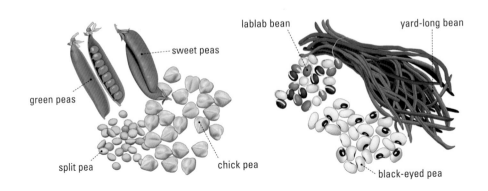

lablab bean

yard-long bean

sweet peas

green peas

split pea

chick pea

black-eyed pea

In the botanical sense, the fruit is the organ that contains small plant embryos, or seeds. This means that olives, nuts, and cucumbers are fruits. Even the inedible samaras of maple trees are fruits. In everyday usage, fruits are considered sweet foods, like apples and cherries, and are usually eaten as a snack or dessert.

BERRIES

cross-section of a strawberry

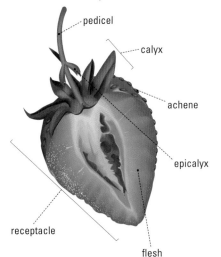

pedicel

calyx

achene

epicalyx

receptacle

flesh

cross-section of a grape

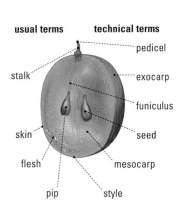

usual terms   technical terms

pedicel

stalk

exocarp

funiculus

skin

seed

flesh

mesocarp

pip

style

FOOD

EXAMPLES OF BERRIES

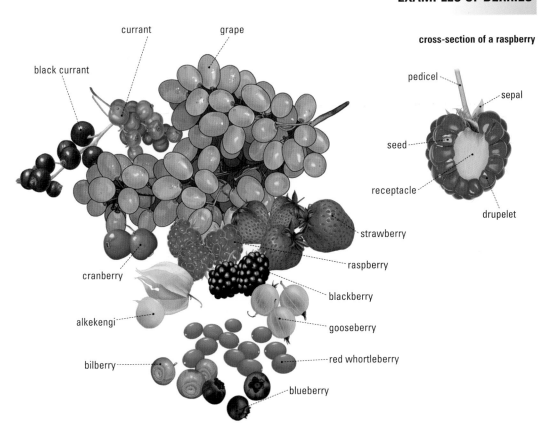

currant

grape

black currant

cranberry

alkekengi

bilberry

strawberry

raspberry

blackberry

gooseberry

red whortleberry

blueberry

cross-section of a raspberry

pedicel

sepal

seed

receptacle

drupelet

STONE FRUITS

cross-section of a peach

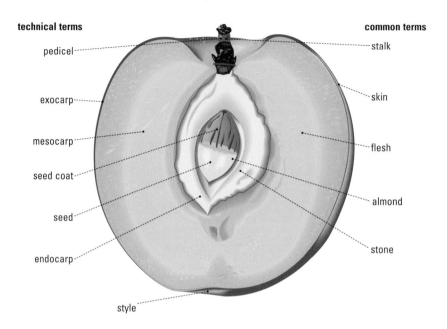

technical terms

pedicel

exocarp

mesocarp

seed coat

seed

endocarp

style

common terms

stalk

skin

flesh

almond

stone

EXAMPLES OF STONE FRUITS

date

nectarine

peach

plum

cherry

apricot

FOOD

POME FRUITS

cross-section of an apple

technical terms

common terms

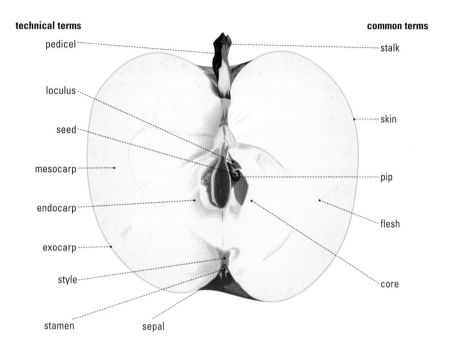

pedicel

stalk

loculus

skin

seed

mesocarp

pip

endocarp

flesh

exocarp

style

core

stamen

sepal

EXAMPLES OF POME FRUITS

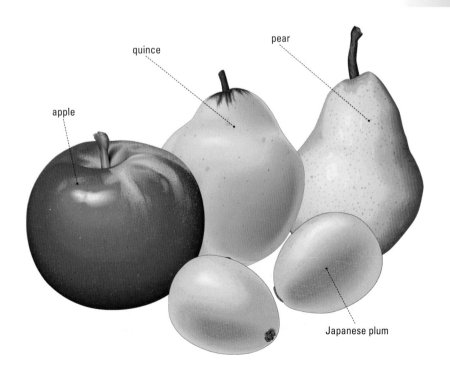

quince

pear

apple

Japanese plum

CITRUS FRUITS

cross-section of an orange

technical terms

common terms

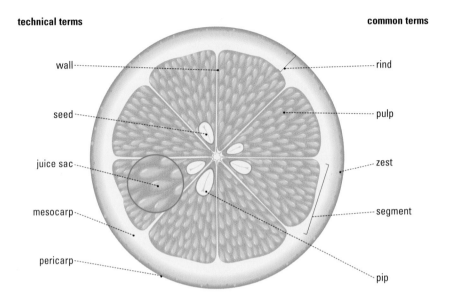

wall

seed

juice sac

mesocarp

pericarp

rind

pulp

zest

segment

pip

EXAMPLES OF CITRUS FRUITS

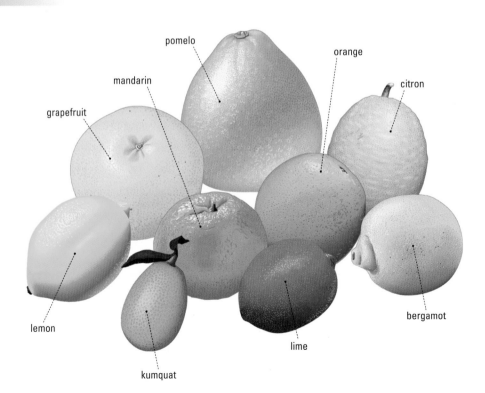

pomelo

orange

mandarin

citron

grapefruit

lemon

kumquat

lime

bergamot

MELONS

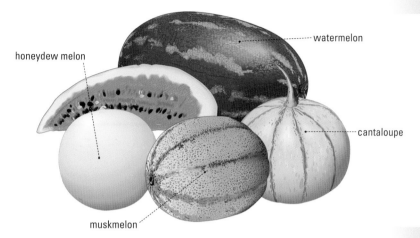

watermelon

honeydew melon

cantaloupe

muskmelon

DRY FRUITS

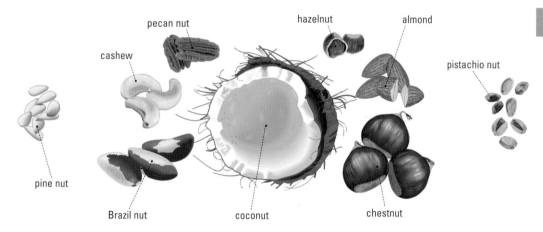

pecan nut

hazelnut

almond

cashew

pistachio nut

pine nut

Brazil nut

coconut

chestnut

TROPICAL FRUITS

pineapple

papaya

mango

pomegranate

kiwi

lychee

carambola

banana

passion fruit

fig

MISCELLANEOUS FOODS

Meals are made up of foods that vary according to the time of day and the part of the world in which they are consumed. Most foods belong to the principal food groups, like fruits and vegetables, cereal products, or dairy products. Because each food provides different nutritional elements to the body, a varied diet is the key to staying healthy.

CEREAL PRODUCTS

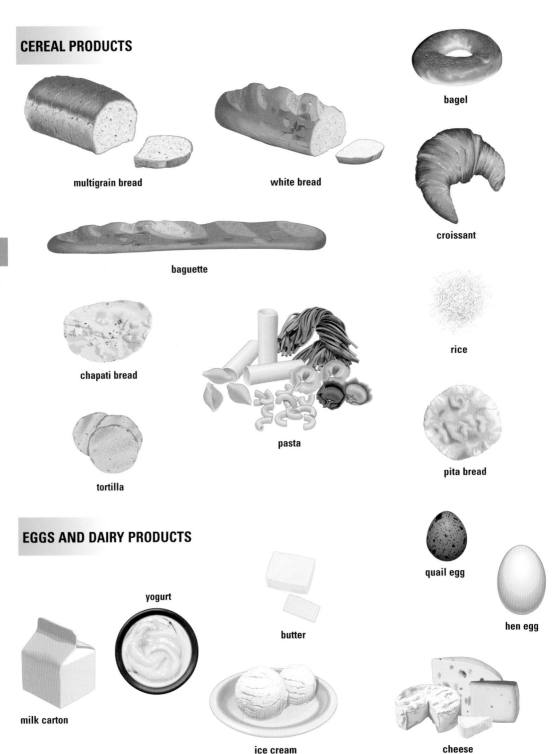

multigrain bread

white bread

bagel

baguette

croissant

chapati bread

pasta

rice

tortilla

pita bread

EGGS AND DAIRY PRODUCTS

quail egg

yogurt

butter

hen egg

milk carton

ice cream

cheese

MEALS

pepperoni

salad

turkey

fish

cooked ham

fish

stew

pizza

steak

spaghetti

sandwich

fruit juice

pie

cookies

cake

baby food

FOOD

Clothing is designed to cover the human body. It is used to protect, hide, warm, or enhance its wearer's appearance. A number of factors determine how people dress: their age, gender, and sometimes occupation. The climate, country, and historical period that a person lives in also play an important role. In developed countries, the clothing industry has a strong influence on many people's seasonal wardrobes.

MEN'S CLOTHING

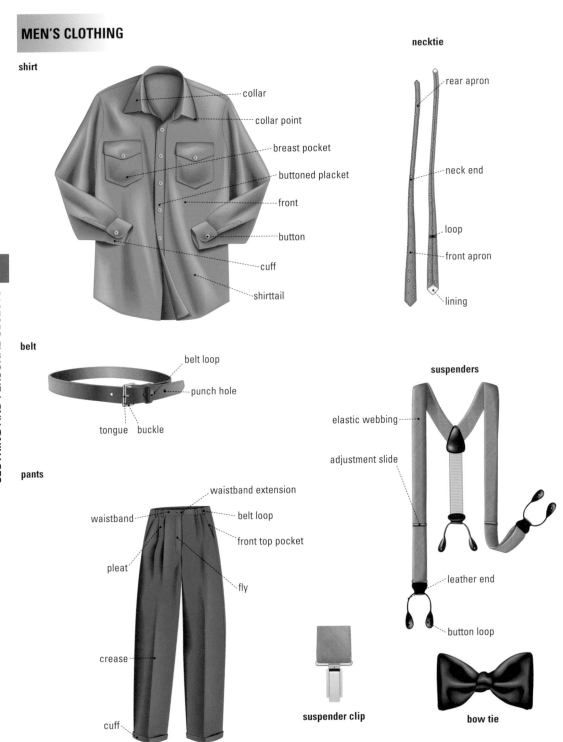

necktie

shirt

- collar
- collar point
- breast pocket
- buttoned placket
- front
- button
- cuff
- shirttail

- rear apron
- neck end
- loop
- front apron
- lining

belt

- belt loop
- punch hole
- tongue
- buckle

suspenders

- elastic webbing
- adjustment slide
- leather end
- button loop

pants

- waistband extension
- waistband
- belt loop
- front top pocket
- pleat
- fly
- crease
- cuff

suspender clip

bow tie

hood

frog

toggle fastening

duffle coat

windbreaker

double-breasted jacket

snap fastener

elastic waistband

raincoat

jacket

single-breasted jacket

MEN'S UNDERWEAR

briefs

waistband

undershirt

fly

elasticized leg opening

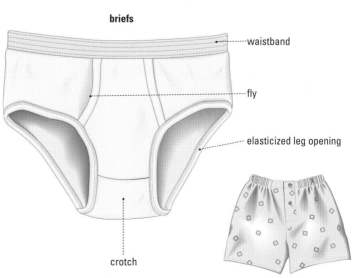

crotch

long underwear

boxer shorts

WOMEN'S CLOTHING

suit

jacket

pea jacket

cape

skirt

polo dress

poncho

princess dress

blouse

ski pants

straight skirt

sarong

pleated skirt

overcoat

pyjamas

bathrobe

culottes

hose

pantyhose

ankle sock

sock

stocking

WOMEN'S UNDERWEAR

shoulder strap

cup

midriff band

bra

half-slip

body suit

briefs

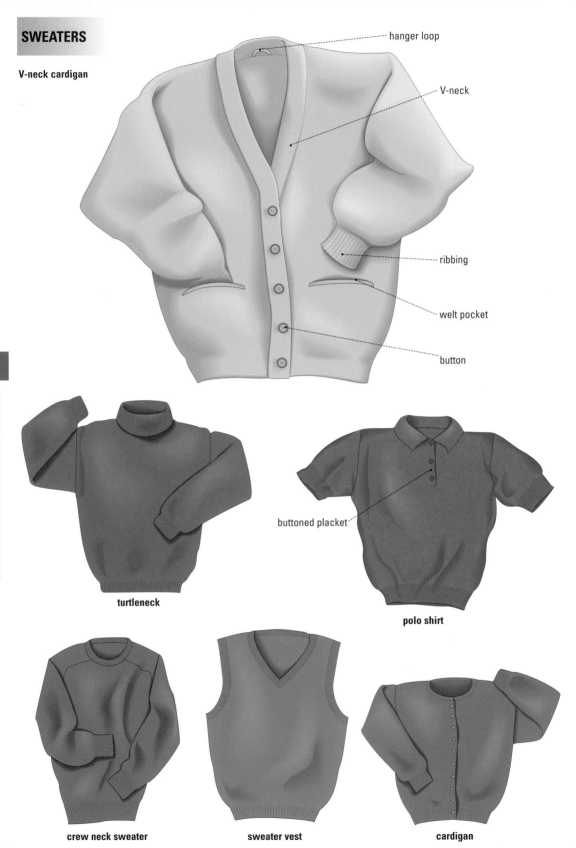

SWEATERS

V-neck cardigan

hanger loop

V-neck

ribbing

welt pocket

button

buttoned placket

turtleneck

polo shirt

crew neck sweater

sweater vest

cardigan

CHILDREN'S CLOTHING

T-shirt dress

jumpsuit

jeans

shorts

pyjamas

bunting bag

overalls

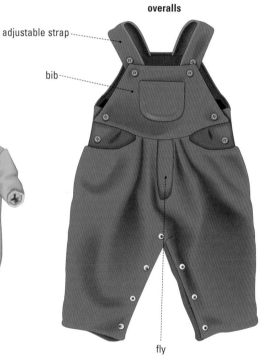

adjustable strap

bib

fly

drawstring hood

fly front closing

snowsuit

rompers

sleepers

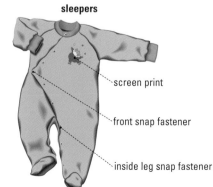

screen print

front snap fastener

inside leg snap fastener

CLOTHING AND PERSONAL OBJECTS

SPORTSWEAR

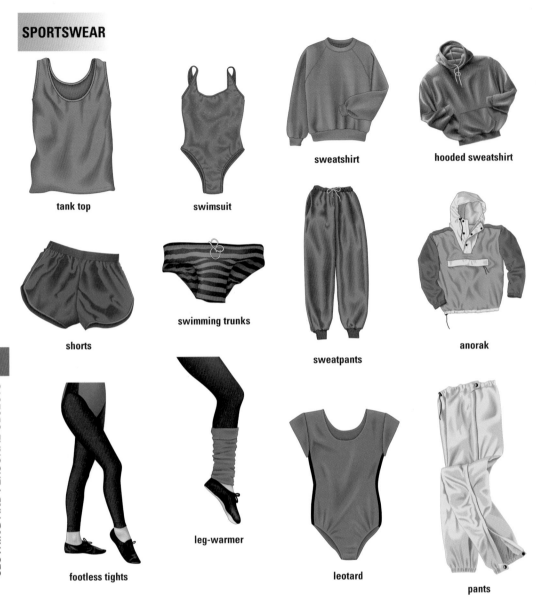

tank top

swimsuit

sweatshirt

hooded sweatshirt

shorts

swimming trunks

sweatpants

anorak

footless tights

leg-warmer

leotard

pants

running shoe

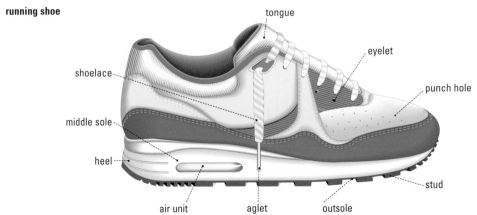

tongue

eyelet

shoelace

punch hole

middle sole

heel

stud

air unit

aglet

outsole

Many accessories have a practical use. A wide-brimmed hat, for example, protects the head from the sun, while a pair of gloves or mittens keeps hands warm. Other accessories, such as a belt and matching handbag, serve to complete an outfit in a visually pleasing way. Added to these accessories is a multitude of practical objects used daily in the care of the body.

MEN'S GLOVES

back of a glove

palm of a glove

glove finger

thumb

palm

mitten

stitching

snap fastener

driving glove

WOMEN'S GLOVES

wrist-length glove

short glove

gauntlet

evening glove

mitt

gauntlet

HEADGEAR

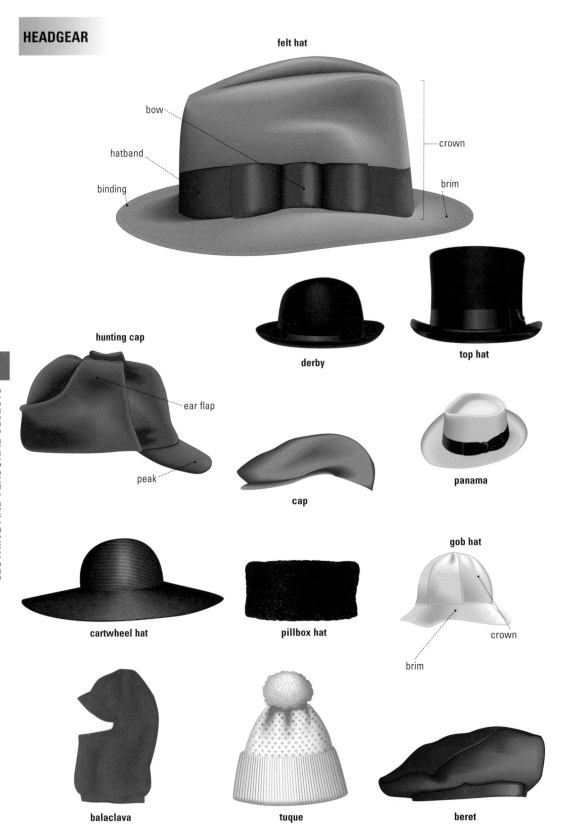

felt hat

bow

hatband

binding

crown

brim

derby

top hat

hunting cap

ear flap

peak

cap

panama

cartwheel hat

pillbox hat

gob hat

crown

brim

balaclava

tuque

beret

SHOES

parts of a shoe

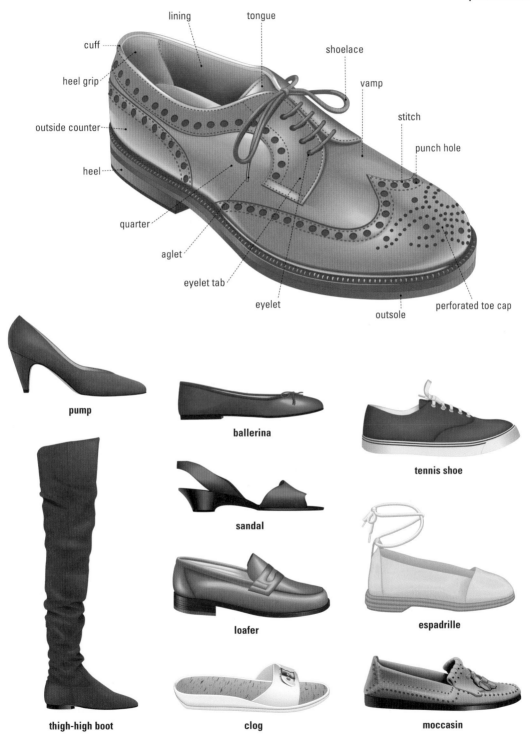

lining

tongue

cuff

shoelace

heel grip

vamp

outside counter

stitch

punch hole

heel

quarter

aglet

eyelet tab

eyelet

outsole

perforated toe cap

pump

ballerina

tennis shoe

sandal

loafer

espadrille

thigh-high boot

clog

moccasin

LEATHER GOODS

attaché case

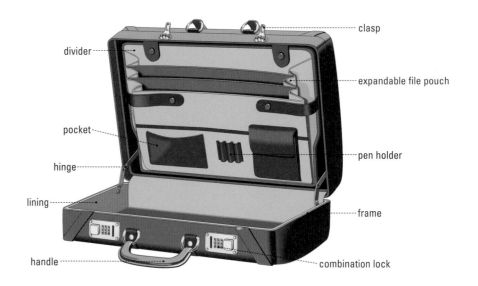

divider · · · · · clasp

· · · · · expandable file pouch

pocket · · · · ·

pen holder

hinge · · · · ·

lining · · · · · frame

handle · · · · · combination lock

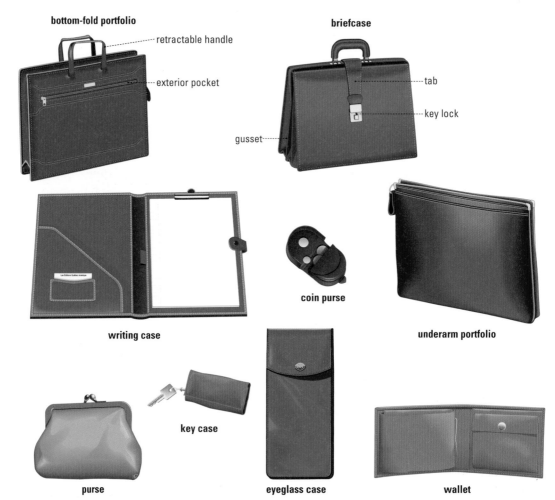

bottom-fold portfolio

retractable handle

exterior pocket

briefcase

tab

key lock

gusset

writing case

coin purse

underarm portfolio

purse

key case

eyeglass case

wallet

LUGGAGE AND HANDBAGS

latch

hasp

trunk

tray

handle

cornerpiece

fittings

zipper

garment bag

suitcase

handle

frame

pull strap

buckle

shoulder strap

wheel

trim

identification tag

shoulder bag

carrier bag

eyelet

drawstring

front pocket

drawstring bag

men's bag

drawstring bag

EYEGLASSES

eyeglass parts

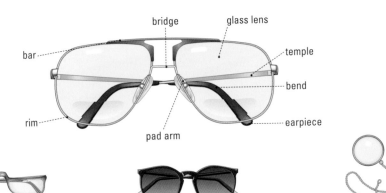

bridge

glass lens

bar

temple

bend

rim

earpiece

pad arm

half-glasses

sunglasses

monocle

UMBRELLA AND WALKING STICK

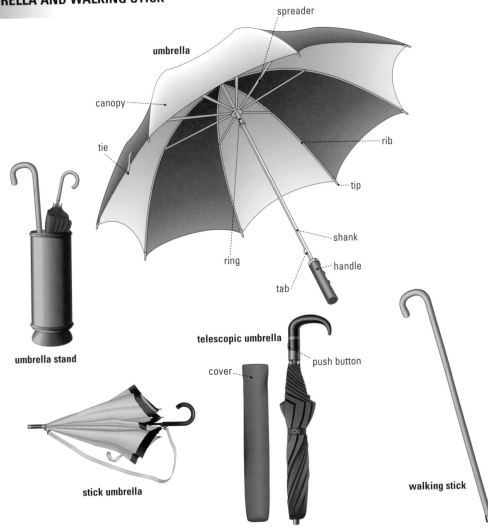

spreader

umbrella

canopy

rib

tie

tip

shank

ring

handle

tab

umbrella stand

telescopic umbrella

push button

cover

stick umbrella

walking stick

hoop earrings

band ring

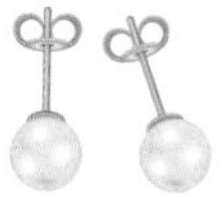

pierced earrings

JEWELLERY

stone

setting

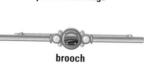

claw

bezel

locket

brooch

rope

charm bracelet

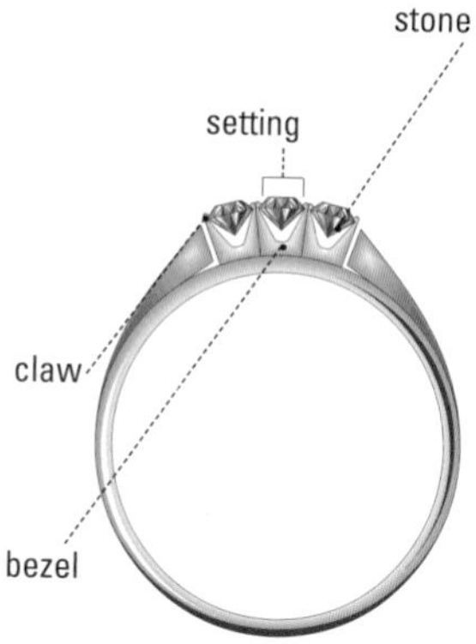

parts of a ring

bangle

matinee-length necklace

pendant

signet ring

semiprecious stones

amethyst

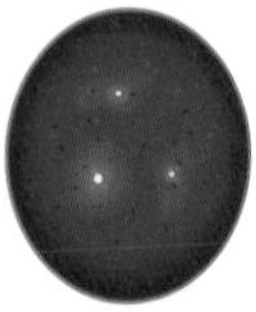

lapis lazuli

aquamarine

topaz

tourmaline

opal

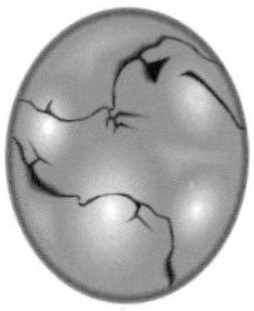

turquoise

garnet

precious stones

emerald

sapphire

diamond

ruby

HAIRDRESSING

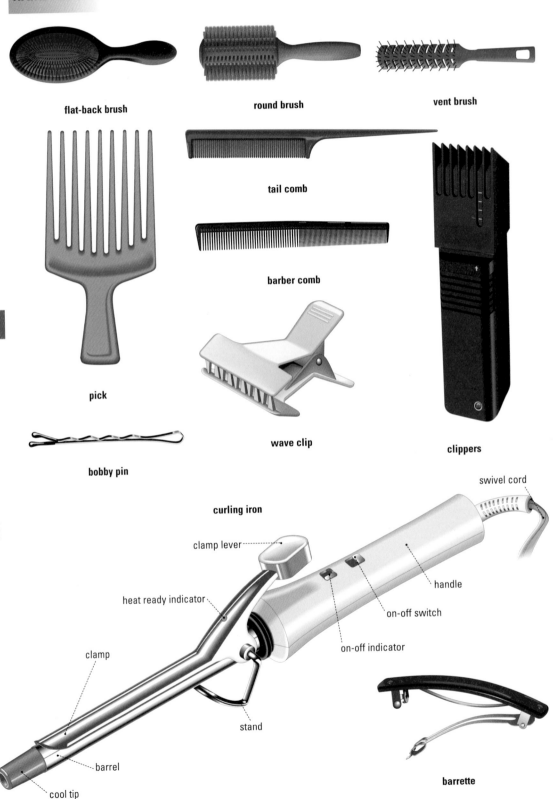

flat-back brush

round brush

vent brush

tail comb

barber comb

pick

wave clip

clippers

bobby pin

curling iron

swivel cord

clamp lever

heat ready indicator

handle

clamp

on-off switch

on-off indicator

stand

barrel

cool tip

barrette

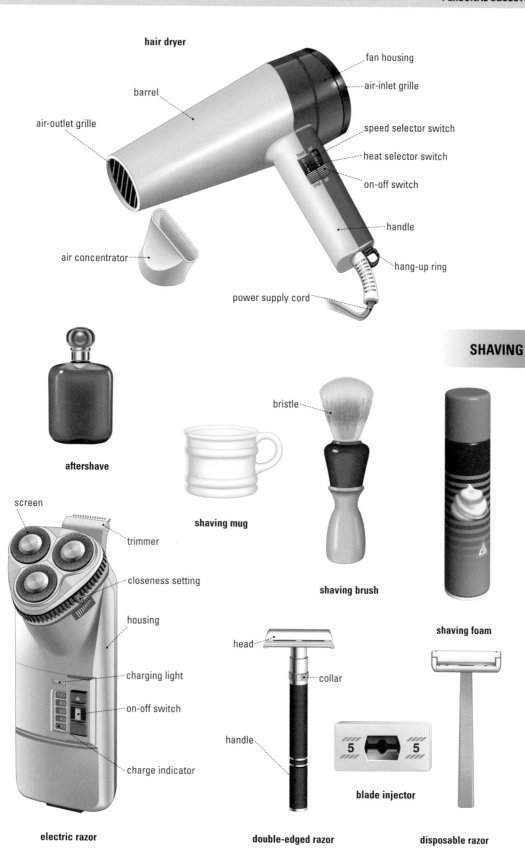

hair dryer

fan housing

air-inlet grille

barrel

air-outlet grille

speed selector switch

heat selector switch

on-off switch

handle

air concentrator

hang-up ring

power supply cord

CLOTHING AND PERSONAL OBJECTS

bristle

aftershave

shaving mug

shaving brush

shaving foam

screen

trimmer

closeness setting

housing

charging light

on-off switch

charge indicator

head

collar

handle

100
80
60
40
20

5   5

blade injector

electric razor

double-edged razor

disposable razor

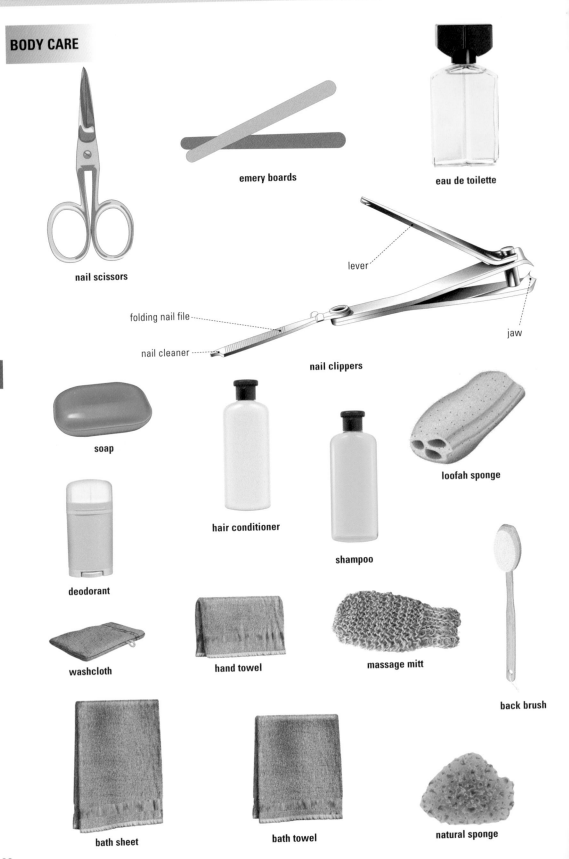

BODY CARE

emery boards

eau de toilette

nail scissors

lever

folding nail file

nail cleaner

jaw

nail clippers

soap

hair conditioner

shampoo

loofah sponge

deodorant

washcloth

hand towel

massage mitt

back brush

bath sheet

bath towel

natural sponge

DENTAL CARE

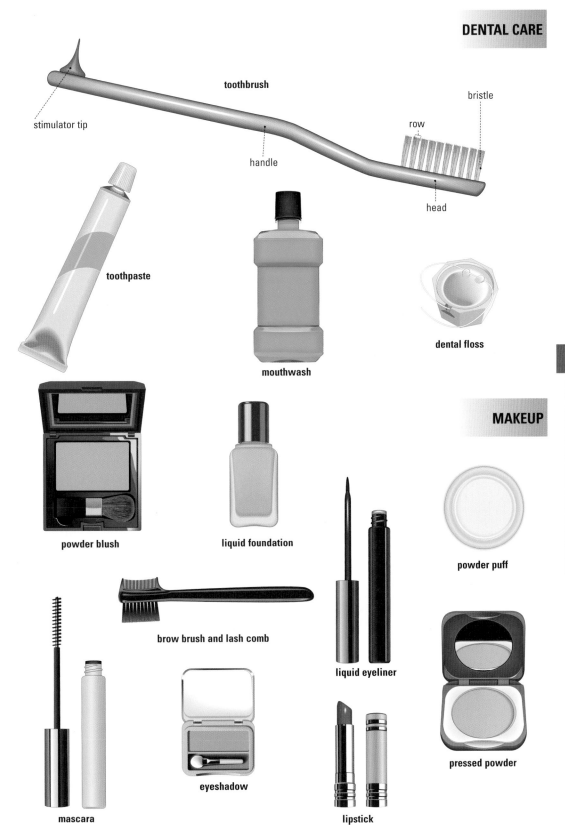

toothbrush

stimulator tip

bristle

row

handle

head

toothpaste

mouthwash

dental floss

MAKEUP

powder blush

liquid foundation

powder puff

brow brush and lash comb

liquid eyeliner

pressed powder

mascara

eyeshadow

lipstick

The materials used to cover the building, the flat or peaked shape of the roof, the addition of a garage, and the number of floors are all factors that help to determine the outside appearance of a house. The surrounding land is also an important part of the overall appearance, whether it consists of a narrow flower bed or is large enough for a swimming pool, a vegetable garden, and a tool shed.

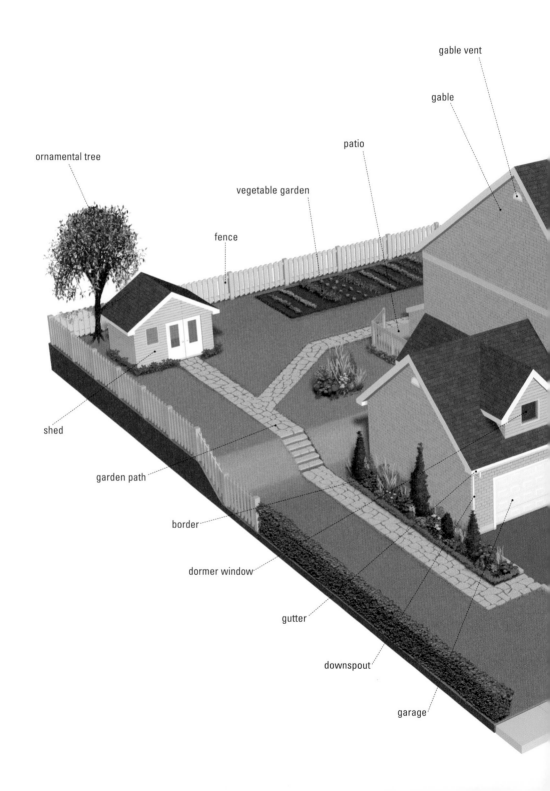

gable vent

gable

patio

ornamental tree

vegetable garden

fence

shed

garden path

border

dormer window

gutter

downspout

garage

above-ground swimming pool

in-ground swimming pool

filter

steps

diving board

lightning rod

chimney

roof

cornice

skylight

steps

site plan

hedge

lawn

basement window

flower bed

sidewalk

porch

driveway

ELEMENTS OF A HOUSE

Whether constructed of wood, brick, or straw, every house is made up of basic elements like a roof and walls. Some walls have a door cut into them to allow people to enter or exit the house. Openings like windows are made to allow light and fresh air to enter. Modern houses have many doors and windows in different styles.

DOOR

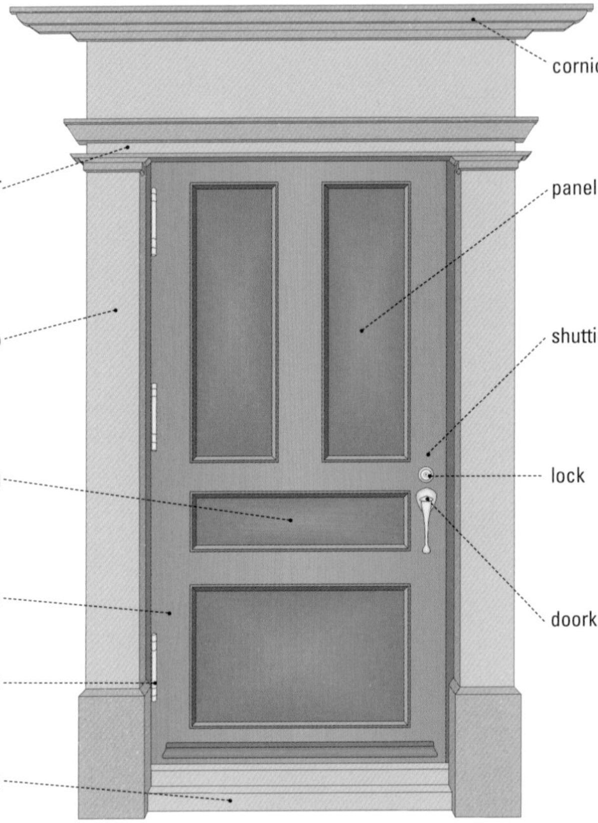

cornice
header
panel
jamb
shutting stile
lock
middle panel
doorknob
hanging stile
hinge
threshold

lock

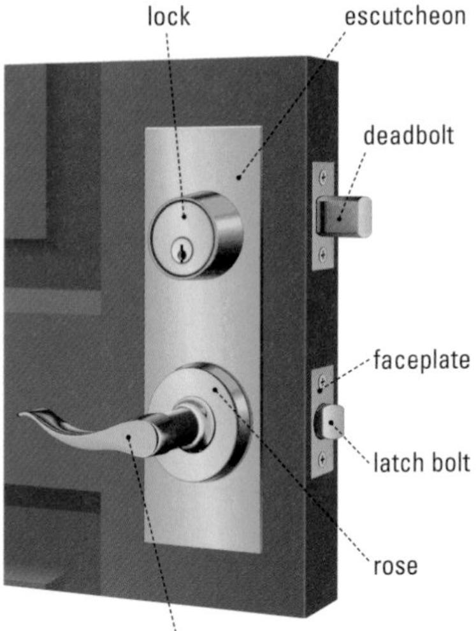

lock
escutcheon
deadbolt
faceplate
latch bolt
rose
doorknob

examples of doors

sliding door

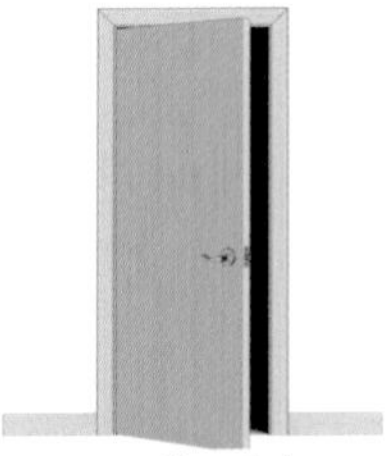

conventional door

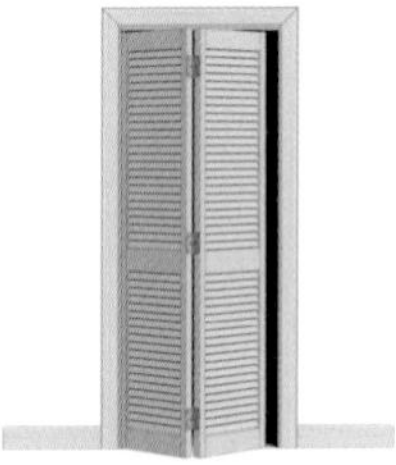

folding door

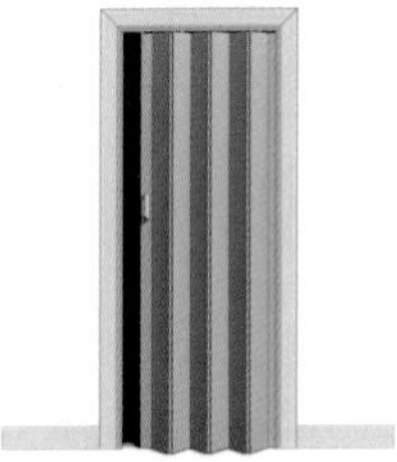

sliding folding door

HOUSE

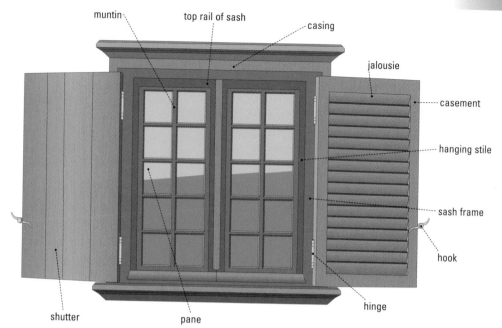

muntin

top rail of sash

casing

jalousie

casement

hanging stile

sash frame

hook

hinge

shutter

pane

HOUSE

examples of windows

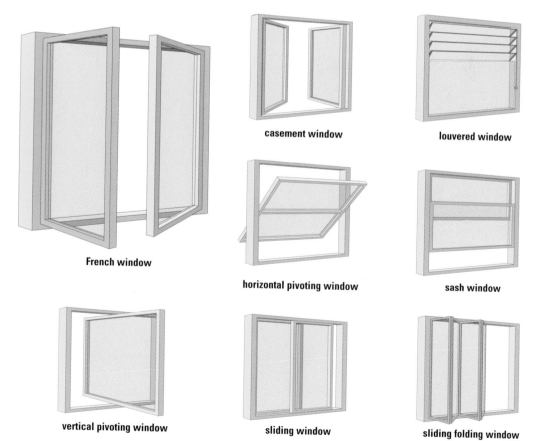

French window

casement window

louvered window

horizontal pivoting window

sash window

vertical pivoting window

sliding window

sliding folding window

MAIN ROOMS

The rooms in a house may all be situated on one level or they may be spread over several floors. The number of rooms can vary a lot from one house to another depending on the needs and the budget of the residents. Most modern houses usually have a kitchen, dining room, living room, bathroom, and at least one bedroom.

ELEVATION

loft

second floor

first floor

basement

FIRST FLOOR

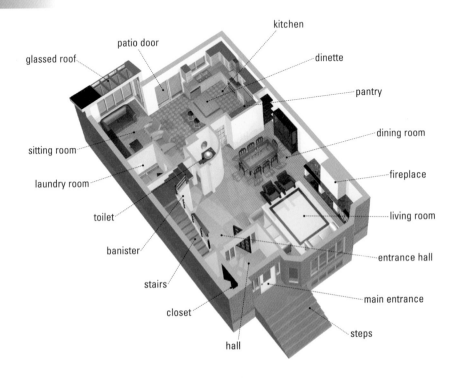

kitchen

patio door

glassed roof

dinette

pantry

dining room

sitting room

fireplace

laundry room

living room

toilet

banister

entrance hall

stairs

main entrance

closet

steps

hall

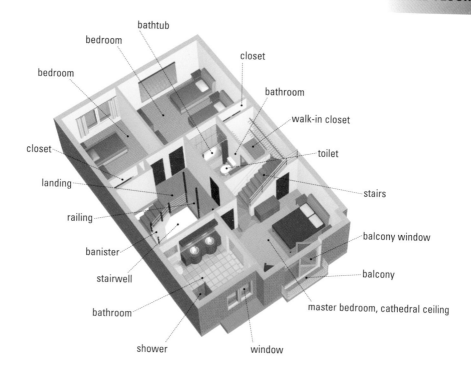

bathtub

bedroom

bedroom

closet

bathroom

walk-in closet

closet

toilet

landing

stairs

railing

banister

balcony window

stairwell

balcony

bathroom

master bedroom, cathedral ceiling

shower

window

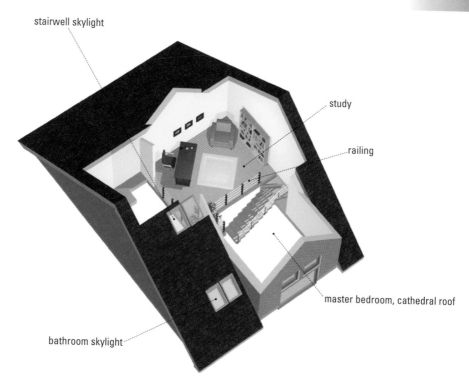

stairwell skylight

study

railing

master bedroom, cathedral roof

bathroom skylight

HOUSE FURNITURE

The furniture in a house consists of movable objects that its occupants use for sitting, lying down, and displaying or storing objects. The type of furniture found in a home reflects the culture of the people living there, the way they live, and the period in history to which they belong. Desert nomads are never burdened by extra furniture. Meanwhile, many people in developing countries are too poor to own furniture.

SEATS, SIDECHAIRS, AND ARMCHAIRS

parts of a sidechair

ear

top rail

cross rail

stile

apron

spindle

rear leg

front leg

back

seat

support

rocking chair

stool

bar stool

armchair

bean bag chair

club chair

love seat

ottoman

bench

sofa

folding chair

chaise longue

HOUSE

140

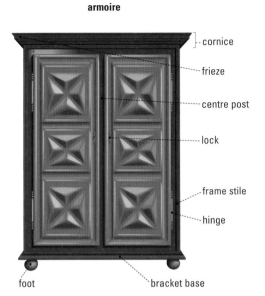

armoire

cornice

frieze

centre post

lock

frame stile

hinge

foot

bracket base

dresser

chiffonier

change table

high chair

back

tray

waist belt

footrest

leg

crib

barrier

headboard

slat

mattress

drawer

caster

booster seat

HOUSE

BED

parts

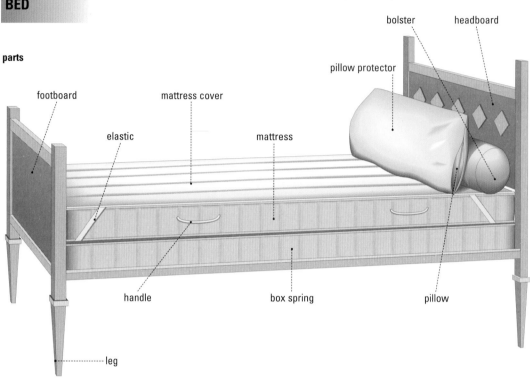

footboard

mattress cover

elastic

mattress

bolster

headboard

pillow protector

handle

box spring

pillow

leg

linen

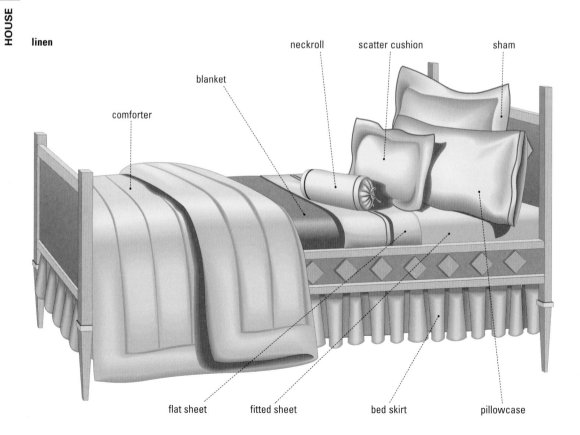

neckroll

scatter cushion

sham

blanket

comforter

flat sheet

fitted sheet

bed skirt

pillowcase

Whether limited to a corner or occupying a vast room, the kitchen is the place where meals are prepared. The modern kitchen is equipped with a refrigerator, stove, and an entire range of small electrical appliances and utensils. Cooks today have a variety of tools at their disposal to help them prepare and cook food in a fast and efficient way.

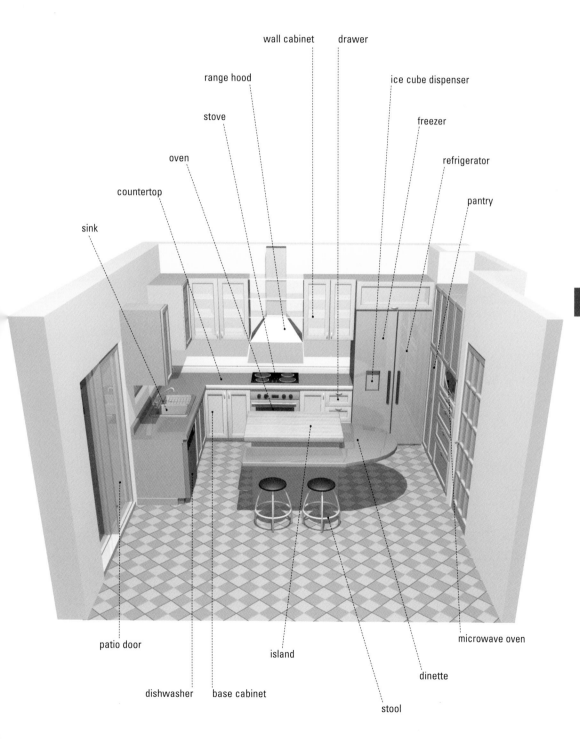

wall cabinet

drawer

range hood

ice cube dispenser

stove

freezer

oven

refrigerator

countertop

pantry

sink

patio door

island

microwave oven

dishwasher

base cabinet

dinette

stool

HOUSE

GLASSWARE

tumbler; glass

burgundy glass

white wine glass

champagne glass

champagne flute

decanter

carafe

beer mug

DINNERWARE

teacup and saucer

demitasse

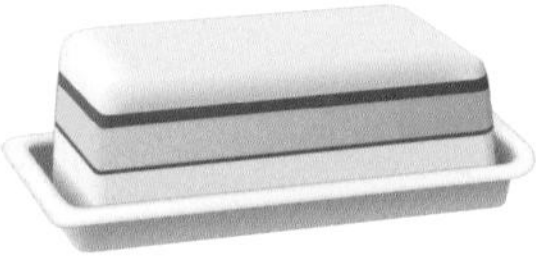

butter dish

sugar bowl

coffee mug

ramekin

creamer

pepper shaker

salt shaker

gravy boat

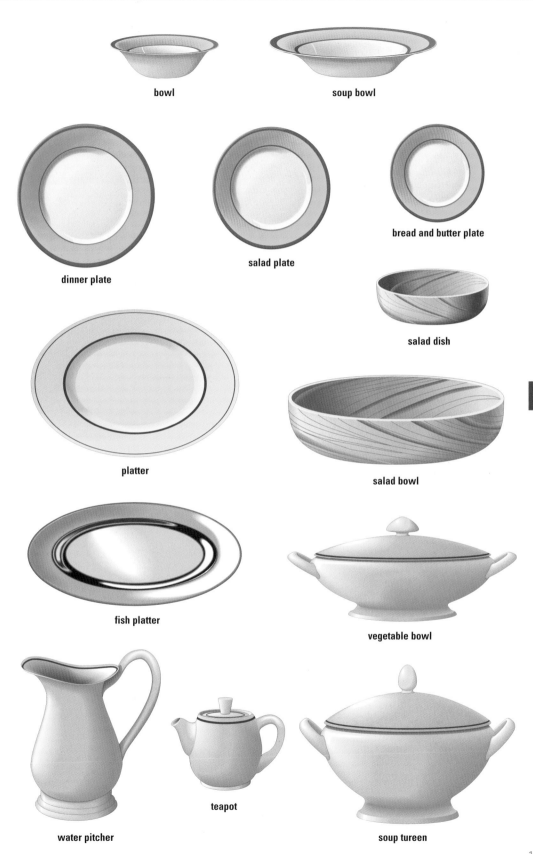

bowl

soup bowl

dinner plate

salad plate

bread and butter plate

salad dish

platter

salad bowl

fish platter

vegetable bowl

water pitcher

teapot

soup tureen

SILVERWARE

butter knife

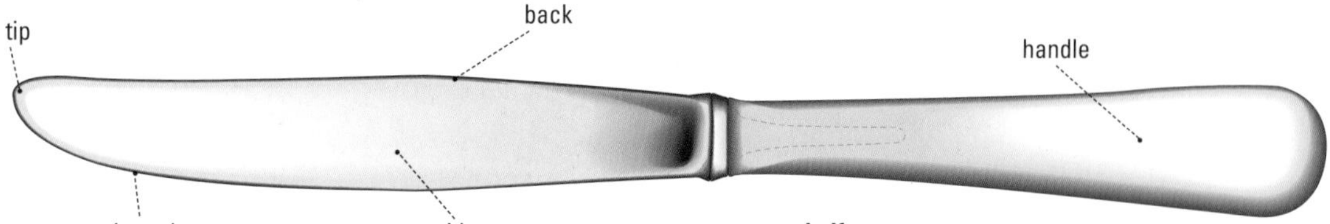

tip

back

handle

cutting edge

side

knife

steak knife

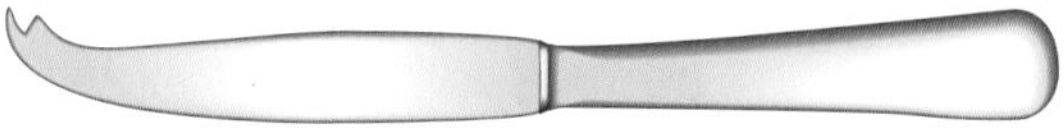

cheese knife

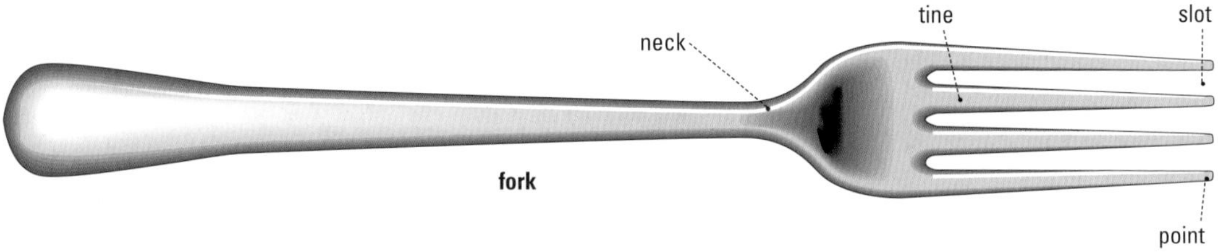

neck

tine

slot

fork

point

fondue fork

spoon

inside

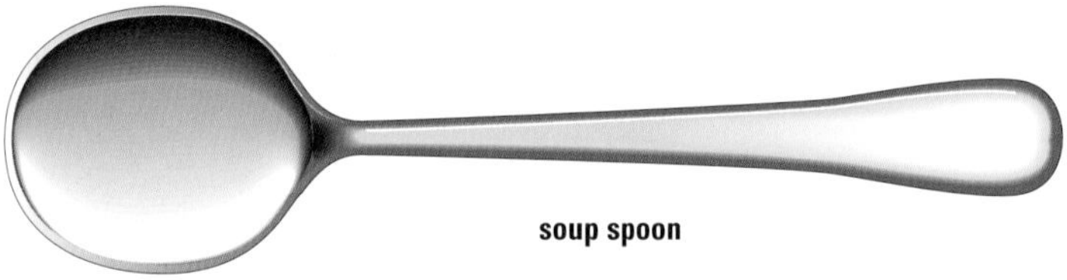

soup spoon

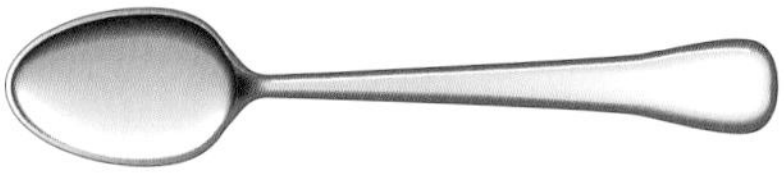

coffee spoon

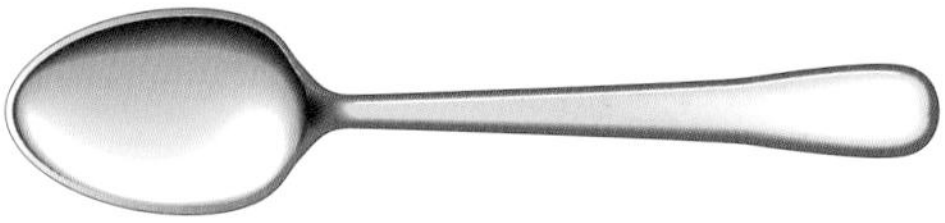

teaspoon

kitchen scale

citrus juicer

grater

salad spinner

colander

apple corer

peeler

melon baller

vegetable brush

can opener

corkscrew

nutcracker

bottle opener

muffin pan

funnel

measuring cup

cookie cutters

measuring spoons

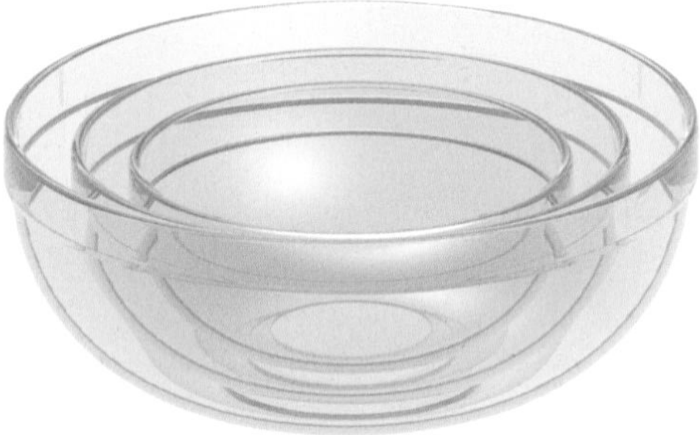

mixing bowls

whisk

egg beater

baster

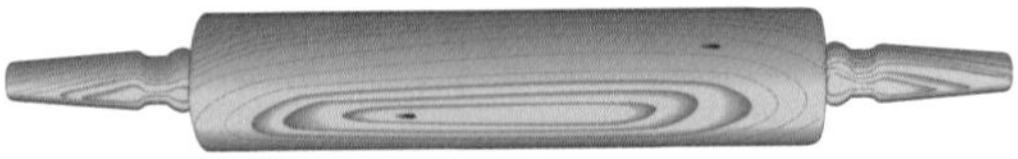

rolling pin

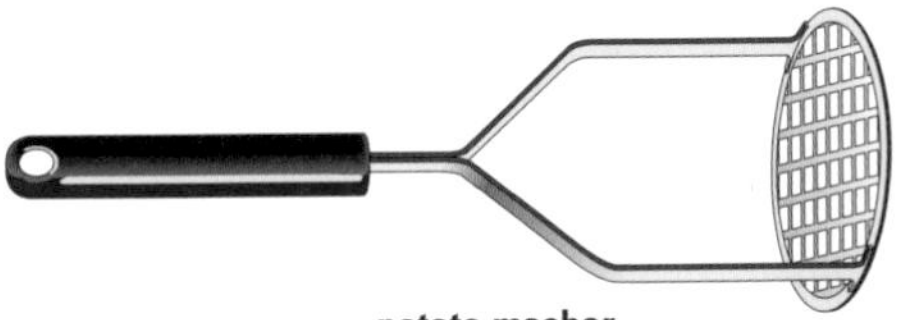

potato masher

cook's knife

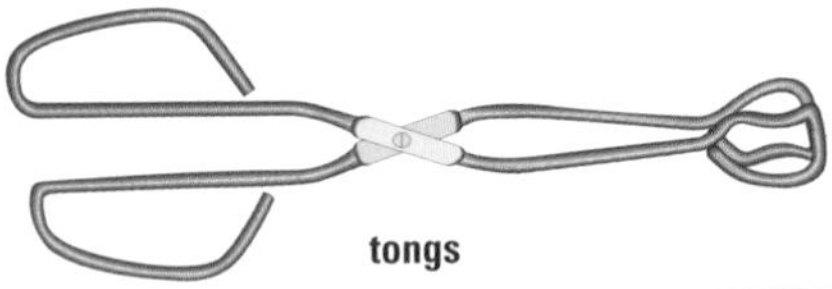

tongs

spatula

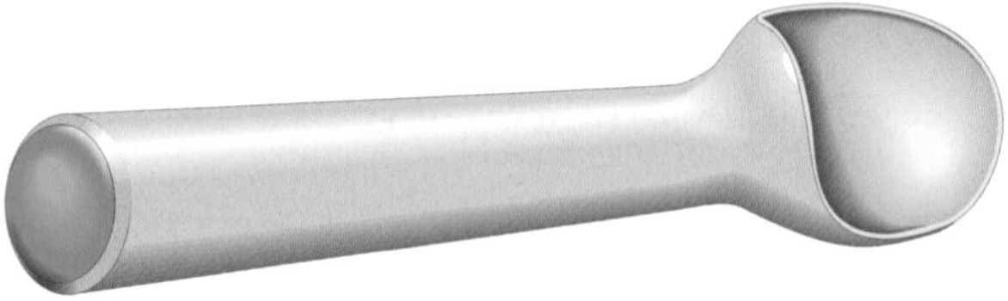

ladle

ice cream scoop

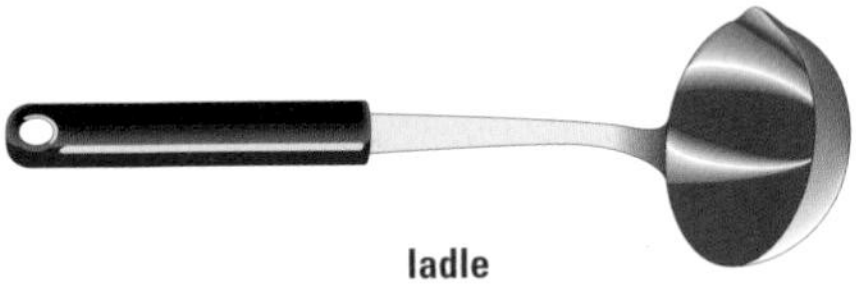

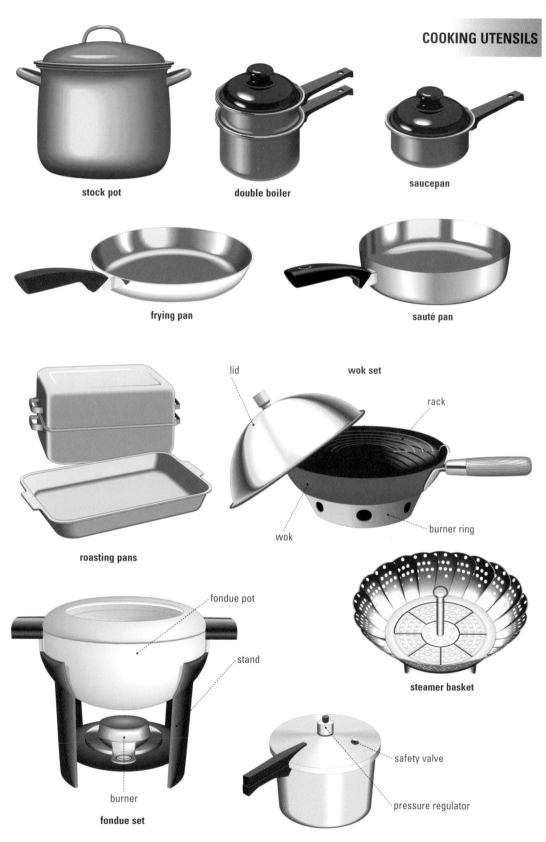

COOKING UTENSILS

stock pot

double boiler

saucepan

frying pan

sauté pan

wok set

lid

rack

wok

burner ring

roasting pans

fondue pot

stand

burner

fondue set

steamer basket

safety valve

pressure regulator

pressure cooker

HOUSE

149

DOMESTIC APPLIANCES

food processor

blender

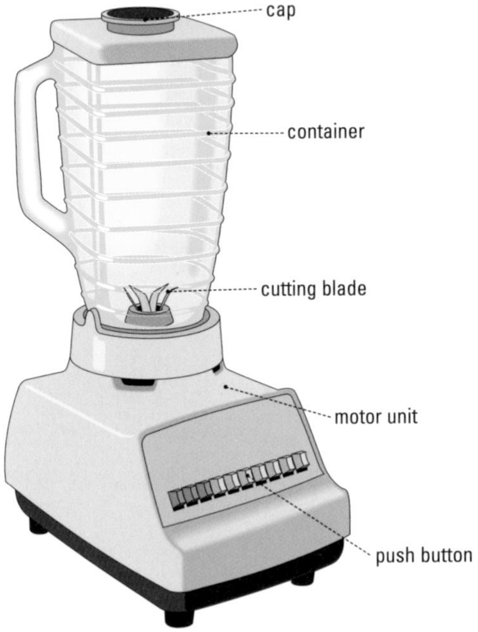

cap

container

cutting blade

motor unit

push button

pusher

feed tube

lid

blade

bowl

speed selector

motor unit

spindle

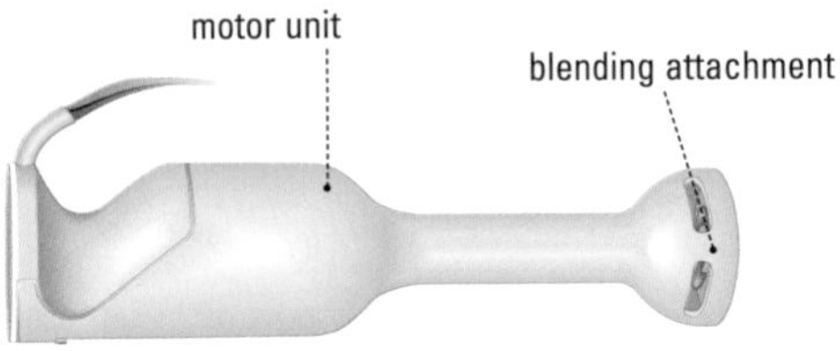

motor unit

blending attachment

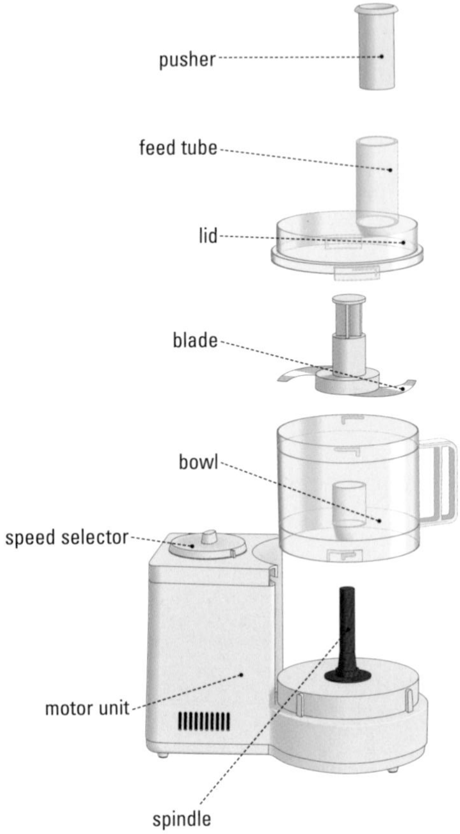

hand blender

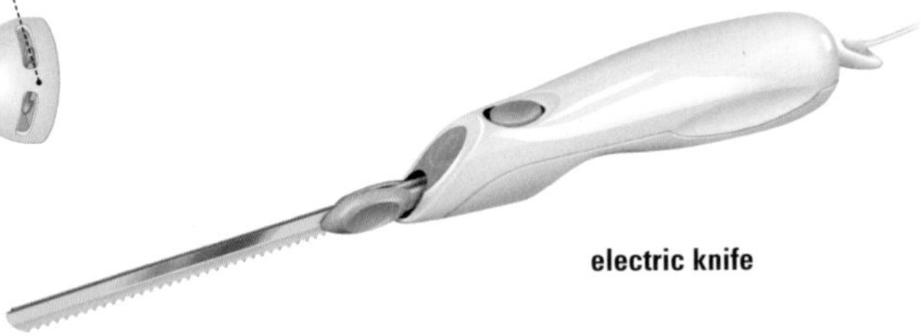

electric knife

hand mixer

electric can opener

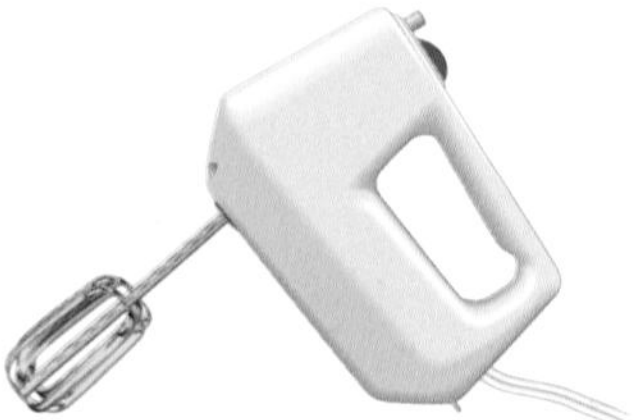

waffle iron

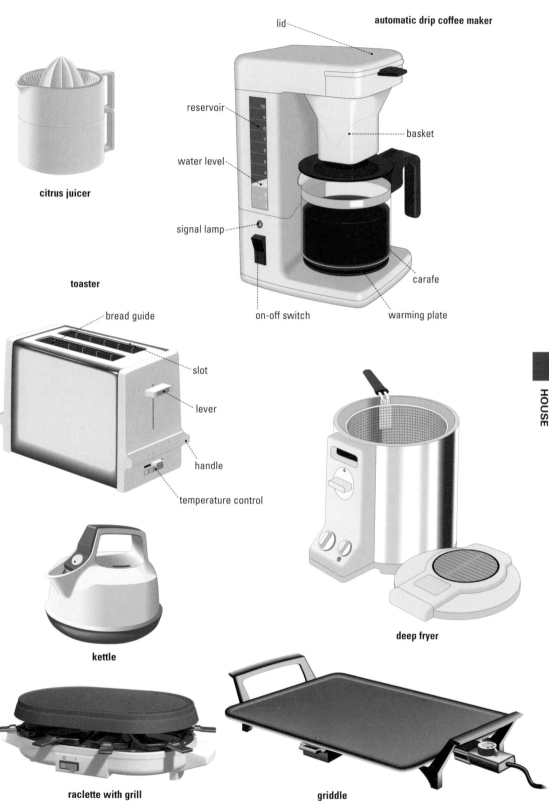

automatic drip coffee maker

lid

reservoir

water level

signal lamp

on-off switch

basket

carafe

warming plate

citrus juicer

toaster

bread guide

slot

lever

handle

temperature control

kettle

deep fryer

raclette with grill

griddle

refrigerator

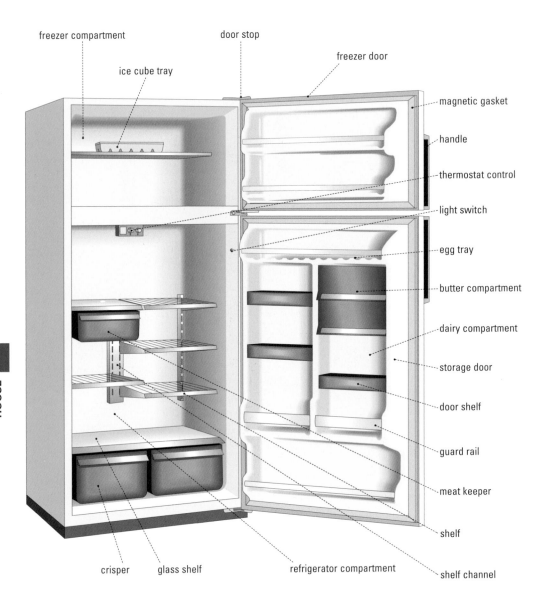

freezer compartment

ice cube tray

door stop

freezer door

magnetic gasket

handle

thermostat control

light switch

egg tray

butter compartment

dairy compartment

storage door

door shelf

guard rail

meat keeper

shelf

crisper

glass shelf

refrigerator compartment

shelf channel

HOUSE

microwave oven

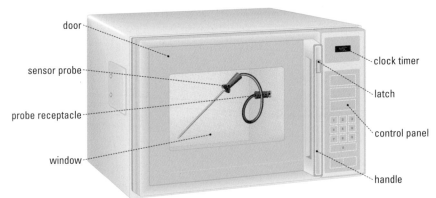

door

sensor probe

probe receptacle

window

clock timer

latch

control panel

handle

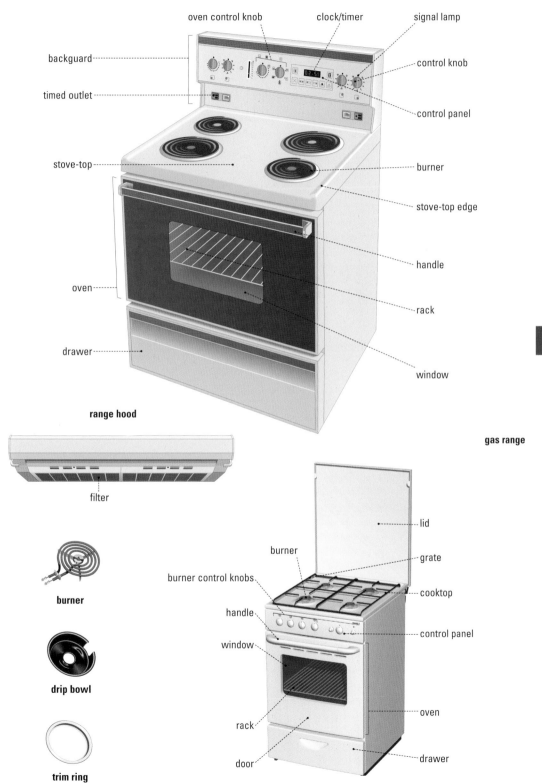

electric range

oven control knob

clock/timer

signal lamp

backguard

control knob

timed outlet

control panel

stove-top

burner

stove-top edge

handle

rack

oven

drawer

window

range hood

gas range

filter

lid

burner

grate

burner control knobs

cooktop

burner

handle

window

control panel

drip bowl

oven

rack

drawer

trim ring

door

HOUSE

BATHROOM

Taking a bath is an activity as old as civilization. It was not until the 19th century, however, that the first bathroom with running water appeared. In modern houses, this room is often equipped with a toilet, sink, shower, and bathtub. Small or large, simple or luxurious, the bathroom is above all a place dedicated to hygiene.

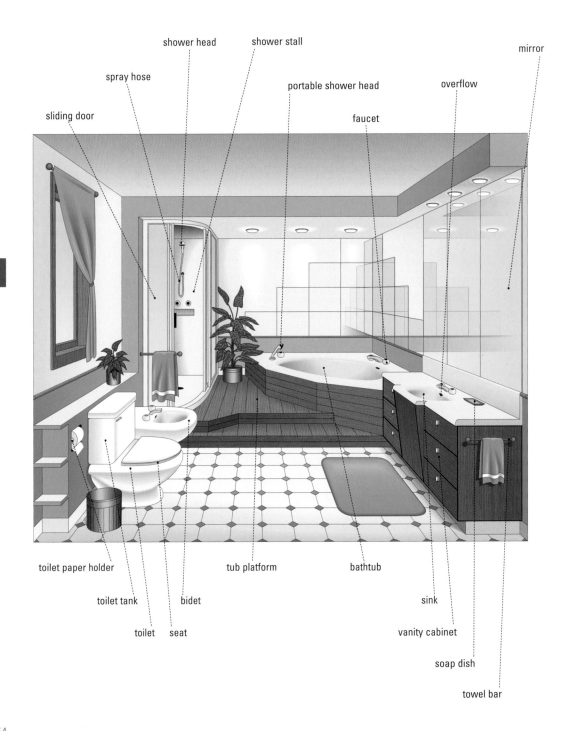

shower head

shower stall

mirror

spray hose

portable shower head

overflow

sliding door

faucet

toilet paper holder

tub platform

bathtub

toilet tank

bidet

sink

toilet

seat

vanity cabinet

soap dish

towel bar

Light and temperature conditions contribute to the comfort of a dwelling. Using different kinds of fixtures and lamps, lighting can be adapted to suit the purpose of any room. Whether direct, as in the case of a fireplace, or indirect, as in a central system that sends heat to every room from a single point, heating should maintain a comfortable temperature.

LIGHTING

HOUSE

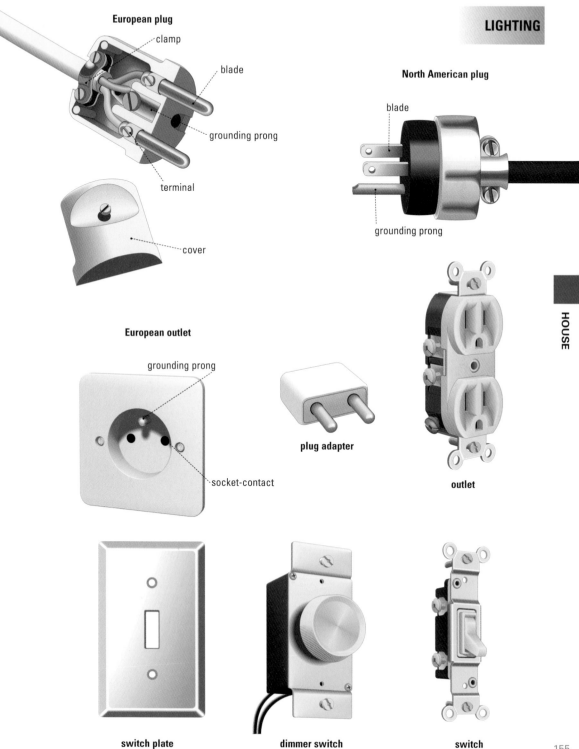

European plug

clamp

blade

grounding prong

terminal

cover

North American plug

blade

grounding prong

European outlet

grounding prong

socket-contact

plug adapter

outlet

switch plate

dimmer switch

switch

HOUSE

incandescent light bulb

filament

inert gas

lead-in wire

bulb

base

energy-saving bulb

bulb

fluorescent tube

tube retention clip

mounting plate

electronic ballast

housing

base

screw base

bayonet base

lamp socket

fluorescent tube

lead-in wire

phosphorescent coating

bulb

pin base

electrode

gas

pin

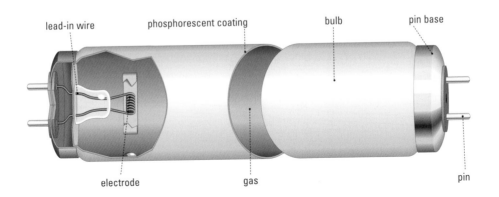

adjustable lamp

on-off switch

arm

transformer

spot

shade

track lighting

spring

hanging pendant

adjustable clamp

chandelier

ceiling fitting

HOUSE

clamp spotlight

shade

desk lamp

base

stand

floor lamp

light post

table lamp

HEATING

fire irons

log holder

fireplace

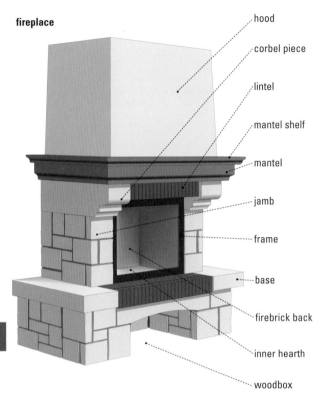

hood

corbel piece

lintel

mantel shelf

mantel

jamb

frame

base

firebrick back

inner hearth

woodbox

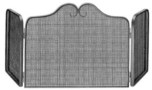

fireplace screen

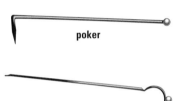

poker

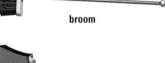

log tongs

broom

radiant heater

fan heater

shovel

electric baseboard heater

room thermostat

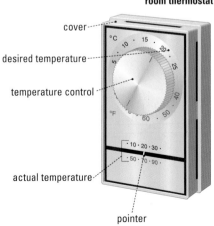

cover

desired temperature

temperature control

actual temperature

pointer

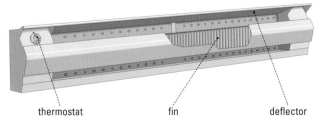

thermostat

fin

deflector

Up until the invention of electricity, performing household tasks depended on muscular force. People swept, washed, and dusted by hand. The earliest electrical appliances, the electric iron being the first, turned electricity into heat. With the invention of the motor, electricity could be turned into movement. This led to the development of a new generation of appliances like the clothes washer and dryer.

scouring pad

kitchen towel

pouring spout

handle

steam iron

brush

pail

mop

hand-held vacuum cleaner

lid

canister vacuum cleaner

handle

upright vacuum cleaner

garbage can

dustpan

broom

HOUSE

washer

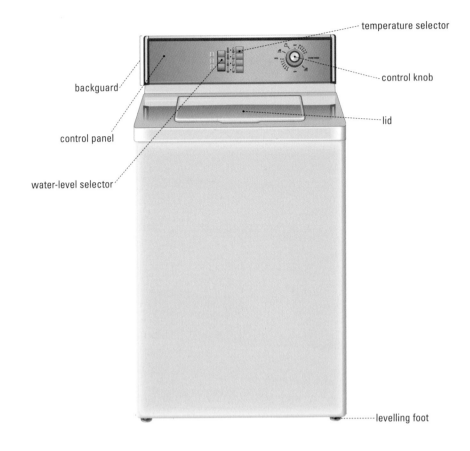

temperature selector

backguard

control knob

control panel

lid

water-level selector

levelling foot

dryer

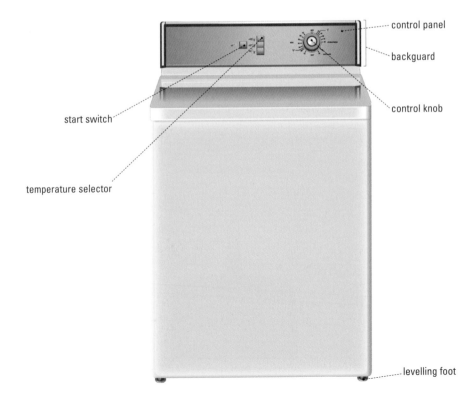

control panel

backguard

control knob

start switch

temperature selector

levelling foot

HOUSE

Painting a room, changing a fuse, or repairing a leaky faucet does not require the services of a professional. Any clever and inventive person can carry out these small manual tasks and become a devoted do-it-yourselfer. Even if the home handyperson can make do with whatever is at hand, selecting the right materials, using the correct method, and having good tools makes the job easier.

CARPENTRY TOOLS

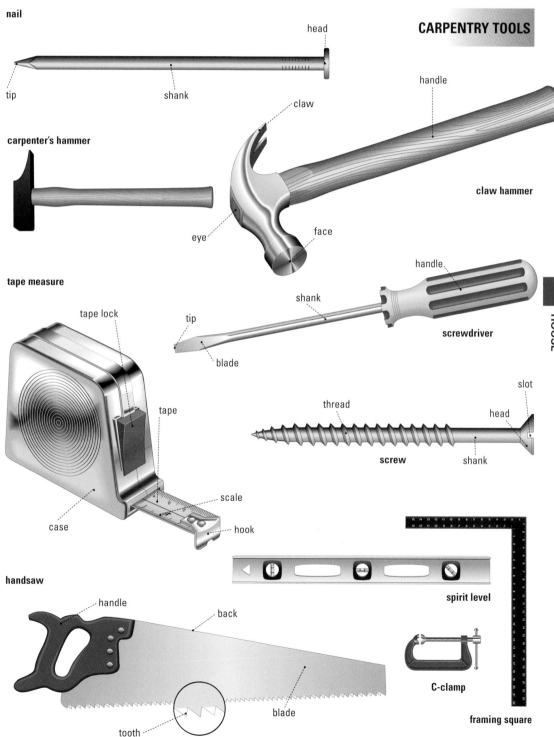

nail
head
tip
shank

carpenter's hammer

claw hammer
handle
claw
eye
face

tape measure
tape lock
tip
blade
shank
handle
screwdriver

tape
scale
case
hook

screw
thread
head
slot
shank

handsaw
handle
back
blade
tooth

spirit level

C-clamp

framing square

HOUSE

crescent wrench

curved jaw

fixed jaw

handle

handle

slip joint

movable jaw

thumbscrew

slip joint pliers

locking pliers

adjusting screw

spring

adjustable channel

lever

toothed jaw

rib joint pliers

release lever

ELECTRICAL TOOLS

circular saw blade

tooth

circular saw

upper blade guard

handle

trigger switch

motor

blade tilting mechanism

knob handle

tip

base plate

blade

electric drill

trigger switch

housing

pistol grip handle

chuck

solid centre auger bit

jaw

cable sleeve

auxiliary handle

cable

twist bit

PAINTING SUPPLIES

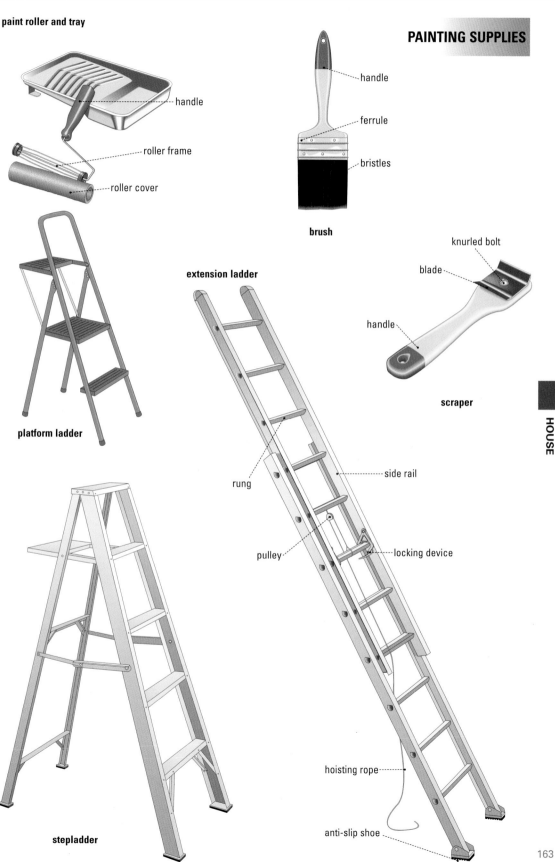

paint roller and tray

handle

roller frame

roller cover

handle

ferrule

bristles

brush

knurled bolt

blade

handle

scraper

extension ladder

platform ladder

rung

side rail

pulley

locking device

stepladder

hoisting rope

anti-slip shoe

GARDENING

Whether cultivating an ornamental garden, growing a vegetable plot, or arranging a modest flower box, gardening is an increasingly popular pastime. Gardens vary in appearance according to their gardeners' tastes, the amount of space available, and environmental conditions. A good knowledge of cultivated plants and a wise choice of tools help the gardener get the best out of his or her plot of land.

wheelbarrow

handle

tray

leg

wheel

small hand cultivator

trowel

pruning shears

weeder

hedge shears

sprayer

gardening gloves

shovel

lawn edger

spreader

lawn mower

speed control

handle

ignition key

safety handle

grassbox

starter

motor

filler cap

spray nozzle

hose trolley

watering can

lawn rake

bow rake

compost bin

Scientific researchers working in laboratories use equipment specially adapted for different types of experiments. Microbiologists use microscopes to observe the microorganisms that have developed in their Petri dishes. Chemists mix their materials in various kinds of measuring containers, like beakers, Erlenmeyer flasks, and pipettes.

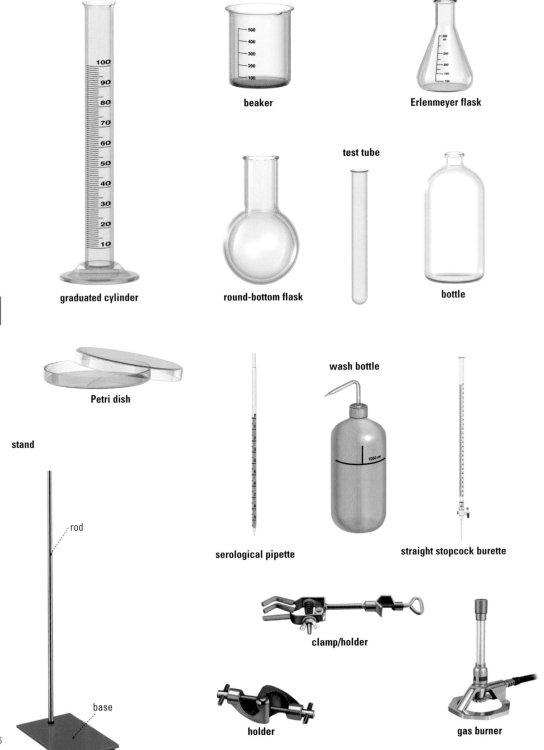

beaker

Erlenmeyer flask

test tube

graduated cylinder

round-bottom flask

bottle

Petri dish

wash bottle

stand

rod

serological pipette

straight stopcock burette

clamp/holder

base

holder

gas burner

MAGNIFYING GLASS AND MICROSCOPES

microscope

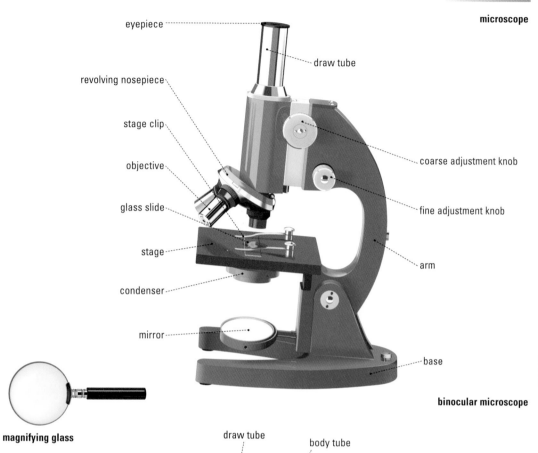

eyepiece

draw tube

revolving nosepiece

stage clip

objective

glass slide

stage

condenser

mirror

coarse adjustment knob

fine adjustment knob

arm

base

magnifying glass

binocular microscope

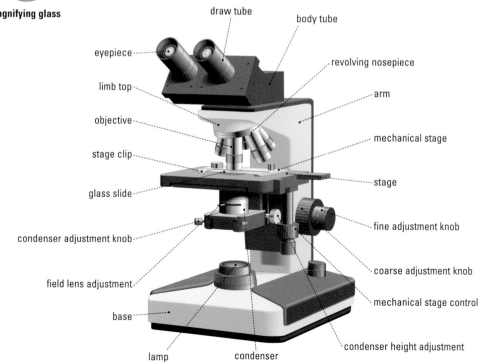

draw tube

body tube

eyepiece

revolving nosepiece

limb top

arm

objective

mechanical stage

stage clip

stage

glass slide

fine adjustment knob

condenser adjustment knob

coarse adjustment knob

field lens adjustment

mechanical stage control

base

condenser height adjustment

lamp

condenser

From the beginning, people have invented different kinds of instruments to help them take measurements. The first instrument for measuring the passage of time, the sundial, goes back at least 3,000 years.

In exact sciences like physics, chemistry, and mathematics, precise measurements are extremely important. This need has resulted in the invention of a wide variety of measuring instruments.

SCIENCE

MEASURE OF TIME

stopwatch

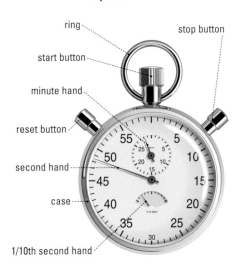

ring
stop button
start button
minute hand
reset button
55 5
25 5
50 20 10 10
second hand
15
45 15
case
40 20
1/10th second hand
35 25
30

sundial

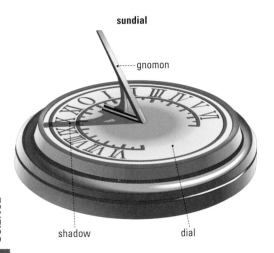

gnomon

shadow
dial

digital watch

liquid crystal display

grandfather clock

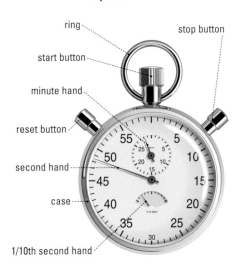

pediment
body
moon dial
hour hand
minute hand
dial
weight
pendulum
chain
plinth

analog watch

dial

crown

strap

mechanical watch

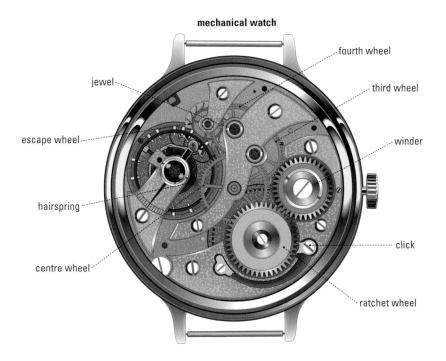

fourth wheel

jewel

third wheel

escape wheel

winder

hairspring

centre wheel

click

ratchet wheel

MEASURE OF TEMPERATURE

thermometer

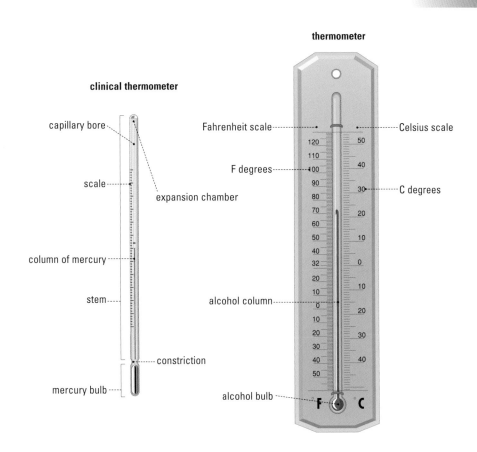

clinical thermometer

capillary bore

Fahrenheit scale

Celsius scale

F degrees

scale

C degrees

expansion chamber

column of mercury

stem

alcohol column

constriction

mercury bulb

alcohol bulb

MEASURE OF WEIGHT

steelyard

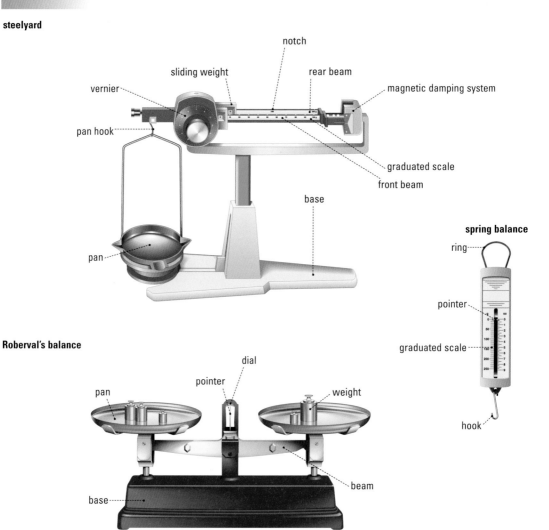

notch

sliding weight

rear beam

vernier

magnetic damping system

pan hook

graduated scale

front beam

base

pan

SCIENCE

spring balance

ring

pointer

graduated scale

hook

Roberval's balance

dial

pointer

pan

weight

beam

base

electronic scale

weight

display

unit price

total

platform

printout

numeric keyboard

function keys

product code

bathroom scale

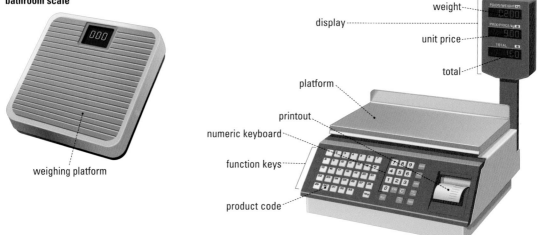

weighing platform

Geometry is a branch of mathematics that studies points, lines, flat surfaces like circles or squares, as well as solid objects like spheres and cubes. Geometry offers a variety of clever methods for measuring both two- and three-dimensional forms. By studying objects as they appear on flat planes as well as in space, geometry is at the heart of many disciplines, such as engineering and architecture.

GEOMETRICAL SHAPES

parts of a circle

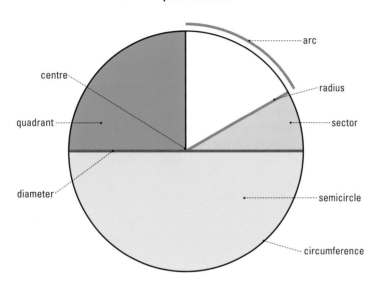

examples of angles

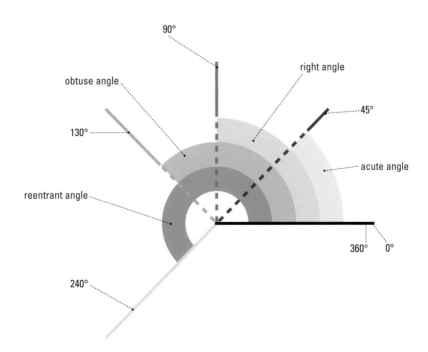

polygons

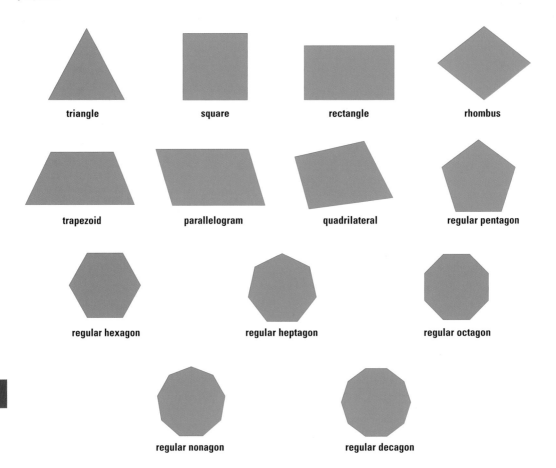

triangle

square

rectangle

rhombus

trapezoid

parallelogram

quadrilateral

regular pentagon

regular hexagon

regular heptagon

regular octagon

regular nonagon

regular decagon

solids

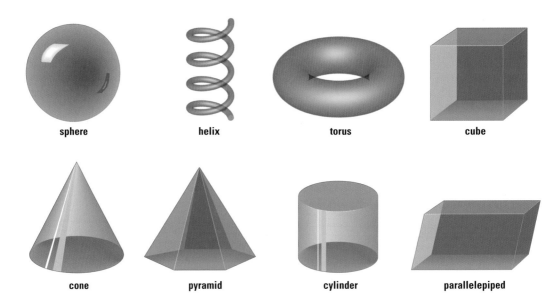

sphere

helix

torus

cube

cone

pyramid

cylinder

parallelepiped

Good weather or bad, our planet receives large quantities of energy from the Sun every day. Essential to life on Earth, solar energy can be captured by special cells and used to heat water and the insides of homes and dwellings. This never-ending and non-polluting source of energy can also be transformed into electricity with the help of solar cells.

SOLAR CELL SYSTEM

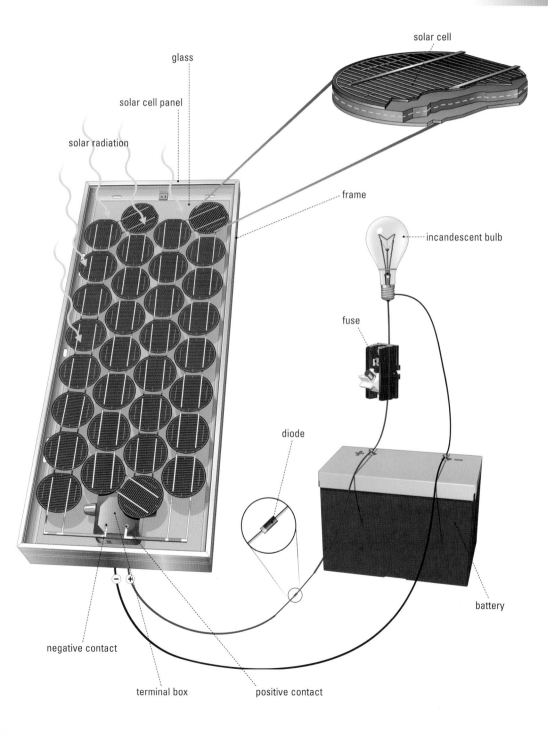

solar cell

glass

solar cell panel

solar radiation

frame

incandescent bulb

fuse

diode

negative contact

terminal box

positive contact

battery

HYDROELECTRICITY

Like everything in motion, running water possesses energy. Hydroelectric power stations use water's energy and transform it into electricity. The water runs through several kinds of dams built to collect it or build up its pressure. Arriving at the power station, the water is channelled to power turbines, which in turn drive machinery that produces an electrical current.

HYDROELECTRIC COMPLEX

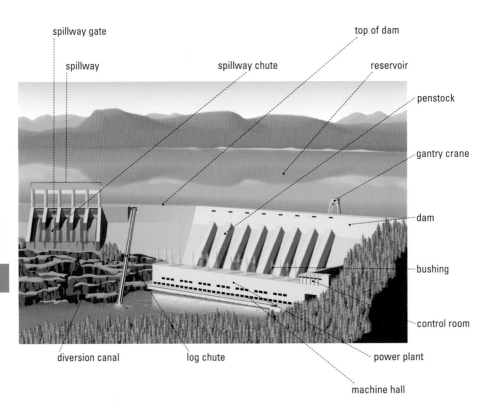

spillway gate

top of dam

spillway

spillway chute

reservoir

penstock

gantry crane

dam

bushing

control room

diversion canal

log chute

power plant

machine hall

examples of dams

embankment dam   **gravity dam**   **arch dam**   **buttress dam**

cross-section of a hydroelectric power plant

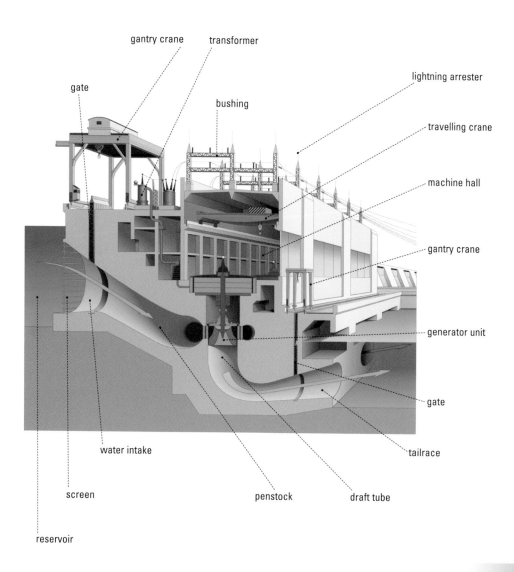

gantry crane

transformer

gate

bushing

lightning arrester

travelling crane

machine hall

gantry crane

generator unit

gate

water intake

tailrace

screen

penstock

draft tube

reservoir

ELECTRIC CIRCUIT

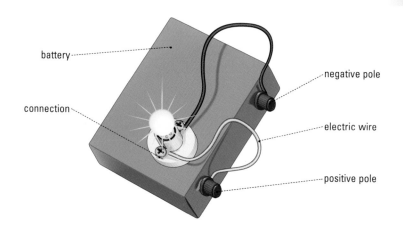

battery

connection

negative pole

electric wire

positive pole

STEPS IN THE PRODUCTION OF ELECTRICITY

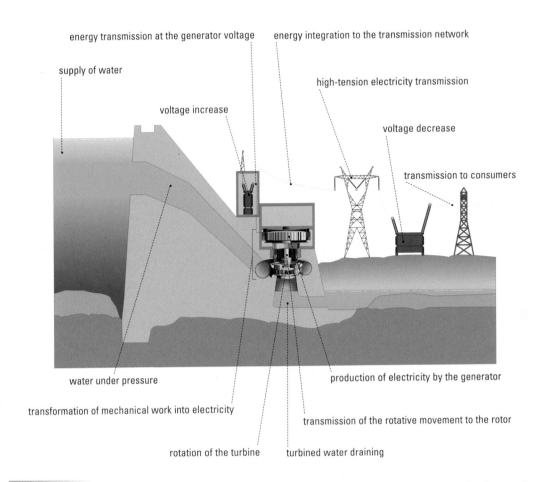

energy transmission at the generator voltage

energy integration to the transmission network

supply of water

high-tension electricity transmission

voltage increase

voltage decrease

transmission to consumers

water under pressure

production of electricity by the generator

transformation of mechanical work into electricity

transmission of the rotative movement to the rotor

rotation of the turbine

turbined water draining

ELECTRICITY TRANSMISSION

overhead connection

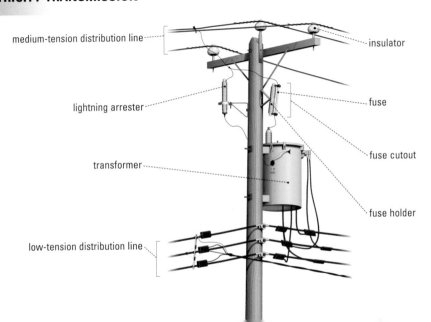

medium-tension distribution line

insulator

lightning arrester

fuse

fuse cutout

transformer

fuse holder

low-tension distribution line

Nuclear energy is produced by splitting apart the nucleus in certain atoms. The split uranium nucleus, for example, releases an enormous amount of energy that can be transformed into electricity at a nuclear power station. These stations are equipped with safety devices to prevent dangerous radioactive substances from escaping into the environment.

NUCLEAR GENERATING STATION

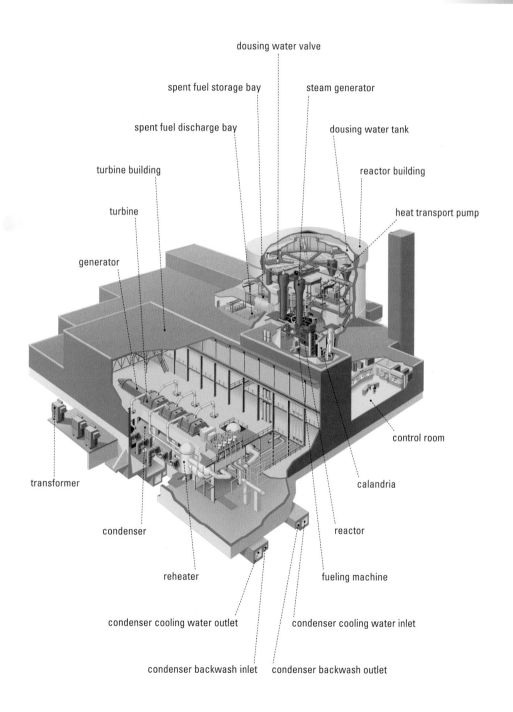

dousing water valve

spent fuel storage bay

steam generator

spent fuel discharge bay

dousing water tank

turbine building

reactor building

turbine

heat transport pump

generator

transformer

control room

condenser

calandria

reheater

reactor

condenser cooling water outlet

fueling machine

condenser cooling water inlet

condenser backwash inlet

condenser backwash outlet

ENERGY

PRODUCTION OF ELECTRICITY FROM NUCLEAR ENERGY

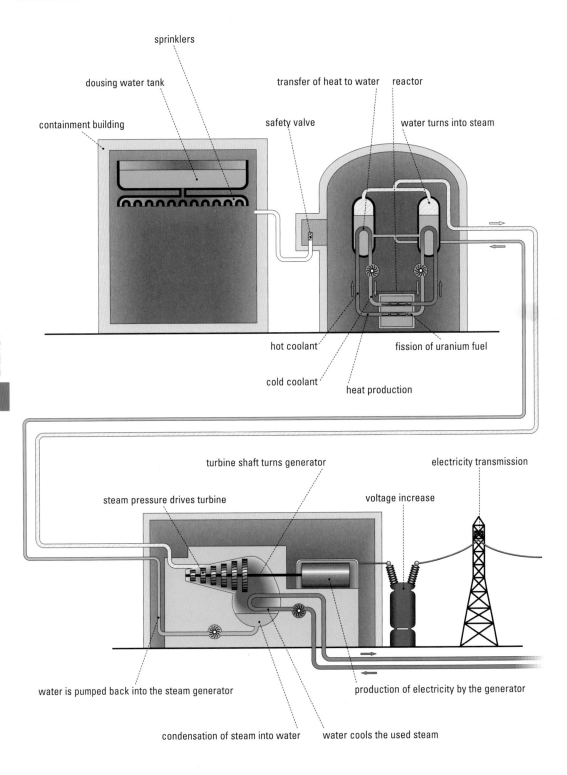

sprinklers

dousing water tank

transfer of heat to water   reactor

containment building

safety valve

water turns into steam

hot coolant

fission of uranium fuel

cold coolant

heat production

turbine shaft turns generator

electricity transmission

steam pressure drives turbine

voltage increase

water is pumped back into the steam generator

production of electricity by the generator

condensation of steam into water   water cools the used steam

Wind energy is also known as aeolian energy, after Aeolus, the Greek god of the winds. Long before motors were invented, the wind was used to propel sailboats and to power windmills for grinding grain.

For more than a century, this natural force has also been harnessed to help create electrical energy using turbines. Pushed by the wind, the blades of the turbine drive a generator that produces electricity.

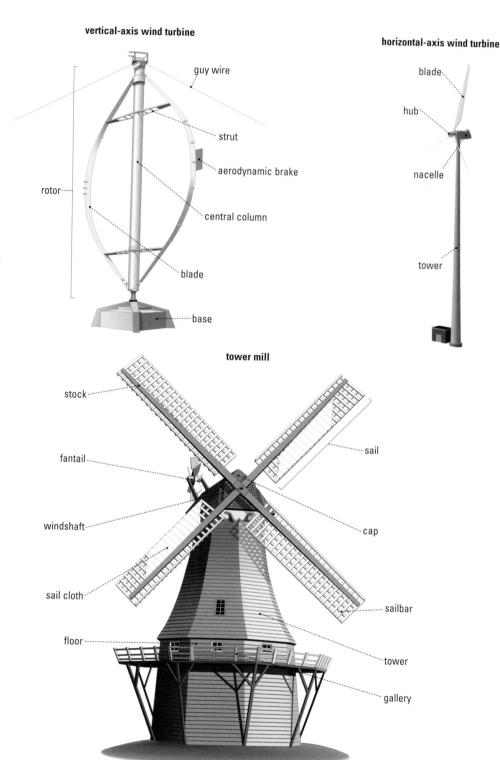

vertical-axis wind turbine

guy wire

strut

aerodynamic brake

rotor

central column

blade

base

horizontal-axis wind turbine

blade

hub

nacelle

tower

ENERGY

tower mill

stock

fantail

windshaft

sail cloth

floor

sail

cap

sailbar

tower

gallery

179

Oil, coal, and natural gas originate in the residue of partially fossilized organisms that lived millions of years ago. These combustible fossils are found in limited quantities under the ground. Refining allows crude oil to be turned into more than 500 different consumer products. One of the most valuable, gasoline, is used to fuel engines, giving crude oil the nickname "black gold."

OIL

ENERGY

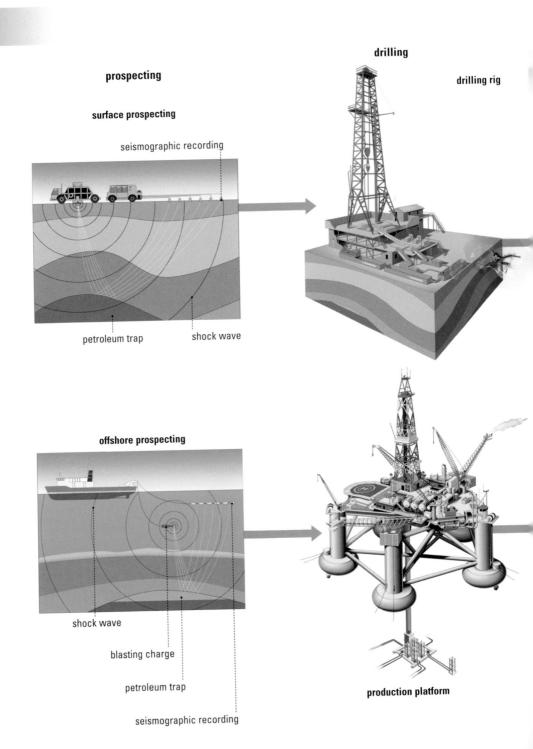

drilling

drilling rig

prospecting

surface prospecting

seismographic recording

petroleum trap

shock wave

offshore prospecting

shock wave

blasting charge

petroleum trap

seismographic recording

production platform

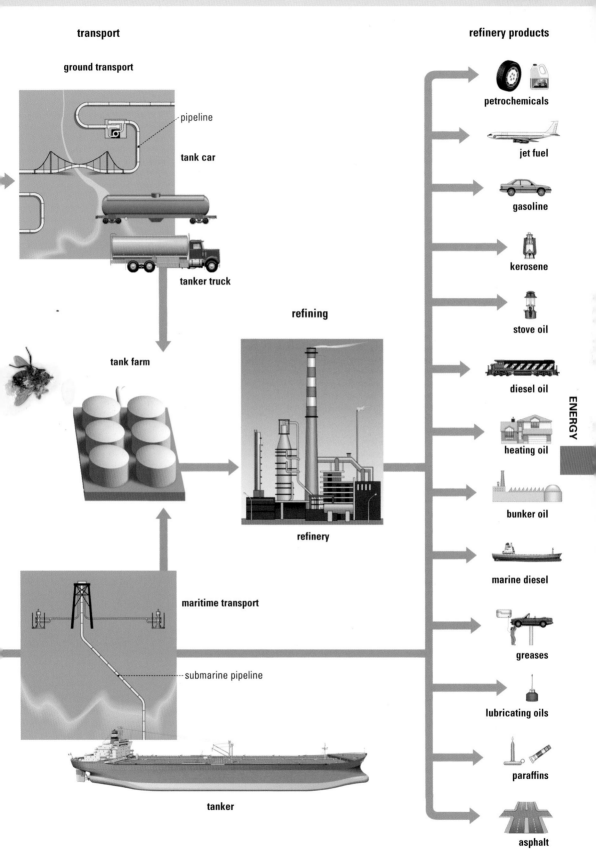

transport

ground transport

pipeline

tank car

tanker truck

tank farm

refining

refinery

maritime transport

submarine pipeline

tanker

refinery products

petrochemicals

jet fuel

gasoline

kerosene

stove oil

diesel oil

heating oil

bunker oil

marine diesel

greases

lubricating oils

paraffins

asphalt

ENERGY

ROAD TRANSPORT

The bicycle, followed by the motorcycle and the automobile, were made possible by the invention of the wheel. These forms of transportation allowed people to travel farther and faster than they ever had before. The automobile has never stopped growing in popularity since its arrival in the 19th century. The millions of motor vehicles in use today has led to an ever-growing system of roads to handle the increased traffic.

ROAD SYSTEM

cloverleaf

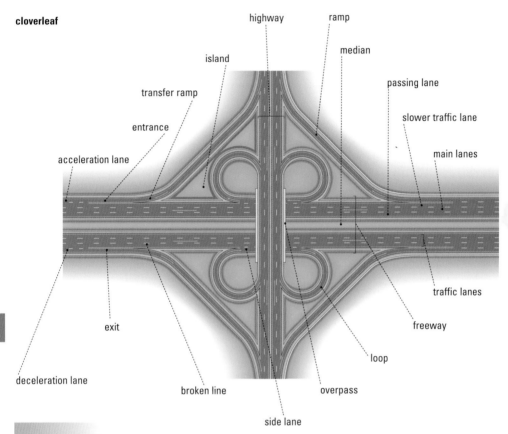

highway
ramp
median
island
passing lane
transfer ramp
slower traffic lane
entrance
main lanes
acceleration lane
traffic lanes
exit
freeway
deceleration lane
loop
broken line
overpass
side lane

ROAD TUNNEL

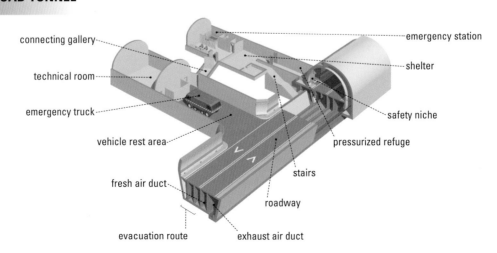

connecting gallery
emergency station
technical room
shelter
emergency truck
safety niche
vehicle rest area
pressurized refuge
fresh air duct
stairs
evacuation route
roadway
exhaust air duct

FIXED BRIDGES

suspension bridge

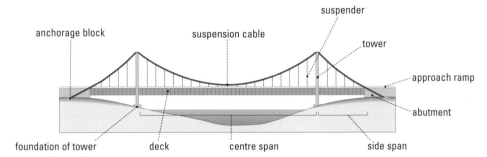

anchorage block — suspension cable — suspender — tower — approach ramp — abutment — foundation of tower — deck — centre span — side span

beam bridge

arch bridge

cable-stayed bridge

cantilever bridge

MOVABLE BRIDGES

swing bridge

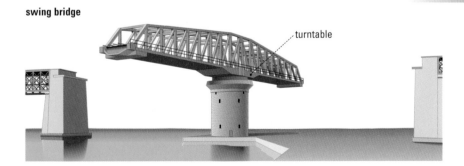

turntable

floating bridge

manrope — pontoon

double-leaf bascule bridge

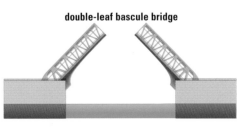

AUTOMOBILE

body

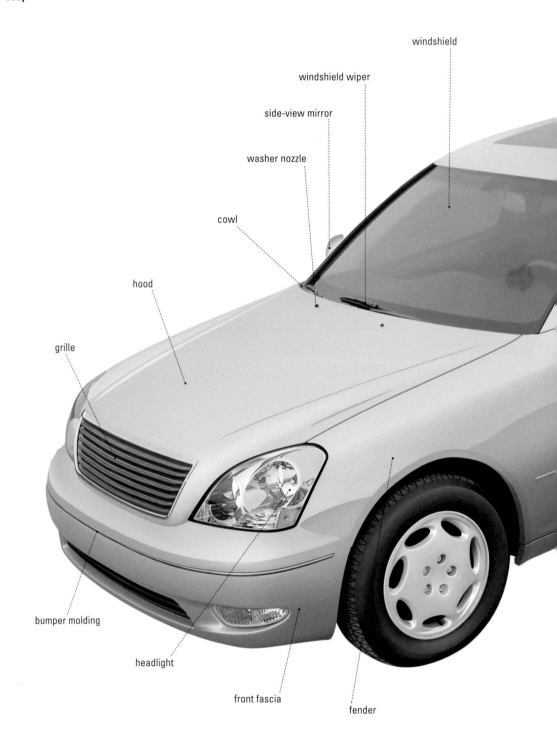

windshield

windshield wiper

side-view mirror

washer nozzle

cowl

hood

grille

bumper molding

headlight

front fascia

fender

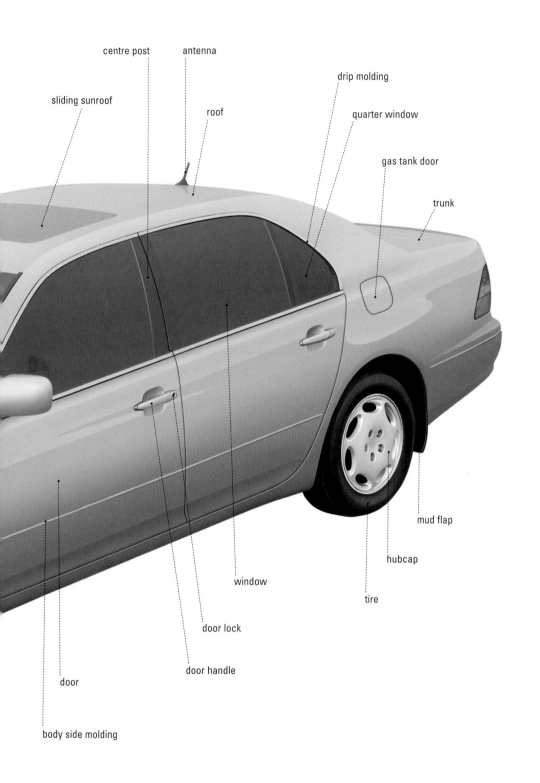

centre post

antenna

drip molding

sliding sunroof

roof

quarter window

gas tank door

trunk

sliding sunroof

window

door lock

door handle

door

body side molding

mud flap

hubcap

tire

types of cars

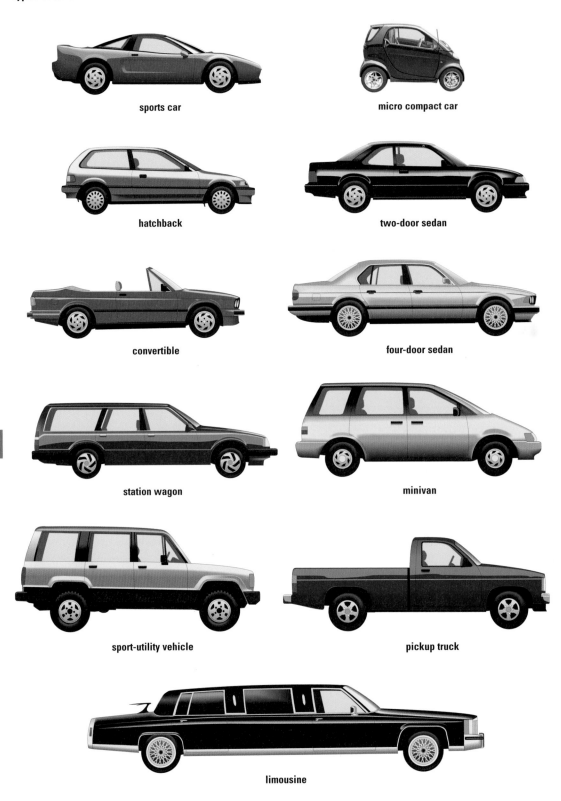

sports car

micro compact car

hatchback

two-door sedan

convertible

four-door sedan

station wagon

minivan

sport-utility vehicle

pickup truck

limousine

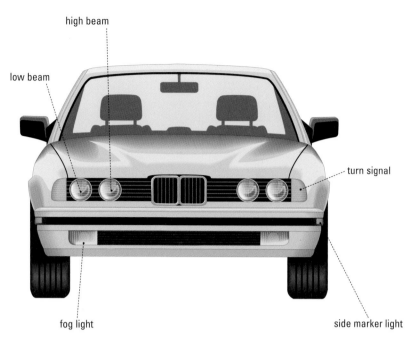

headlights

high beam

low beam

turn signal

fog light

side marker light

TRANSPORTATION AND HEAVY MACHINERY

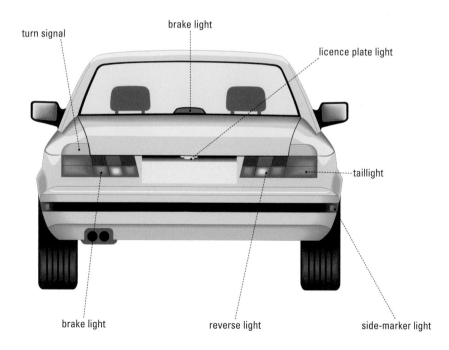

taillights

turn signal

brake light

licence plate light

taillight

brake light

reverse light

side-marker light

TRANSPORTATION AND HEAVY MACHINERY

dashboard

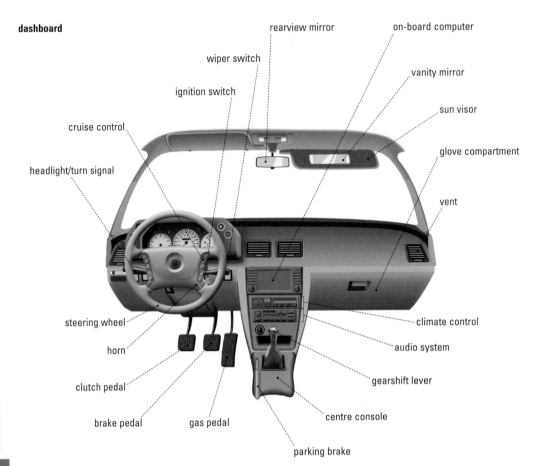

rearview mirror

on-board computer

wiper switch

vanity mirror

ignition switch

sun visor

cruise control

glove compartment

headlight/turn signal

vent

steering wheel

climate control

horn

audio system

clutch pedal

gearshift lever

brake pedal

gas pedal

centre console

parking brake

instrument panel

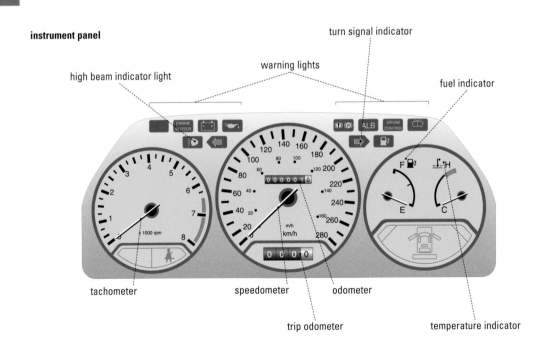

turn signal indicator

warning lights

high beam indicator light

fuel indicator

tachometer

speedometer

odometer

trip odometer

temperature indicator

roof

screen door

canopy

bunk

window

spare tire

body

stabilizer jack

tent trailer

luggage rack

air conditioner

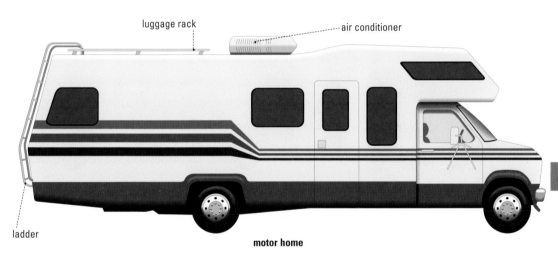

ladder

motor home

trailer

BUSES

school bus

double-decker bus

city bus

minibus

coach

articulated bus

protective helmet

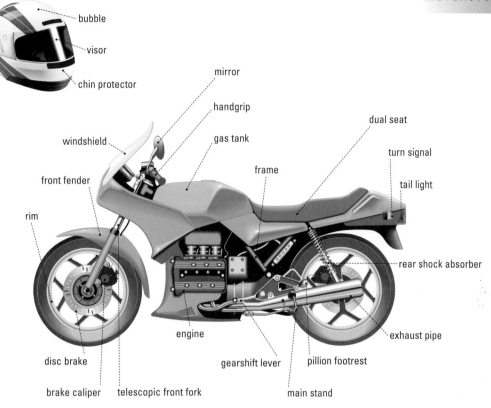

bubble

visor

chin protector

mirror

handgrip

dual seat

windshield

gas tank

turn signal

front fender

frame

tail light

rim

rear shock absorber

engine

exhaust pipe

disc brake

gearshift lever

pillion footrest

brake caliper

telescopic front fork

main stand

examples of motorcycles

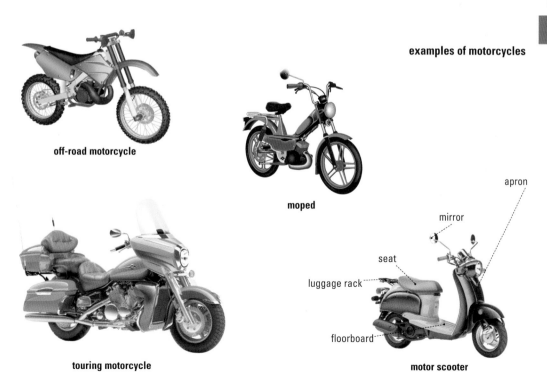

off-road motorcycle

moped

apron

mirror

seat

luggage rack

floorboard

touring motorcycle

motor scooter

TRUCKING

TRANSPORTATION AND HEAVY MACHINERY

truck tractor

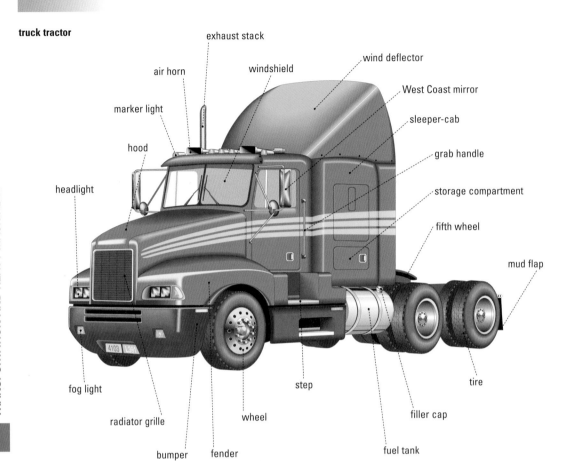

exhaust stack

air horn

windshield

wind deflector

West Coast mirror

marker light

sleeper-cab

hood

grab handle

headlight

storage compartment

fifth wheel

mud flap

fog light

tire

radiator grille

wheel

filler cap

step

bumper

fender

fuel tank

examples of trucks

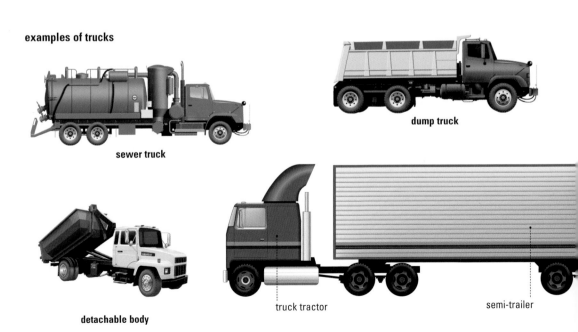

sewer truck

dump truck

detachable body

truck tractor

semi-trailer

tow truck

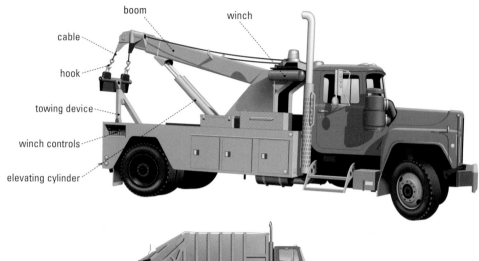

boom

winch

cable

hook

towing device

winch controls

elevating cylinder

garbage truck

tanker truck

snowblower

concrete mixer truck

cube van

tandem tractor trailer

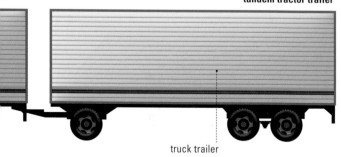

street sweeper

truck trailer

BICYCLE

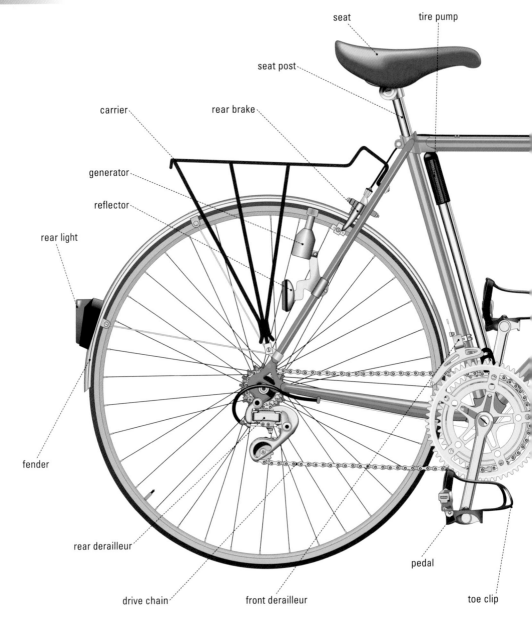

seat

tire pump

seat post

carrier

rear brake

generator

reflector

rear light

fender

rear derailleur

pedal

drive chain

front derailleur

toe clip

accessories

child carrier

protective helmet

lock

bicycle bag

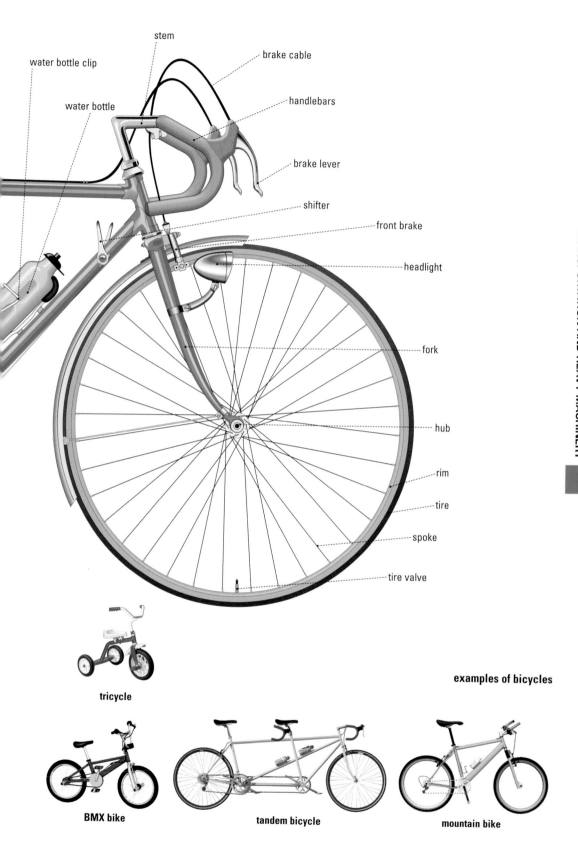

stem

water bottle clip

brake cable

water bottle

handlebars

brake lever

shifter

front brake

headlight

fork

hub

rim

tire

spoke

tire valve

tricycle

examples of bicycles

BMX bike

tandem bicycle

mountain bike

RAIL TRANSPORT

Railways were the most popular form of transportation in the 19th century. Even today, many travellers still prefer the train to the automobile or the airplane. High-performance, high-speed trains carry passengers at more than 300 km/h (180 mph) throughout Europe, America, and Asia. In urban settings, however, rail transportation most often takes the form of subways and streetcars.

PASSENGER TRAIN

diesel-electric locomotive

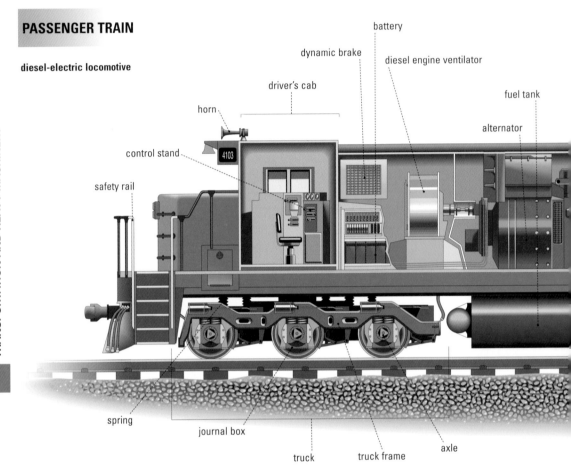

battery
dynamic brake
diesel engine ventilator
driver's cab
fuel tank
horn
alternator
control stand
4103
safety rail
spring
journal box
truck
truck frame
axle

examples of freight cars

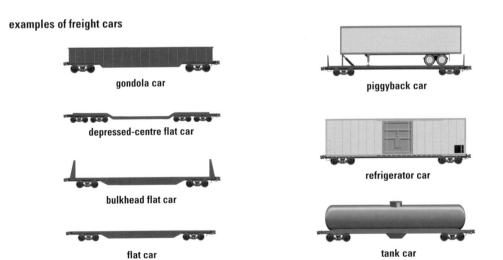

gondola car

piggyback car

depressed-centre flat car

bulkhead flat car

refrigerator car

flat car

tank car

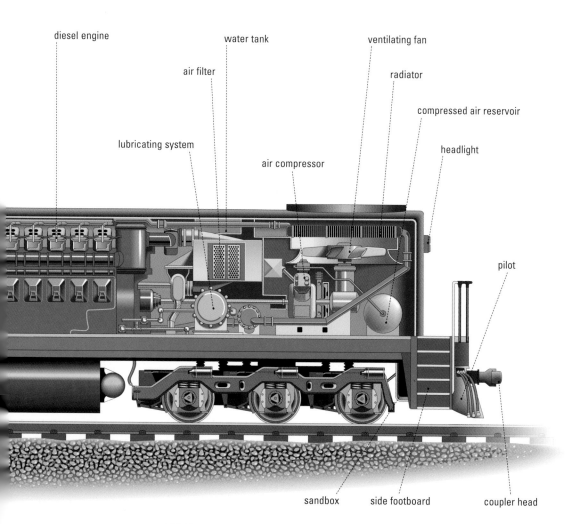

diesel engine

water tank

ventilating fan

air filter

radiator

lubricating system

compressed air reservoir

air compressor

headlight

pilot

sandbox

side footboard

coupler head

caboose

hopper ore car

container car

livestock car

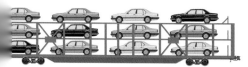

automobile car

box car

TRANSPORTATION AND HEAVY MACHINERY

high-speed train

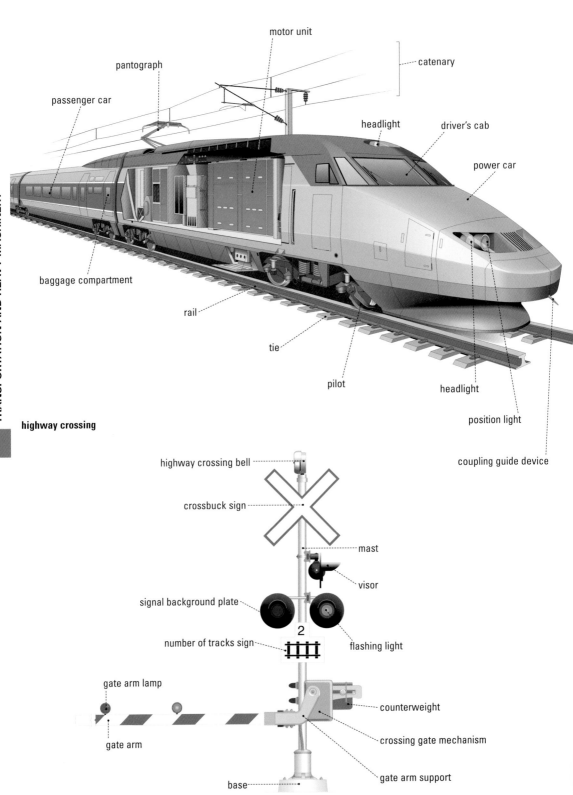

motor unit

catenary

pantograph

passenger car

headlight

driver's cab

power car

baggage compartment

rail

tie

pilot

headlight

position light

coupling guide device

highway crossing

highway crossing bell

crossbuck sign

mast

visor

signal background plate

flashing light

number of tracks sign

2

gate arm lamp

counterweight

gate arm

crossing gate mechanism

base

gate arm support

passenger car

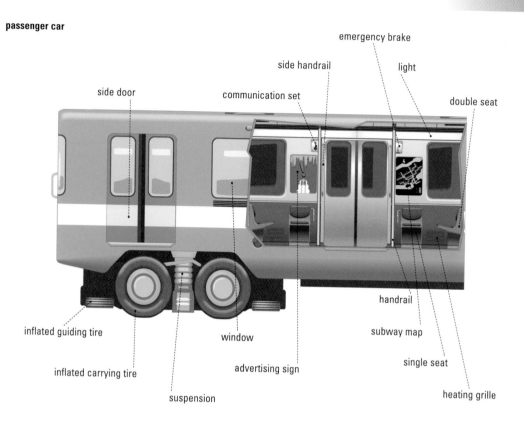

emergency brake

side handrail

light

side door

communication set

double seat

inflated guiding tire

window

handrail

subway map

inflated carrying tire

advertising sign

single seat

suspension

heating grille

subway train

motor car

trailer car

motor car

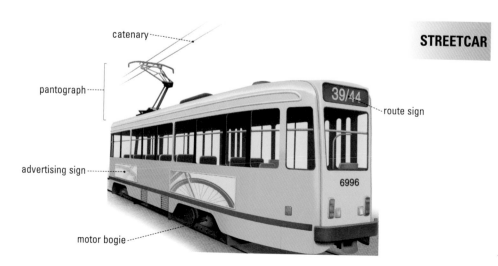

catenary

pantograph

39/44

route sign

advertising sign

6996

motor bogie

TRANSPORTATION AND HEAVY MACHINERY

MARITIME TRANSPORT

Next to the donkey and camel, boats are the oldest form of transportation. By the 14th century, the possibility of trade with unknown lands led to the development of large and efficient sailing ships. By the 19th century, the arrival of immense steamships freed sailors from a dependence on unreliable wind power. Today the world's sea lanes are mainly used to transport merchandise at a low cost.

HARBOUR

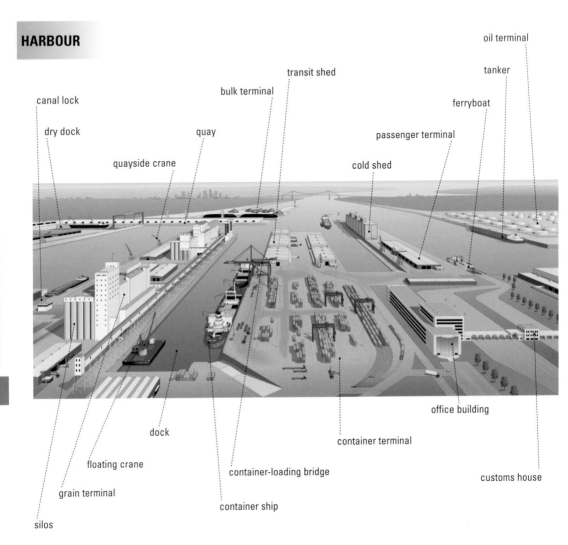

oil terminal

transit shed

tanker

bulk terminal

ferryboat

canal lock

dry dock

quay

passenger terminal

quayside crane

cold shed

office building

dock

container terminal

floating crane

container-loading bridge

customs house

grain terminal

container ship

silos

PASSENGER LINER

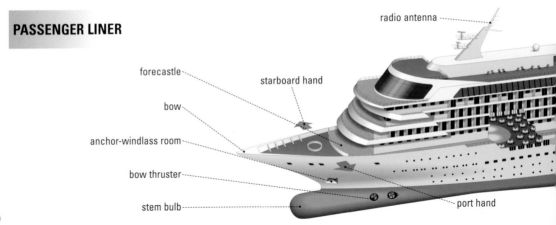

radio antenna

forecastle

starboard hand

bow

anchor-windlass room

bow thruster

stem bulb

port hand

FOUR-MASTED BARQUE

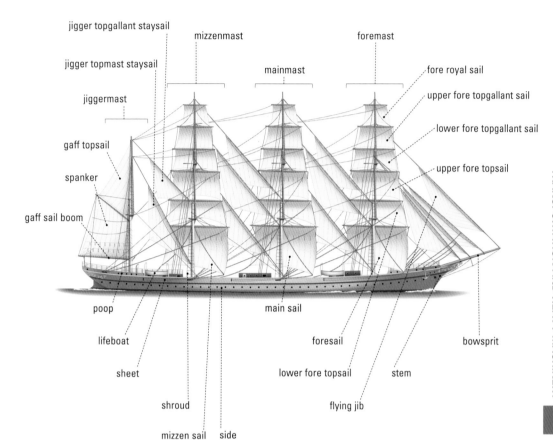

jigger topgallant staysail

jigger topmast staysail

jiggermast

gaff topsail

spanker

gaff sail boom

mizzenmast

mainmast

foremast

fore royal sail

upper fore topgallant sail

lower fore topgallant sail

upper fore topsail

poop

main sail

lifeboat

foresail

bowsprit

sheet

lower fore topsail

stem

shroud

flying jib

mizzen sail

side

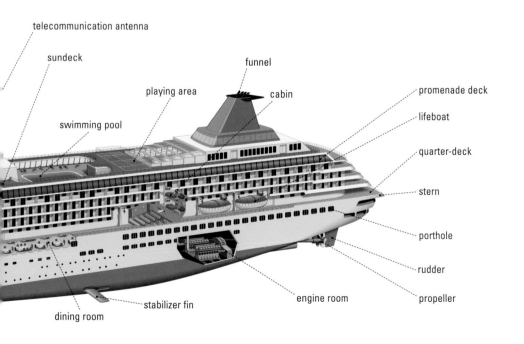

telecommunication antenna

sundeck

funnel

playing area

cabin

promenade deck

lifeboat

swimming pool

quarter-deck

stern

porthole

rudder

dining room

stabilizer fin

engine room

propeller

EXAMPLES OF BOATS AND SHIPS

runabout

motor yacht

houseboat

tug

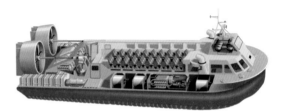

hovercraft

hydrofoil boat

ferry

icebreaker

trawler

TRANSPORTATION AND HEAVY MACHINERY

Before the invention of the helicopter and airplane, taking a train or a boat were the only practical means of travelling long distances. In the 1950s, the jet airplane revolutionized air travel by offering flights that could transport passengers over long distances in a short amount of time. Helicopters are particularly useful in rescue operations because of their ability to take off and land in places inaccessible to airplanes.

HELICOPTER

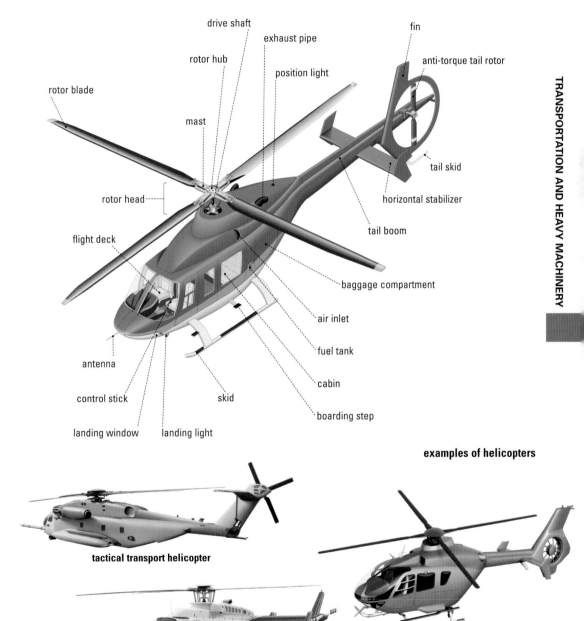

drive shaft

exhaust pipe

rotor hub

position light

fin

anti-torque tail rotor

rotor blade

mast

tail skid

rotor head

horizontal stabilizer

flight deck

tail boom

baggage compartment

air inlet

fuel tank

antenna

cabin

control stick

skid

boarding step

landing window   landing light

examples of helicopters

tactical transport helicopter

ambulance helicopter

water bomber helicopter

AIRPORT

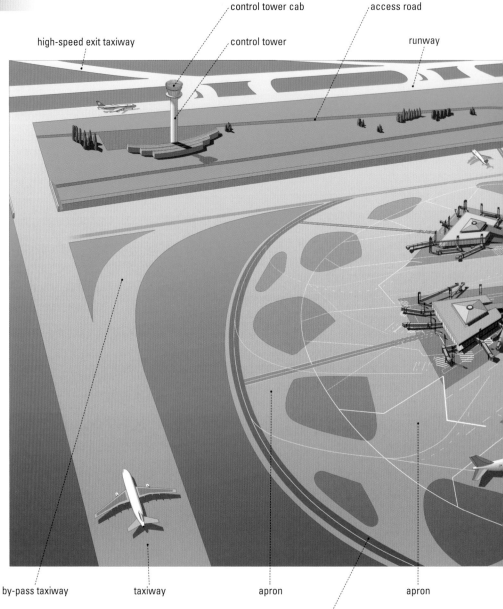

control tower cab

access road

high-speed exit taxiway

control tower

runway

by-pass taxiway

taxiway

apron

apron

service road

ground airport equipment

wheel chock

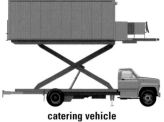

catering vehicle

aircraft maintenance truck

tow bar

passenger terminal

boarding walkway

maintenance hangar

parking area

radial passenger loading area

telescopic corridor

service area

taxiway line

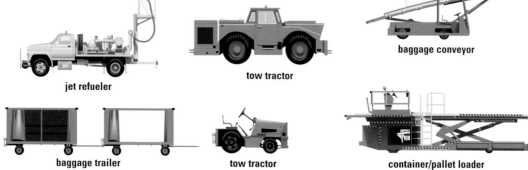

jet refueler

tow tractor

baggage conveyor

baggage trailer

tow tractor

container/pallet loader

TRANSPORTATION AND HEAVY MACHINERY

AIRPLANE

examples of wing shapes

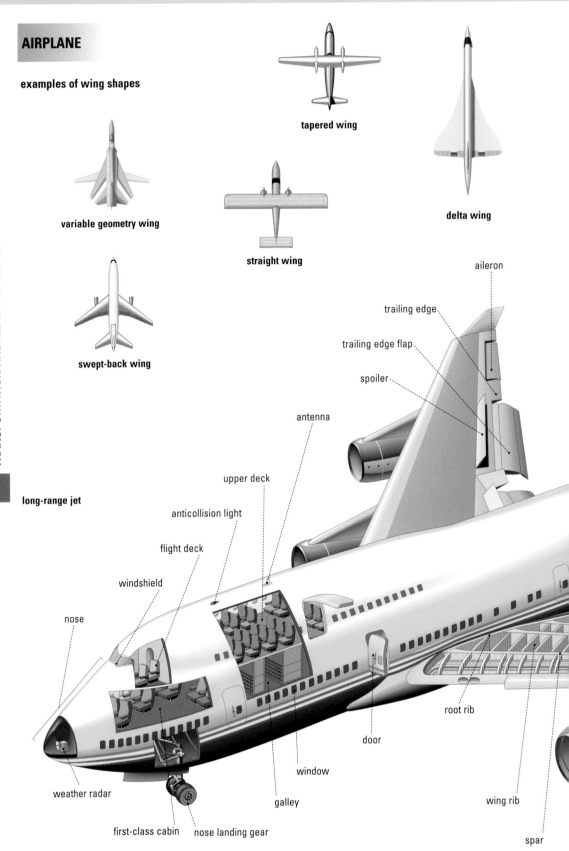

tapered wing

delta wing

variable geometry wing

straight wing

swept-back wing

aileron

trailing edge

trailing edge flap

spoiler

antenna

upper deck

long-range jet

anticollision light

flight deck

windshield

nose

root rib

door

window

weather radar

galley

wing rib

first-class cabin   nose landing gear

spar

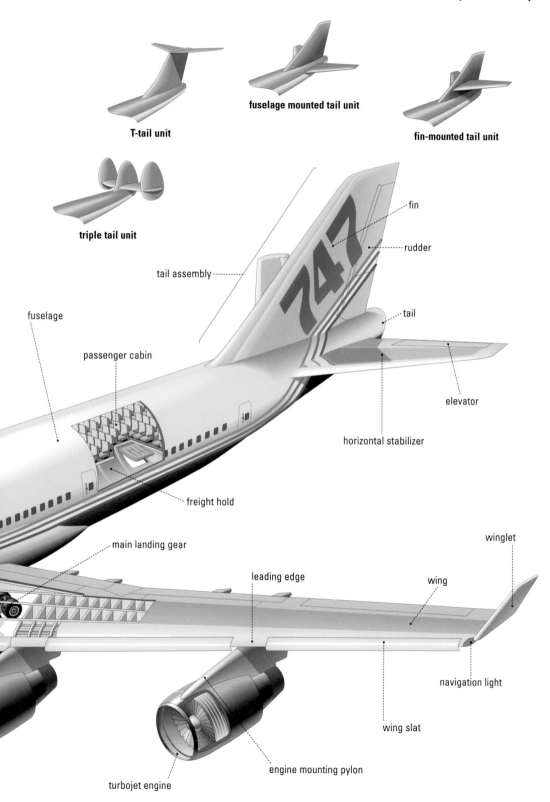

examples of tail shapes

T-tail unit

fuselage mounted tail unit

fin-mounted tail unit

triple tail unit

fin

rudder

tail assembly

fuselage

tail

passenger cabin

elevator

horizontal stabilizer

freight hold

winglet

main landing gear

leading edge

wing

navigation light

wing slat

turbojet engine

engine mounting pylon

examples of airplanes

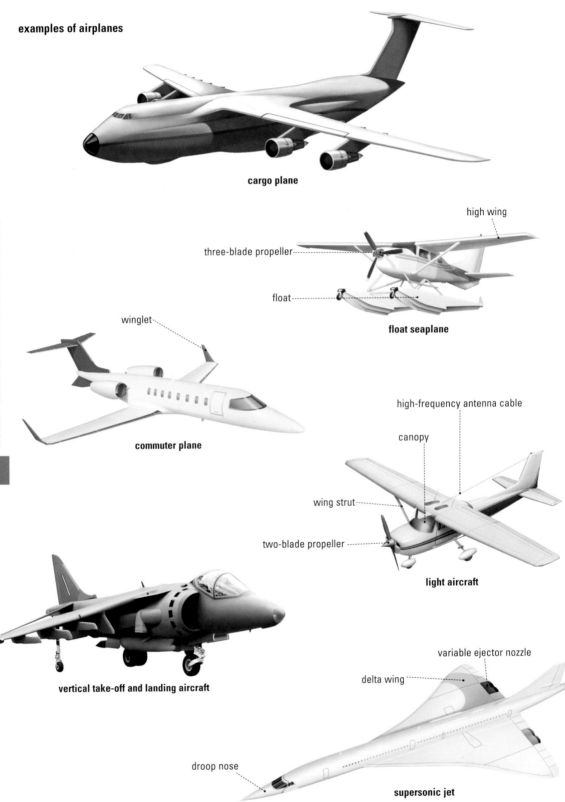

cargo plane

high wing

three-blade propeller

float

float seaplane

winglet

commuter plane

high-frequency antenna cable

canopy

wing strut

two-blade propeller

light aircraft

vertical take-off and landing aircraft

variable ejector nozzle

delta wing

droop nose

supersonic jet

Heavy machinery is a separate category of motor vehicle. Although rarely seen being driven on roads and highways, these vehicles dominate construction sites, quarries, and mines. They are often equipped with caterpillar treads, enabling them to move effortlessly over uneven terrain. Their heavy weight and powerful engines make it possible to dig deep into earth or to move large loads of material from one spot to another.

wheel loader

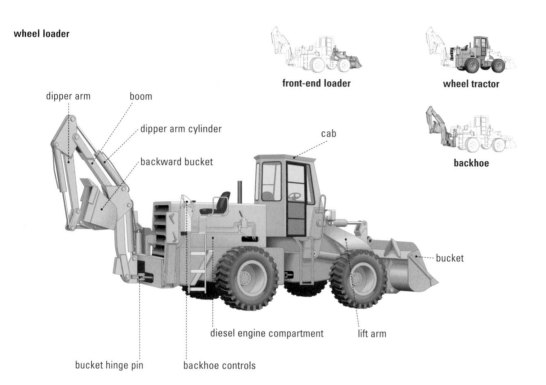

front-end loader

wheel tractor

backhoe

dipper arm

boom

dipper arm cylinder

cab

backward bucket

bucket

diesel engine compartment

lift arm

bucket hinge pin

backhoe controls

TRANSPORTATION AND HEAVY MACHINERY

hydraulic shovel

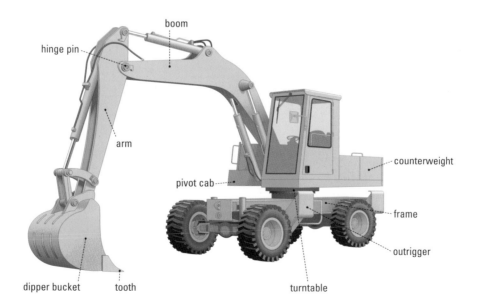

boom

hinge pin

arm

counterweight

pivot cab

frame

outrigger

dipper bucket

tooth

turntable

bulldozer

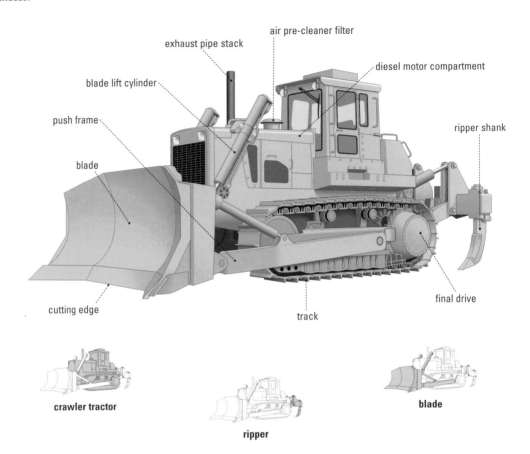

exhaust pipe stack

air pre-cleaner filter

blade lift cylinder

diesel motor compartment

push frame

ripper shank

blade

cutting edge

track

final drive

crawler tractor

ripper

blade

dump truck

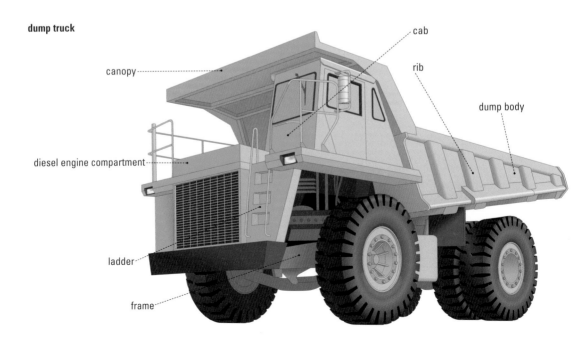

canopy

cab

rib

dump body

diesel engine compartment

ladder

frame

Today, the term "fine arts" is reserved for graphic arts and visual arts. Since the beginning of civilization, people have translated their feelings and perceptions of the world into art, for example, by painting or sculpting. Artists have a wide range of materials and techniques to choose from. Their choice helps them give their work a highly personal style.

PAINTING AND DRAWING

colour circle

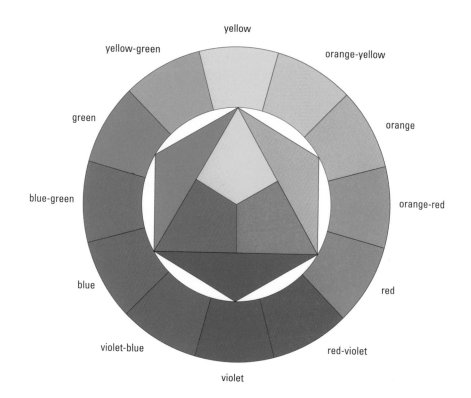

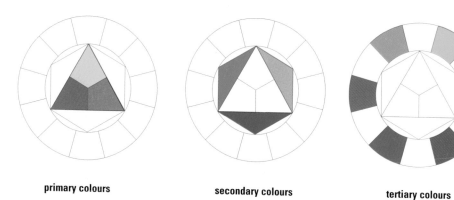

primary colours   **secondary colours**   **tertiary colours**

drawing supplies

felt tip pen

soft pastel

charcoal

oil pastel

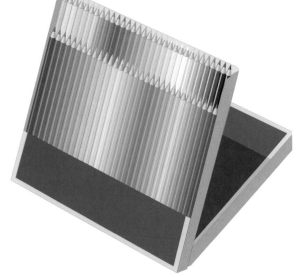

coloured pencils

wax crayons

painting supplies

brush

watercolour/gouache cakes

painting knife

oil paint

fan brush

watercolour/gouache tube

WOOD CARVING

steps

examples of tools

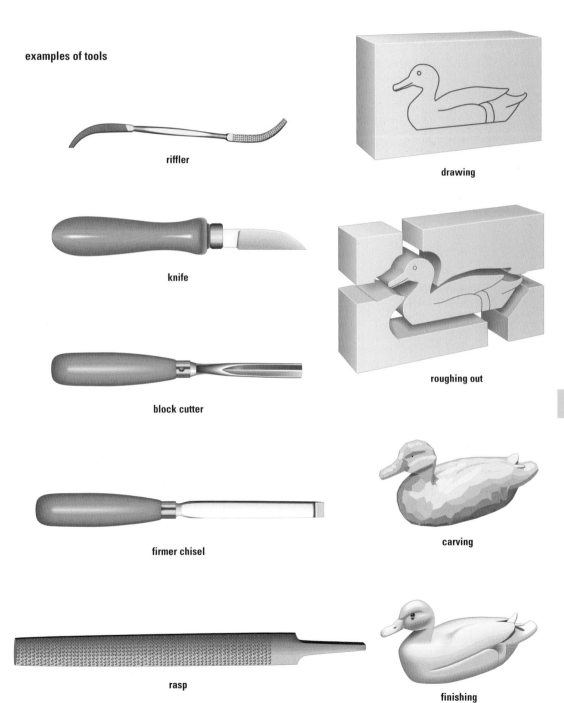

riffler

drawing

knife

roughing out

block cutter

firmer chisel

carving

rasp

finishing

CRAFTS

Sewing and knitting are ancient crafts. Until quite recently, these kinds of activities were generally performed by women. Back in the days when all clothing was made by hand, sewing and knitting served an entirely practical purpose. In modern society, however, these handicrafts have mainly become hobbies for a small number of enthusiasts.

SEWING AND KNITTING

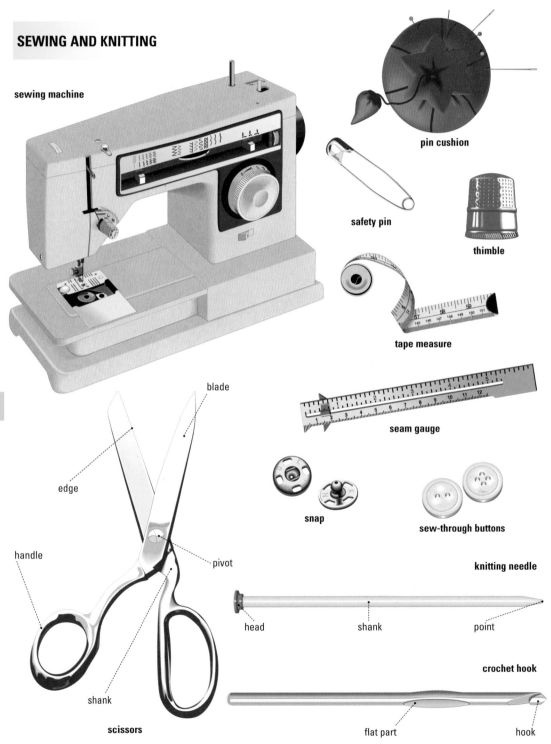

sewing machine

pin cushion

safety pin

thimble

tape measure

seam gauge

blade

edge

handle

pivot

snap

sew-through buttons

knitting needle

head   shank   point

shank

scissors

crochet hook

flat part   hook

All around the world, people construct their shelters from readily available materials. That is why traditional housing can be made from sheet metal, mud, stones, branches, straw, grass, or even snow. Although many houses built locally are of traditional design, modern buildings often resemble one another, whether they are constructed in the East or the West.

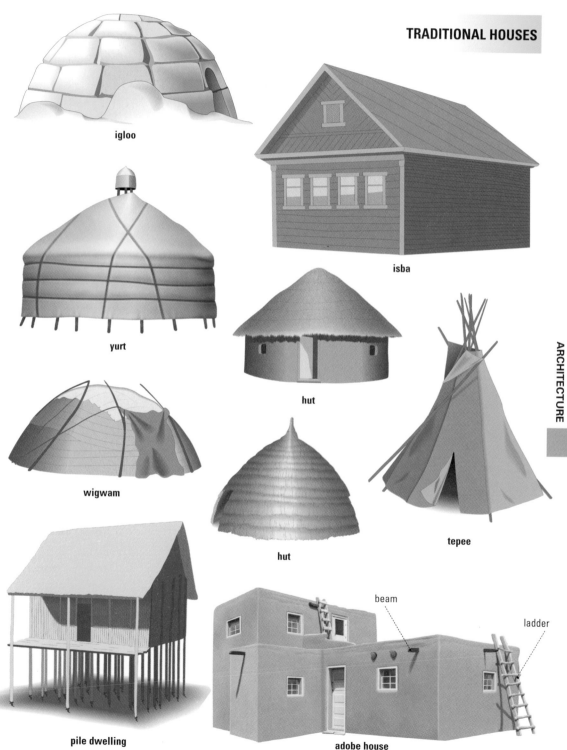

TRADITIONAL HOUSES

igloo

isba

yurt

hut

wigwam

hut

tepee

pile dwelling

adobe house

beam

ladder

CITY HOUSES

semi-detached house

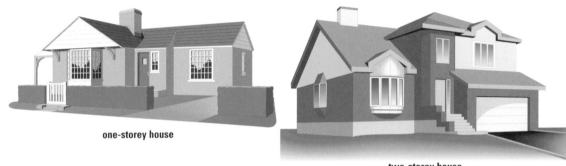

one-storey house

two-storey house

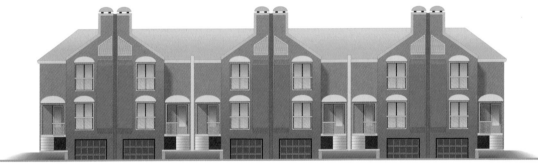

townhouses

high-rise apartment

condominiums

The history of the world can be charted by comparing different styles of architecture and admiring the many masterpieces that mark their respective eras. Whether practical, like the castle keep, or symbolic, like the cathedral bell tower rising up to the heavens, every element in a work of architecture takes into account the intended function of the building.

PYRAMID

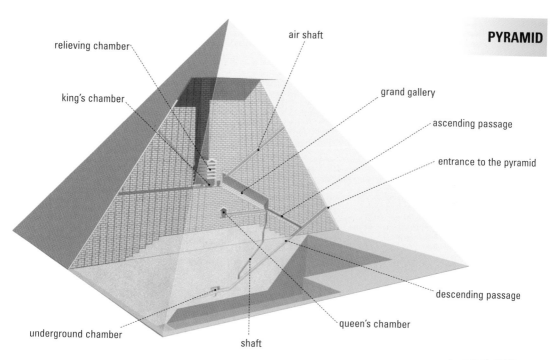

relieving chamber
air shaft
king's chamber
grand gallery
ascending passage
entrance to the pyramid
descending passage
queen's chamber
underground chamber
shaft

GREEK TEMPLE

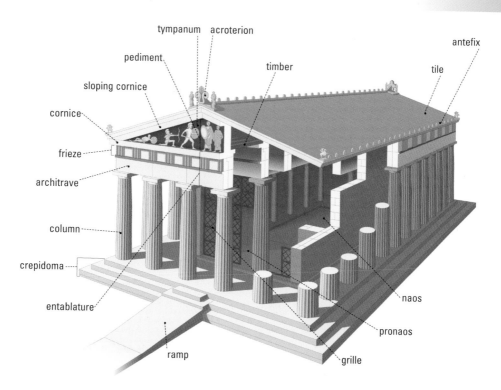

tympanum
acroterion
antefix
pediment
timber
tile
sloping cornice
cornice
frieze
architrave
column
crepidoma
naos
entablature
pronaos
ramp
grille

ROMAN HOUSE

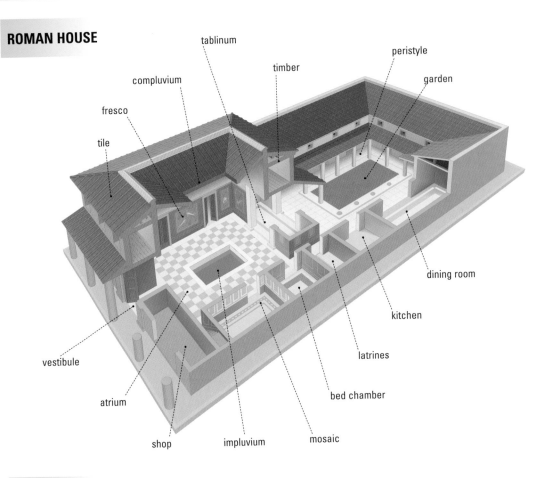

tablinum

compluvium

timber

peristyle

garden

fresco

tile

vestibule

atrium

shop

impluvium

mosaic

bed chamber

latrines

kitchen

dining room

ROMAN AMPHITHEATRE

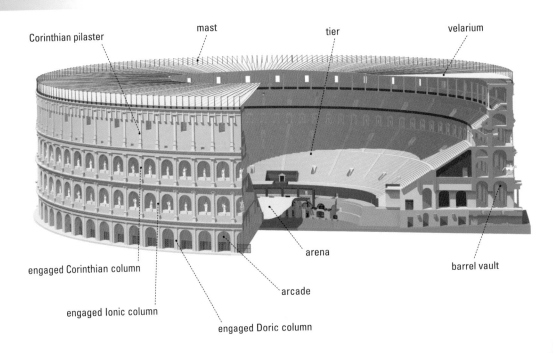

Corinthian pilaster

mast

tier

velarium

engaged Corinthian column

engaged Ionic column

engaged Doric column

arcade

arena

barrel vault

MOSQUE

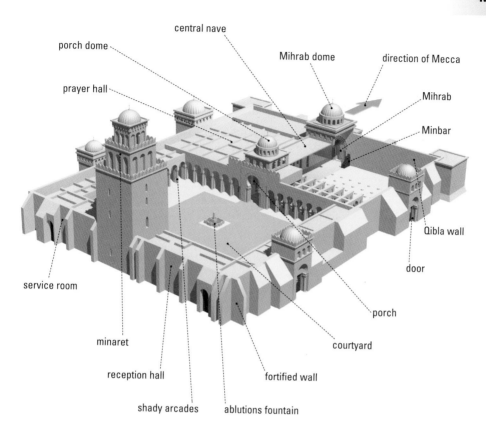

central nave

porch dome

Mihrab dome

direction of Mecca

prayer hall

Mihrab

Minbar

Qibla wall

door

service room

porch

minaret

courtyard

reception hall

fortified wall

shady arcades

ablutions fountain

AZTEC TEMPLE

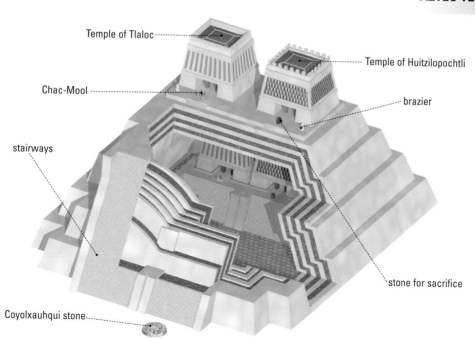

Temple of Tlaloc

Temple of Huitzilopochtli

Chac-Mool

brazier

stairways

stone for sacrifice

Coyolxauhqui stone

CASTLE

machicolation

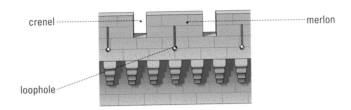

crenel

merlon

loophole

castle

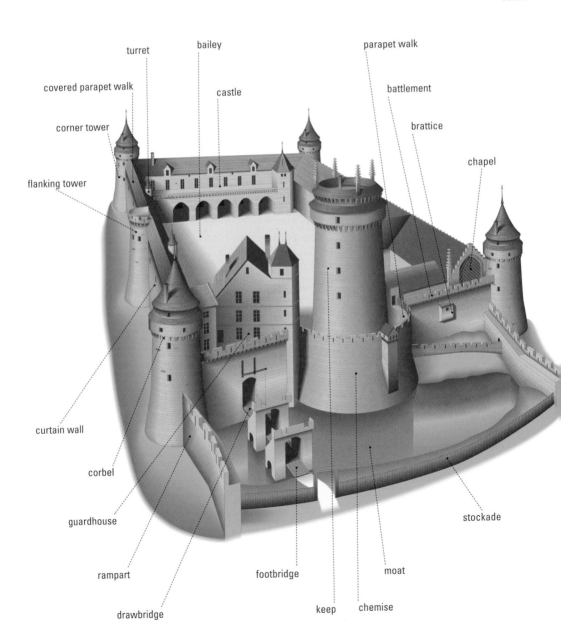

turret

bailey

parapet walk

covered parapet walk

castle

battlement

corner tower

brattice

flanking tower

chapel

curtain wall

corbel

guardhouse

stockade

rampart

footbridge

moat

drawbridge

keep

chemise

facade

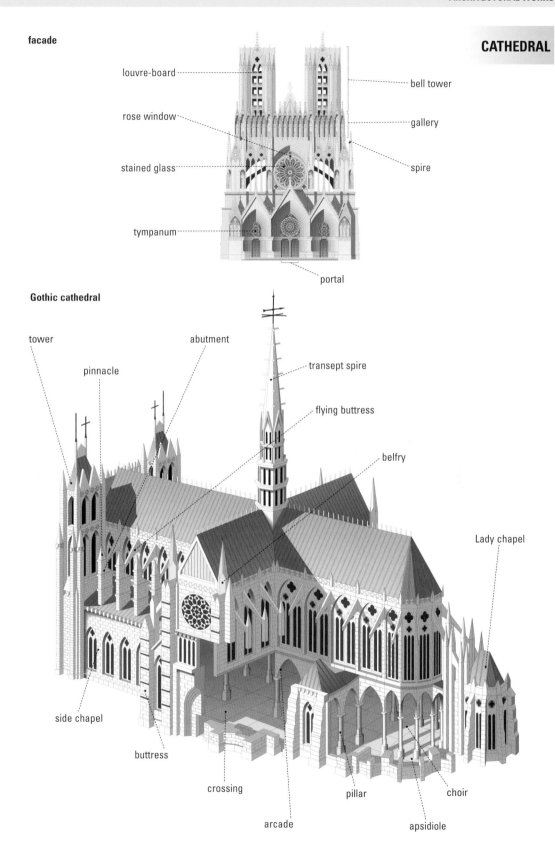

louvre-board

rose window

stained glass

tympanum

bell tower

gallery

spire

portal

Gothic cathedral

tower

pinnacle

abutment

transept spire

flying buttress

belfry

Lady chapel

side chapel

buttress

crossing

arcade

pillar

apsidiole

choir

Musical notation allows the many elements needed to perform a piece of music to be written down on a staff of five lines. With hundreds of different symbols to represent sounds, their pitch, and their duration, musical notation is a precious tool. Its universal language gives musicians of every culture access to the same vast musical library.

staff

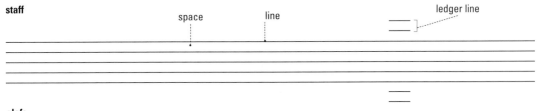

space   line   ledger line

clefs

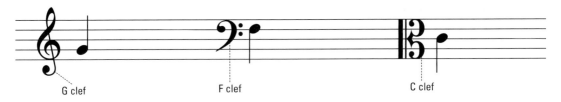

G clef   F clef   C clef

time signatures

three-four time   bar line

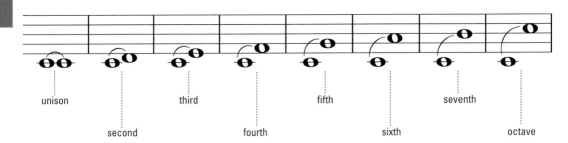

two-two time   four-four time   repeat mark

intervals

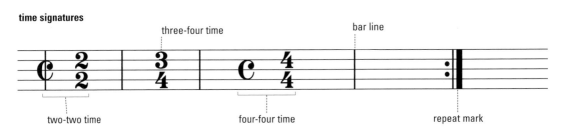

unison   third   fifth   seventh

second   fourth   sixth   octave

scale

C   D   E   F   G   A   B   C

MUSICAL NOTATION

rest symbols

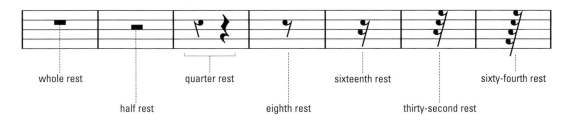

whole rest   quarter rest   sixteenth rest   sixty-fourth rest

half rest   eighth rest   thirty-second rest

ornaments

grace note   trill   turn   mordent

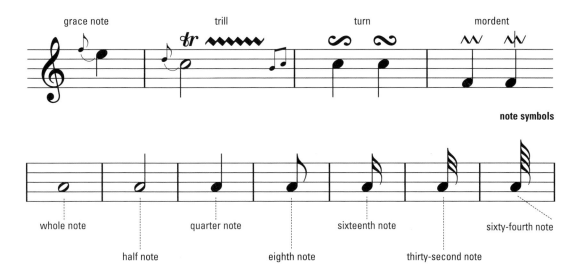

note symbols

whole note   quarter note   sixteenth note   sixty-fourth note

half note   eighth note   thirty-second note

accidentals

flat   double sharp

sharp   double flat

key signature   natural

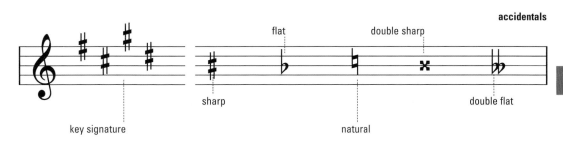

MUSIC

other signs

tie

chord   accent mark   arpeggio   pause

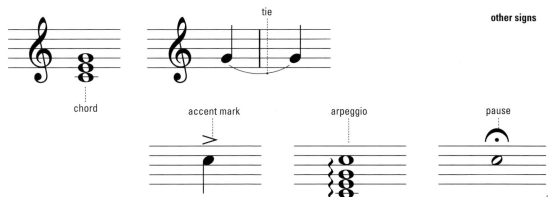

223

MUSICAL INSTRUMENTS

In every civilization, people have found ways to make music with many different kinds of objects. Today, there are thousands of musical instruments, from traditional to electronic, adapted for every style of music. Instruments can be classified in three basic categories: wind, string, and percussion. They can also be grouped according to other criteria, for example, instruments with keyboards.

TRADITIONAL MUSICAL INSTRUMENTS

accordion

bass keyboard

treble register

button

treble keyboard

bass register

key

bellows

grille

bagpipes

drone pipe

blow pipe

windbag

chanter

panpipe

harmonica

banjo

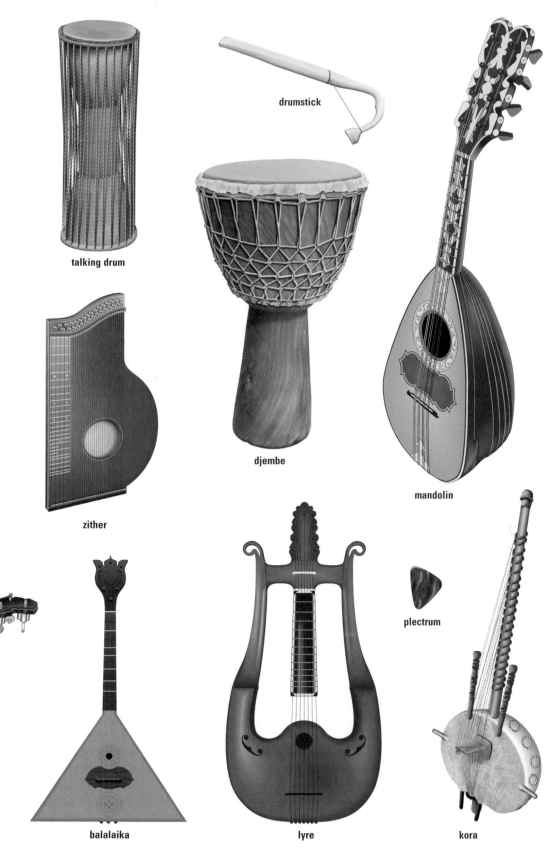

talking drum

drumstick

djembe

mandolin

zither

plectrum

balalaika

lyre

kora

KEYBOARD INSTRUMENTS

upright piano

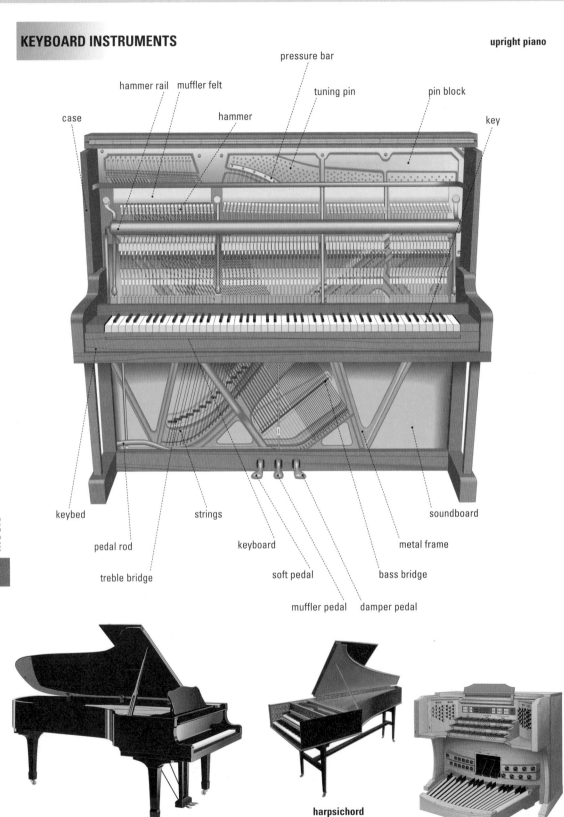

pressure bar

hammer rail   muffler felt

tuning pin

pin block

case

hammer

key

keybed

strings

soundboard

pedal rod

keyboard

metal frame

treble bridge

soft pedal

bass bridge

muffler pedal   damper pedal

concert grand

harpsichord

organ

STRINGED INSTRUMENTS

violin

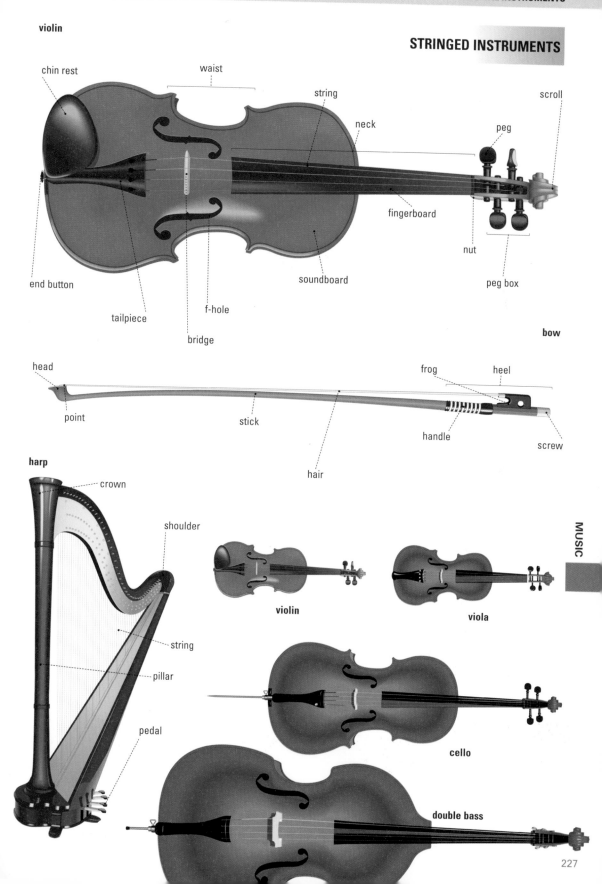

chin rest

waist

string

scroll

neck

peg

fingerboard

nut

end button

soundboard

peg box

tailpiece

f-hole

bridge

bow

head

frog

heel

point

stick

handle

screw

hair

harp

crown

shoulder

violin

viola

string

pillar

pedal

cello

double bass

electric guitar

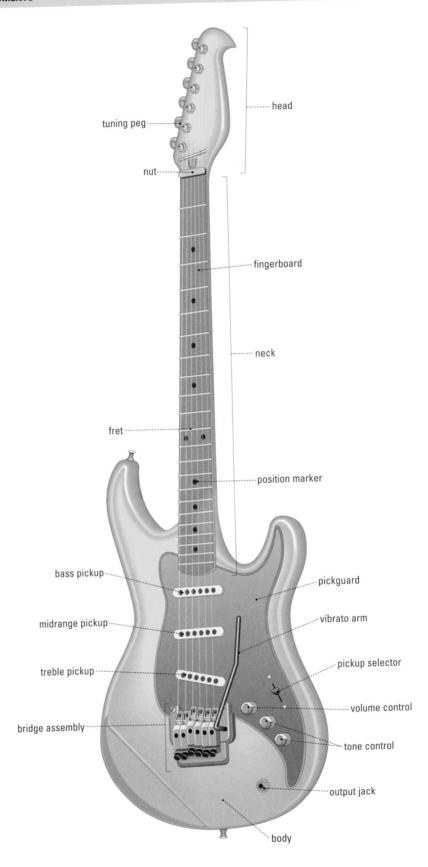

tuning peg

head

nut

fingerboard

neck

fret

position marker

bass pickup

pickguard

midrange pickup

vibrato arm

treble pickup

pickup selector

bridge assembly

volume control

tone control

output jack

body

bass guitar

body

bridge

pickups

strap system

tuning peg

nut

fret

head

neck

fingerboard

position marker

bass tone control

treble tone control

balancer

volume control

acoustic guitar

peg

head

body

neck

soundboard

position marker

nut

fret

heel

purfling

rib

rose

bridge

WIND INSTRUMENTS

trumpet

finger button

little finger hook

mouthpipe

bell

ring

mouthpiece receiver

mouthpiece

tuning slide

first valve slide

third valve slide

water key

thumb hook

valve

valve casing

second valve slide

cornet

bugle

mute

trombone

French horn

saxhorn

tuba

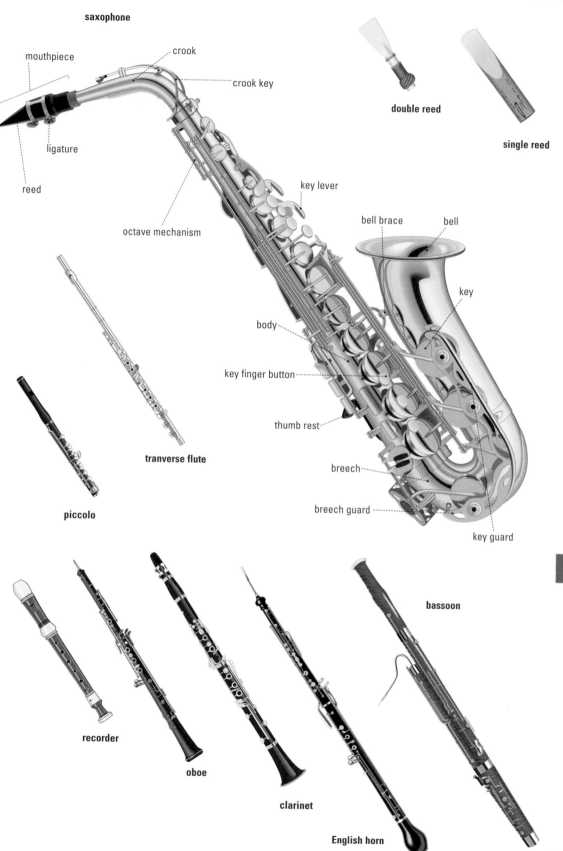

saxophone

mouthpiece

crook

crook key

ligature

reed

double reed

single reed

octave mechanism

key lever

bell brace

bell

key

body

key finger button

thumb rest

breech

breech guard

key guard

transverse flute

piccolo

recorder

oboe

clarinet

English horn

bassoon

PERCUSSION INSTRUMENTS

drums

sticks

tom-tom

cymbal

high-hat cymbal

wire brush

batter head

tenor drum

snare drum

bass drum

tripod stand

mallet

pedal

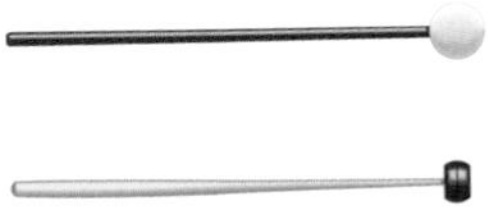

mallets

metal rod

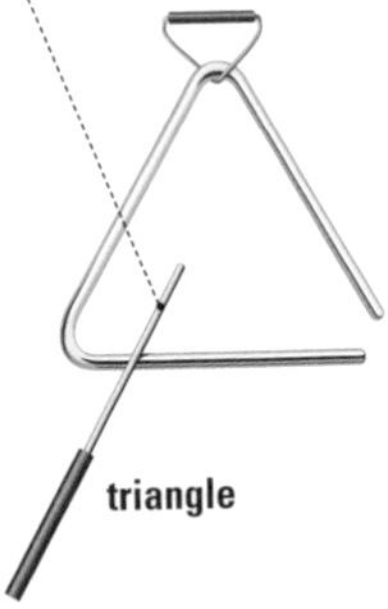

triangle

sleigh bells

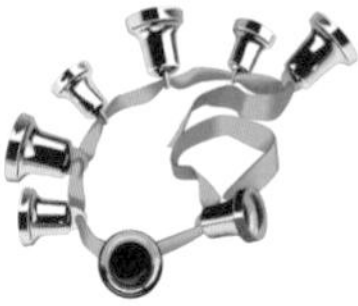

set of bells

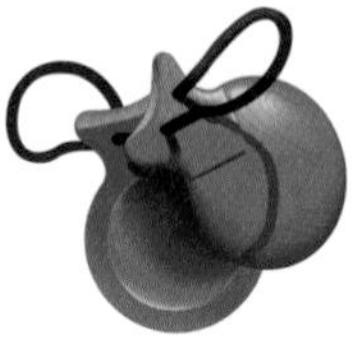

castanets

sistrum

bongos

kettledrum

jingle

tambourine

xylophone

ELECTRONIC INSTRUMENTS

synthesizer

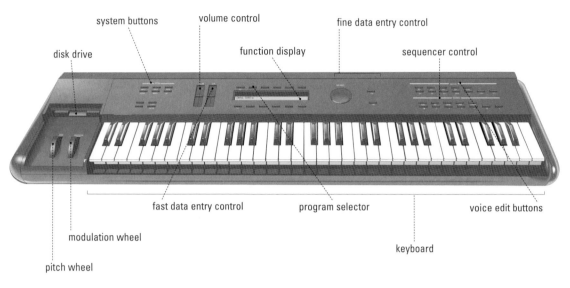

system buttons

volume control

fine data entry control

disk drive

function display

sequencer control

fast data entry control

program selector

voice edit buttons

modulation wheel

keyboard

pitch wheel

electronic drum pad

wind synthesizer controller

mouthpiece

keys

electronic piano

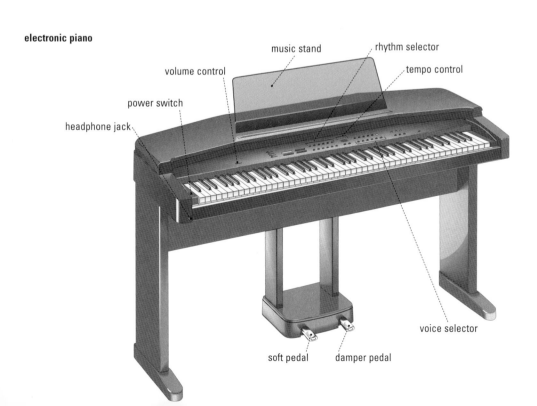

music stand

rhythm selector

volume control

tempo control

power switch

headphone jack

voice selector

soft pedal

damper pedal

233

An orchestra is a group of musicians forming a musical ensemble. There are different types of ensembles, depending on the number and the kind of instruments being brought together. The symphony orchestra, with 100 to 150 instruments distributed in four sections-strings, woodwinds, brass, and percussion-is the biggest kind orchestra. The musicians play under the direction of a conductor.

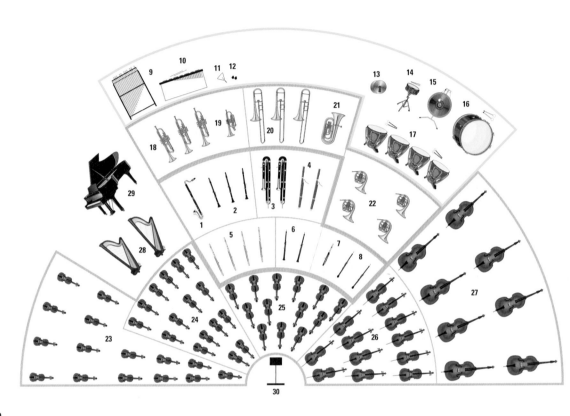

woodwind family	percussion instruments	brass family	violin family
1 bass clarinet	**9** tubular bells	**18** trumpets	**23** first violins
2 clarinets	**10** xylophone	**19** cornet	**24** second violins
3 contrabassoons	**11** triangle	**20** trombones	**25** violas
4 bassoons	**12** castanets	**21** tuba	**26** cellos
5 flutes	**13** cymbals	**22** French horns	**27** double basses
6 oboes	**14** snare drum		
7 piccolo	**15** gong	**28** harps	
8 English horns	**16** bass drum	**29** piano	
	17 timpani	**30** conductor's podium	

When a photograph is taken, an image is produced on the film inside, which is sensitive to light. After it has been exposed to the light, the film is developed and a negative is obtained. When the negative is projected onto white photographic paper, the image of the scene that was photographed appears. There are many different types of cameras available today, the latest being digital.

single-lens reflex (SLR) camera

film rewind button

accessory shoe

control panel

hot-shoe contact

command control dial

film advance mode

film speed

exposure mode

lens cap

remote control terminal

zoom lens

focus mode selector

camera body

shutter release button

objective lens

photographic accessories

electronic flash

flashtube

compact flash memory card

still video film disk

photoelectric cell

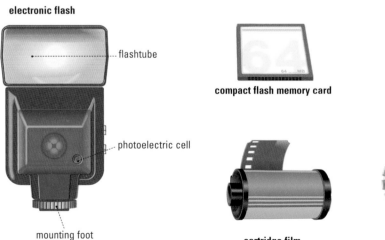

mounting foot

cartridge film

film disk

examples of still cameras

pocket camera

Polaroid® camera

disk camera

zoom camera

underwater camera

digital camera

view camera

disposable camera

COMMUNICATIONS

Radio can broadcast important events directly as they happen, over great distances. During a radio broadcast, the voice of the announcer is transformed into electronic signals with the help of a microphone. These signals are then converted into radio waves by the radio station. When a radio set or a receiver picks up these waves, they are changed back into sounds.

radio (studio and control room)

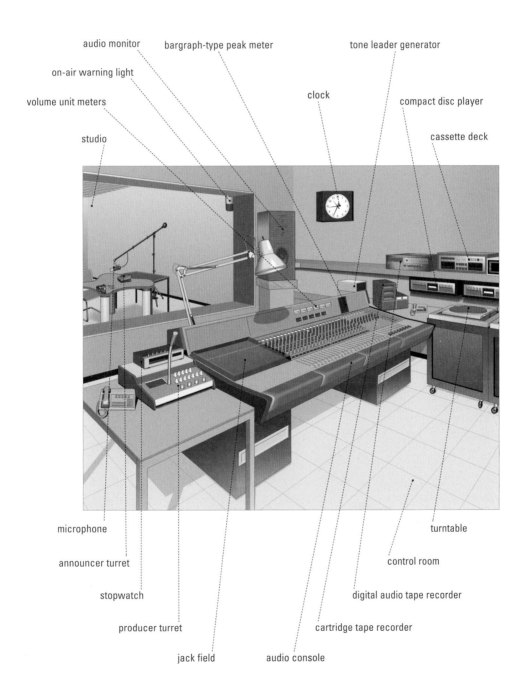

audio monitor

bargraph-type peak meter

tone leader generator

on-air warning light

clock

compact disc player

volume unit meters

cassette deck

studio

microphone

turntable

announcer turret

control room

stopwatch

digital audio tape recorder

producer turret

cartridge tape recorder

jack field

audio console

COMMUNICATIONS

TELEVISION

The video cameras and microphones in a television studio transform images and sounds into electronic signals. These signals are converted into radio waves by the television station, which then broadcasts them. Television programs are sent by satellite, by underground cable, or directly to the viewer. The television set can also receive signals from a video cassette player or DVD player.

studio floor

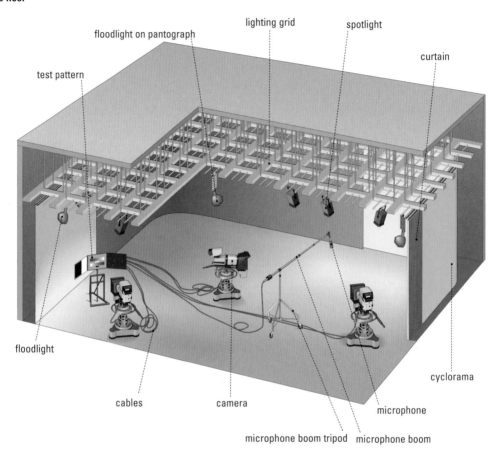

test pattern

floodlight on pantograph

lighting grid

spotlight

curtain

floodlight

cables

camera

microphone

cyclorama

microphone boom tripod

microphone boom

camera

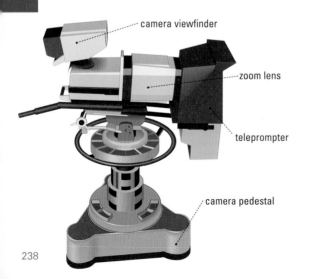

camera viewfinder

zoom lens

teleprompter

camera pedestal

satellite dish

dish

feedhorn

pole

COMMUNICATIONS

television set

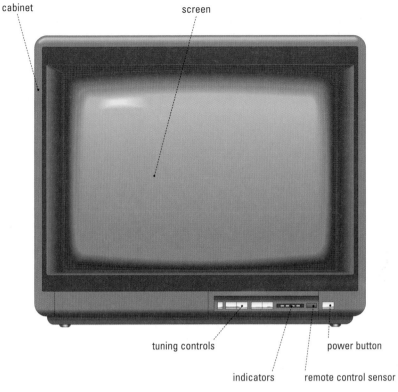

cabinet

screen

tuning controls

power button

indicators

remote control sensor

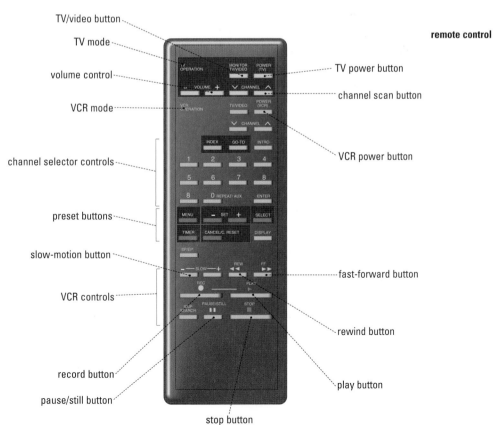

remote control

TV/video button

TV mode

volume control

VCR mode

channel selector controls

preset buttons

slow-motion button

VCR controls

record button

pause/still button

stop button

TV power button

channel scan button

VCR power button

fast-forward button

rewind button

play button

videocassette recorder

videocassette

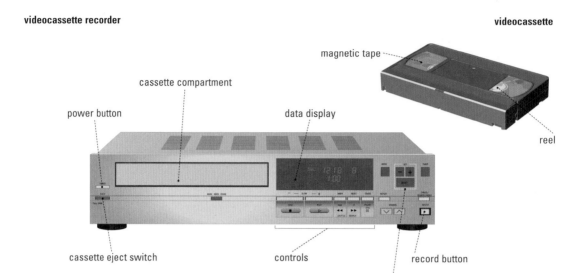

magnetic tape

cassette compartment

power button

data display

reel

cassette eject switch

controls

record button

preset buttons

DVD player

power button

display

disc tray

digital versatile disc (DVD)

analog camcorder

eyecup

edit search button

power/functions switch

electronic viewfinder

videotape operation controls

zoom lens

display panel

nightshot switch

microphone

focus selector

near/far dial

Technological advances in the recording and reproduction of music in the last century have steadily
improved sound quality. Music lovers now have a wide
range of musical equipment to choose from. Cassettes
and compact discs can be played on individual
components or on complete mini-stereo sound systems.
Some homes even have a record player for listening
to old vinyl records.

system components

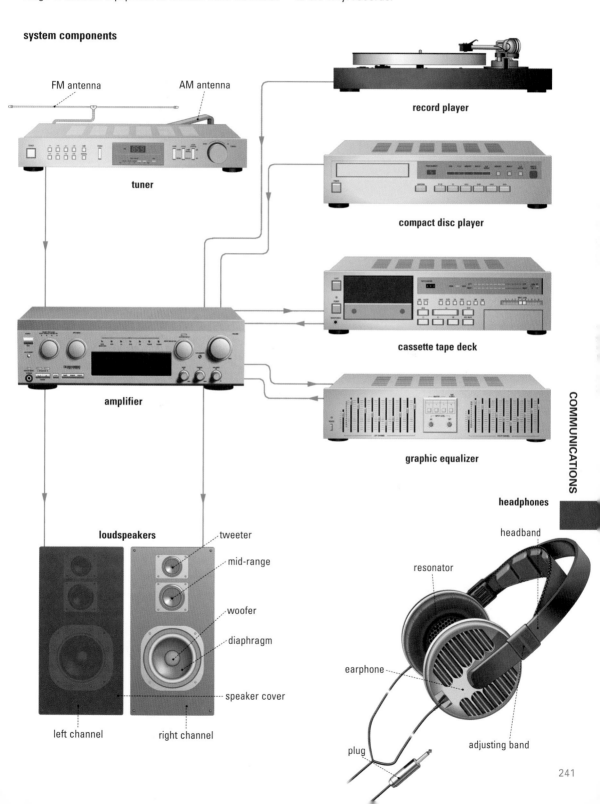

record player

FM antenna

AM antenna

tuner

compact disc player

cassette tape deck

amplifier

graphic equalizer

headphones

loudspeakers

tweeter

mid-range

woofer

diaphragm

speaker cover

left channel

right channel

headband

resonator

earphone

plug

adjusting band

With the miniaturization of electronic components, people can easily listen to their favourite music while on the move. Some sound systems, like the portable CD player, have only one specific function, while other portables resemble miniature sound reproducing systems. The portable CD radio cassette recorder allows one to listen to music that is either being broadcast on a radio station or has been pre-recorded on a cassette or compact disc.

portable CD radio cassette recorder

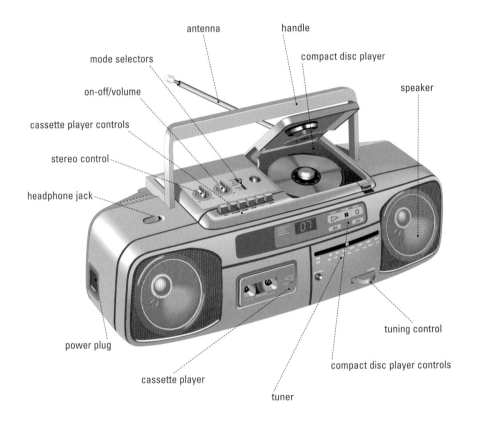

antenna

handle

mode selectors

compact disc player

on-off/volume

speaker

cassette player controls

stereo control

headphone jack

power plug

cassette player

tuner

tuning control

compact disc player controls

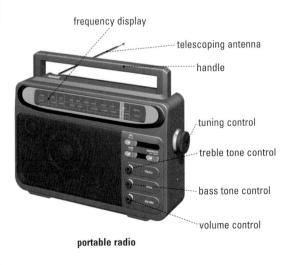

frequency display

telescoping antenna

handle

tuning control

treble tone control

bass tone control

volume control

portable radio

clock radio

compact disc

portable compact disc player

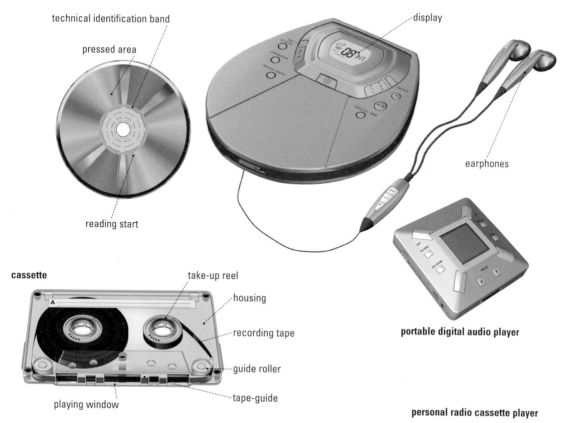

technical identification band

pressed area

reading start

display

earphones

cassette

take-up reel

housing

recording tape

guide roller

tape-guide

playing window

portable digital audio player

personal radio cassette player

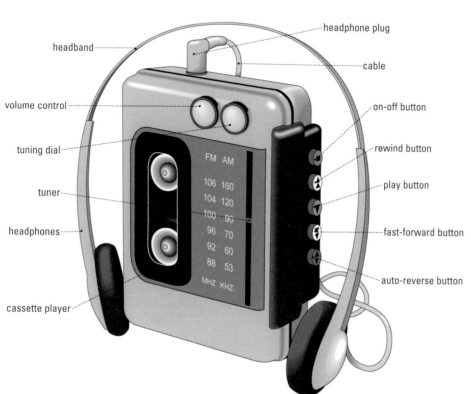

headphone plug

headband

cable

volume control

on-off button

tuning dial

rewind button

tuner

play button

FM AM

106 160
104 120
100 90
96 70
92 60
88 53

MHZ KHZ

headphones

fast-forward button

cassette player

auto-reverse button

Whether portable, fixed, or wireless, the telephone, along with television and radio, is one of the most important forms of telecommunications. Two people separated by thousands of kilometres can have a conversation, communicate in writing over the Internet, or send each other written documents using a fax machine. Thanks to technology like communication satellites, the exchange of information is being conducted at an ever-increasing pace.

telephone set

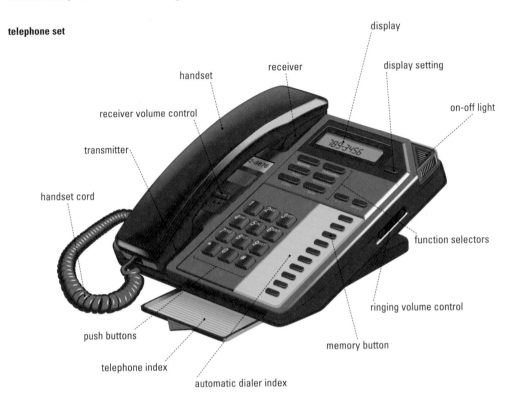

display

receiver

display setting

handset

on-off light

receiver volume control

transmitter

handset cord

function selectors

push buttons

ringing volume control

telephone index

memory button

automatic dialer index

telephone answering machine

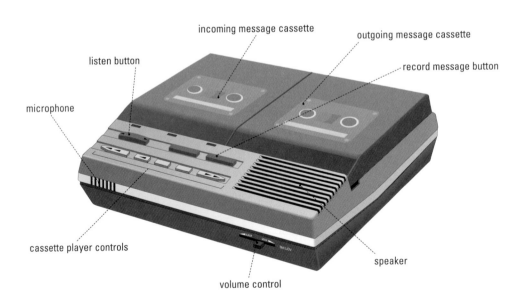

incoming message cassette

outgoing message cassette

listen button

record message button

microphone

cassette player controls

speaker

volume control

pay phone

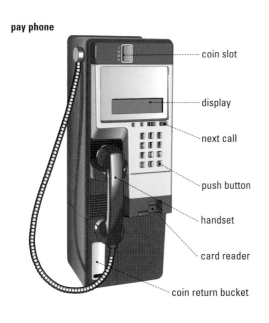

- coin slot
- display
- next call
- push button
- handset
- card reader
- coin return bucket

push-button telephone

cordless telephone

fax machine

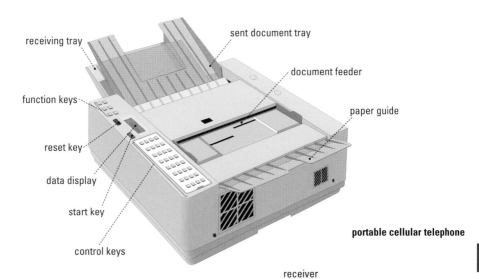

- receiving tray
- sent document tray
- document feeder
- function keys
- paper guide
- reset key
- data display
- start key
- control keys

portable cellular telephone

headset kit

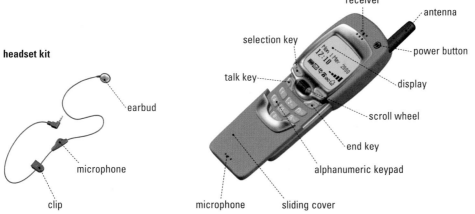

- receiver
- antenna
- selection key
- power button
- talk key
- display
- earbud
- scroll wheel
- microphone
- end key
- clip
- alphanumeric keypad
- microphone
- sliding cover

A computer is an electronic appliance capable of transforming, storing, and sending coded information at an amazing speed. The personal computer has several main elements. They are housed in a central case surrounded by different devices including a mouse, keyboard, monitor, and printer. Whether they are visible or hidden, computers can now be found everywhere.

video monitor

keyboard

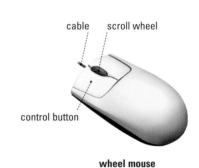

cable   scroll wheel

control button

wheel mouse

mouse pad

diskette

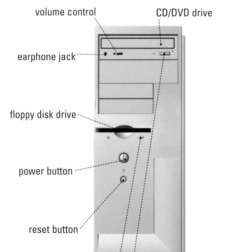

volume control   CD/DVD drive

earphone jack

floppy disk drive

power button

reset button

floppy disk eject button   CD/DVD eject button

tower case

flat screen monitor

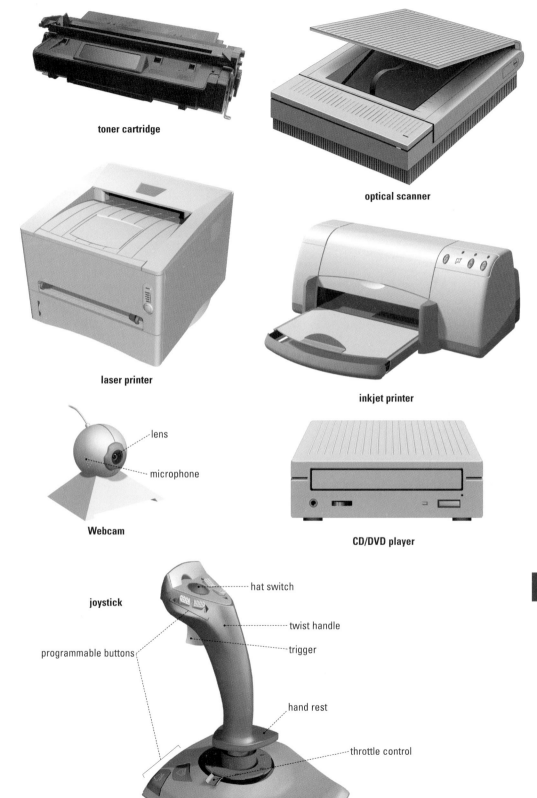

toner cartridge

optical scanner

laser printer

inkjet printer

lens

microphone

Webcam

CD/DVD player

joystick

hat switch

twist handle

trigger

programmable buttons

hand rest

throttle control

base

INTERNET

The Internet is a vast system of international communication. It is made up of a series of computer networks connected by telephone and cable lines that communicate in a common computer language. Developed in 1991 in the United States, the World Wide Web (WWW) has allowed millions of computers and computer users around the world to link together, making communication and the exchange of information easier.

URL (uniform resource locator)

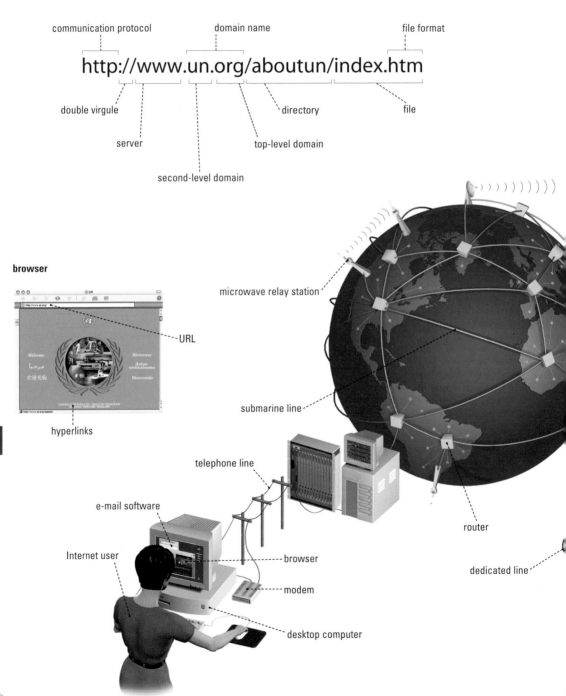

communication protocol

domain name

file format

http://www.un.org/aboutun/index.htm

double virgule

directory

file

server

top-level domain

second-level domain

browser

URL

hyperlinks

microwave relay station

submarine line

telephone line

e-mail software

router

Internet user

browser

dedicated line

modem

desktop computer

Internet uses

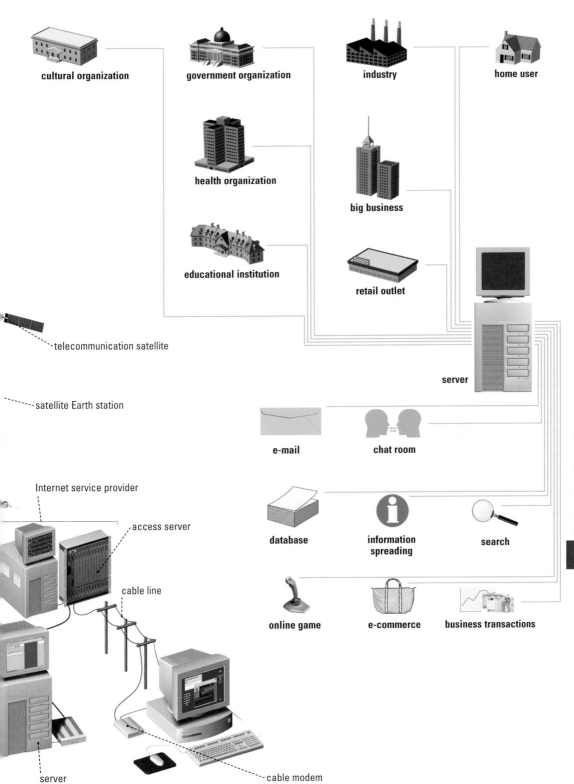

cultural organization

government organization

industry

home user

health organization

big business

educational institution

retail outlet

telecommunication satellite

satellite Earth station

server

e-mail

chat room

Internet service provider

access server

database

information spreading

search

cable line

online game

e-commerce

business transactions

server

cable modem

COMMUNICATIONS

DOWNTOWN

Cities are built-up areas that bring together a large number of people. Most people live in residential neighbourhoods and work in industrial zones on the city's outskirts or in large office buildings downtown.

The heart of a typical city also includes a business district as well as establishments that offer a variety of goods and services. These establishments may include a city hall, universities, and museums, to name a few.

cathedral

convention centre

office tower

median strip

square

park

railroad station

planetarium

railroad track

freeway

street

delivery ramp

traffic island

boulevard

hotel

skyscraper

high-rise apartment

restaurant

church

office building

museum

stadium

parking lot

streetlamp

store

TERMINAL AND STATIONS

In every city, there are areas specially reserved for the arrival and departure of vehicles like trains, airplanes, and subways. Airports are always built outside of large city centres, while subway stations are usually located in urban areas. Stations where trains pick up and drop off passengers can be found in every kind of setting.

PASSENGER TERMINAL

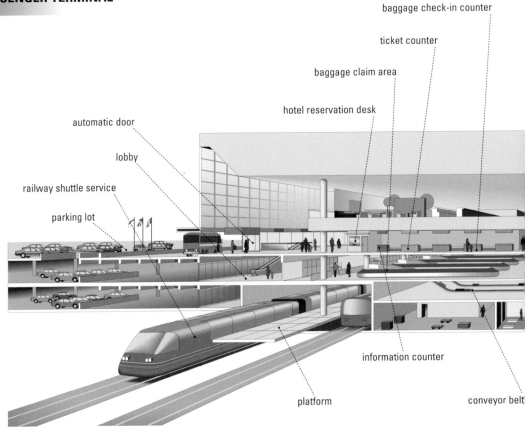

baggage check-in counter

ticket counter

baggage claim area

hotel reservation desk

automatic door

lobby

railway shuttle service

parking lot

information counter

platform

conveyor belt

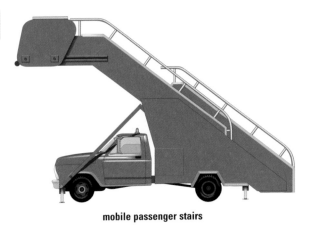

mobile passenger stairs

universal step

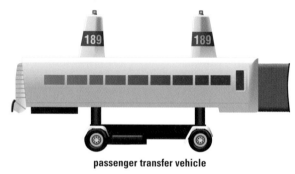

passenger transfer vehicle

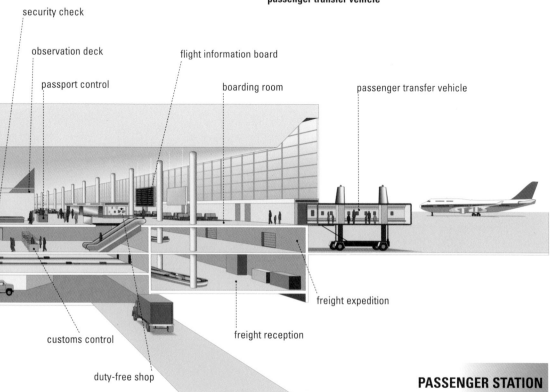

security check

observation deck

flight information board

passport control

boarding room

passenger transfer vehicle

freight expedition

customs control

freight reception

duty-free shop

PASSENGER STATION

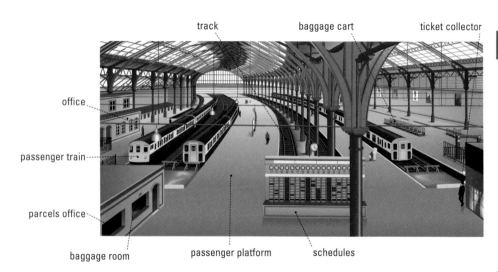

track

baggage cart

ticket collector

office

passenger train

parcels office

baggage room

passenger platform

schedules

SUBWAY STATION

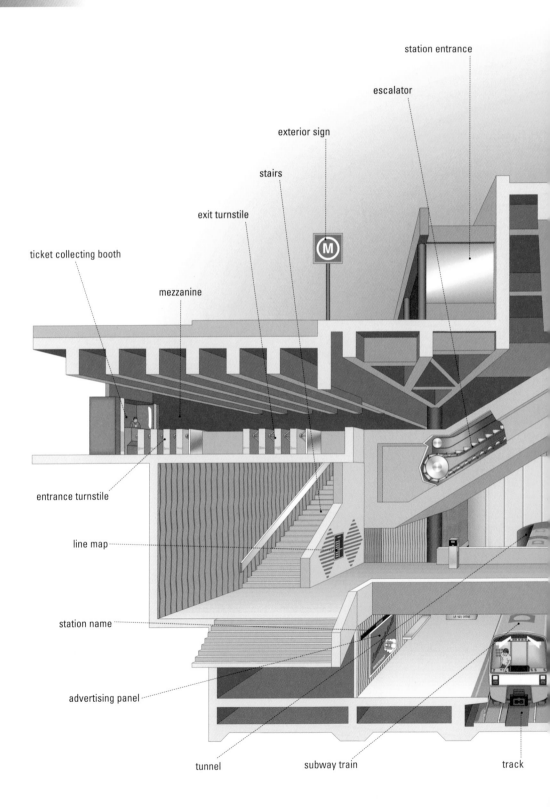

station entrance

escalator

exterior sign

stairs

exit turnstile

ticket collecting booth

mezzanine

entrance turnstile

line map

station name

advertising panel

tunnel

subway train

track

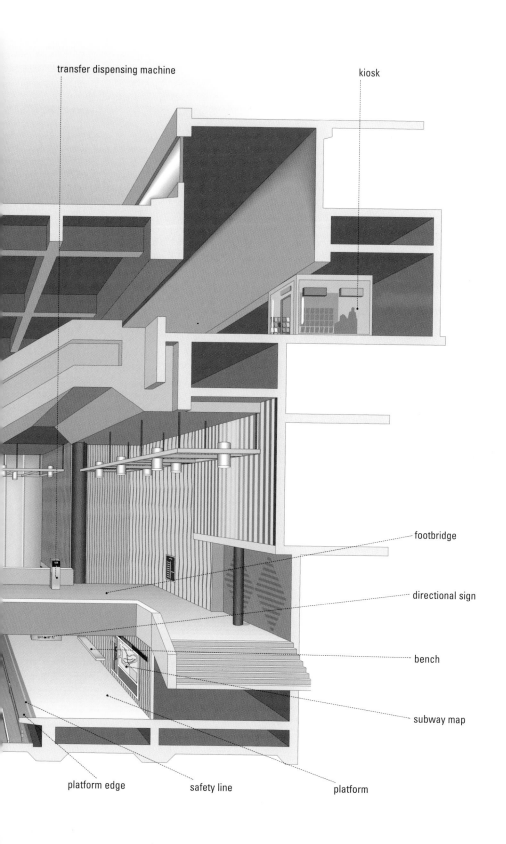

transfer dispensing machine

kiosk

footbridge

directional sign

bench

subway map

platform edge

safety line

platform

COMMERCIAL SERVICES

Every city has a large number of commercial establishments that offer a wide range of goods and services to the public. Supermarkets, shopping malls, restaurants, and service stations are just a few of the businesses that operate in a typical city. In these establishments, one can buy all kinds of consumer goods, including food, clothing, prepared meals, and gasoline.

SUPERMARKET

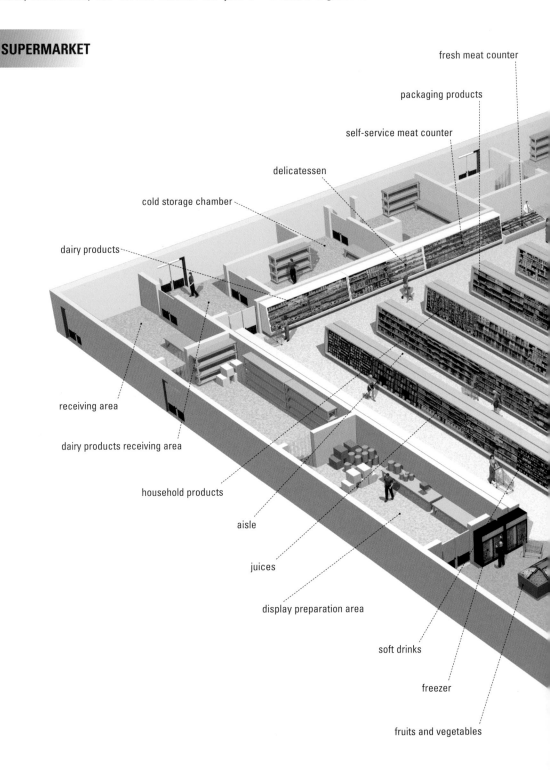

fresh meat counter

packaging products

self-service meat counter

delicatessen

cold storage chamber

dairy products

receiving area

dairy products receiving area

household products

aisle

juices

display preparation area

soft drinks

freezer

fruits and vegetables

checkout

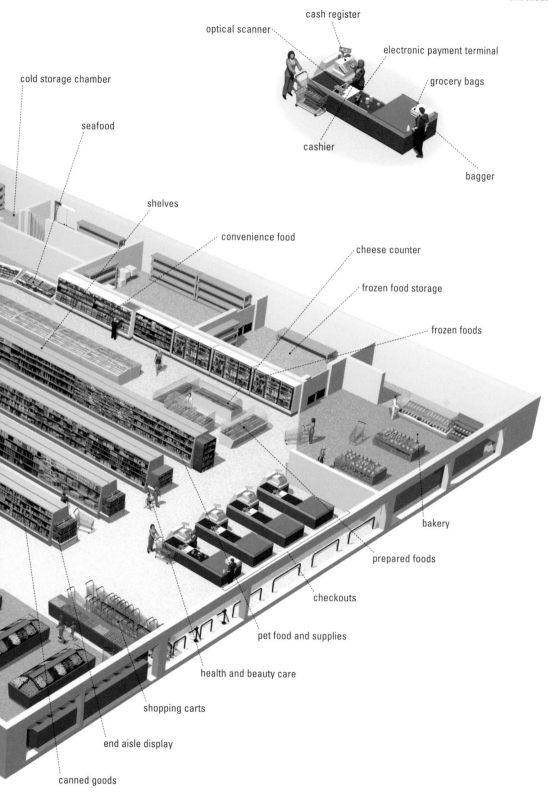

cash register

optical scanner

electronic payment terminal

grocery bags

cold storage chamber

seafood

cashier

bagger

shelves

convenience food

cheese counter

frozen food storage

frozen foods

bakery

prepared foods

checkouts

pet food and supplies

health and beauty care

shopping carts

end aisle display

canned goods

SOCIETY

SHOPPING CENTRE

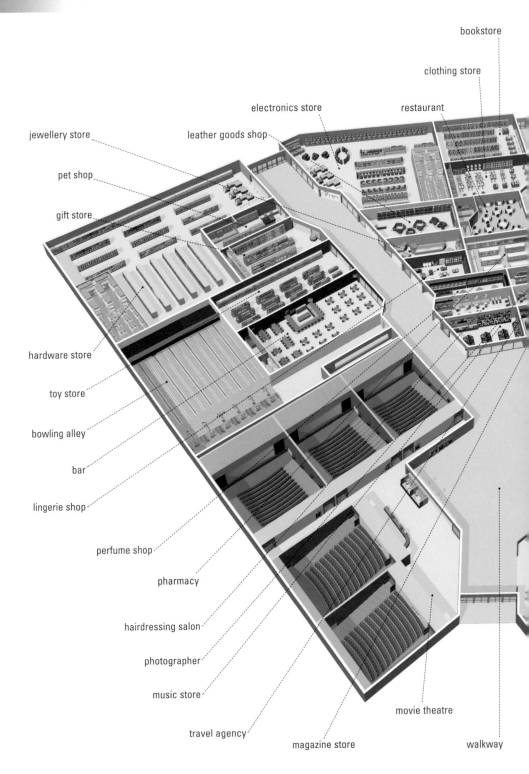

bookstore

clothing store

electronics store

restaurant

jewellery store

leather goods shop

pet shop

gift store

hardware store

toy store

bowling alley

bar

lingerie shop

perfume shop

pharmacy

hairdressing salon

photographer

music store

movie theatre

travel agency

magazine store

walkway

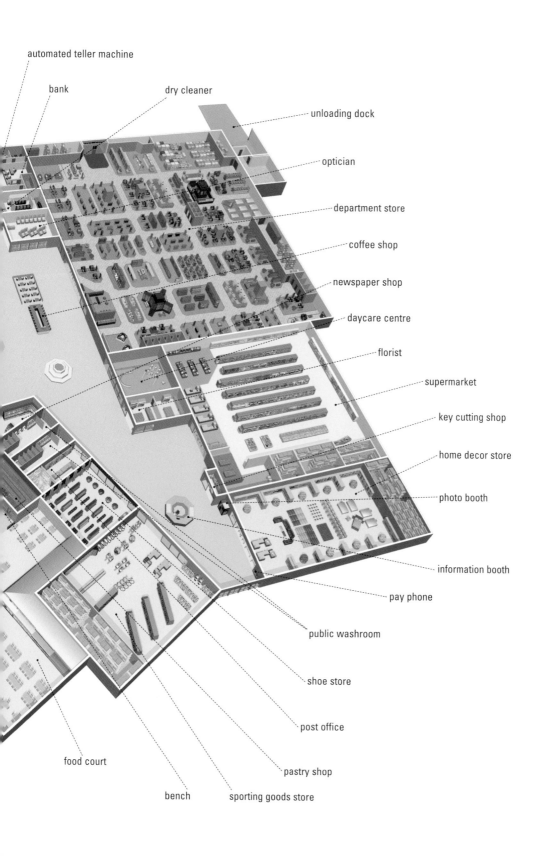

automated teller machine

bank

dry cleaner

unloading dock

optician

department store

coffee shop

newspaper shop

daycare centre

florist

supermarket

key cutting shop

home decor store

photo booth

information booth

pay phone

public washroom

shoe store

post office

food court

pastry shop

bench   sporting goods store

RESTAURANT

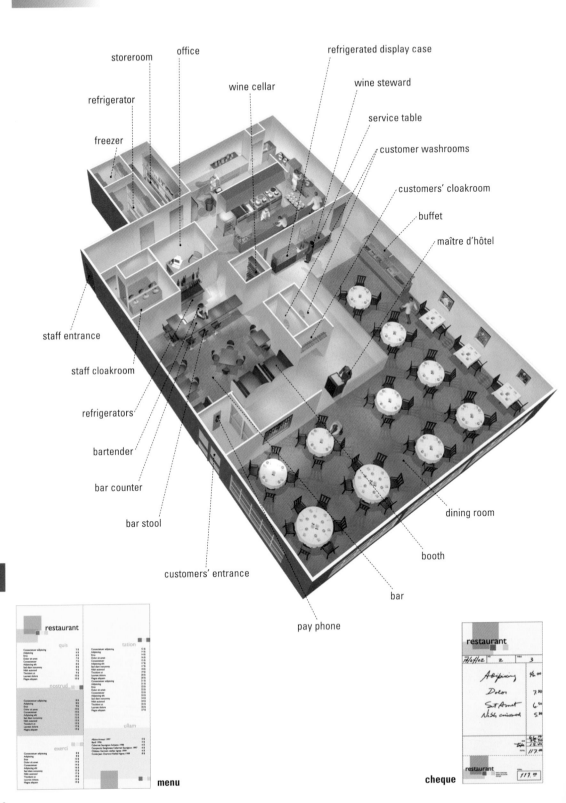

storeroom

office

refrigerated display case

wine cellar

wine steward

refrigerator

service table

freezer

customer washrooms

customers' cloakroom

buffet

maître d'hôtel

staff entrance

staff cloakroom

refrigerators

bartender

bar counter

bar stool

customers' entrance

dining room

booth

bar

pay phone

menu

cheque

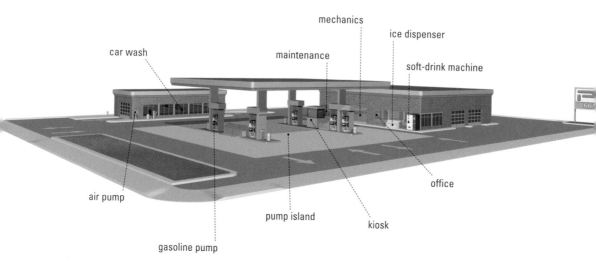

mechanics

ice dispenser

car wash

maintenance

soft-drink machine

air pump

office

pump island

kiosk

gasoline pump

gasoline pump

instructions display

total sale display

card reader slot

volume display

alphanumeric keyboard

price per litre

receipt dispenser

type of fuel

pump number

operating instructions

pump nozzle

gasoline pump hose

In addition to fighting fires and rescuing victims, firefighters look after the public's safety in several ways. Firefighters are among the first to rush to the scene of a road accident or a flooding. The police are also responsible for people's safety. Besides maintaining order, law enforcement officers discourage criminal activity by patrolling and surveying public areas.

FIRE PREVENTION

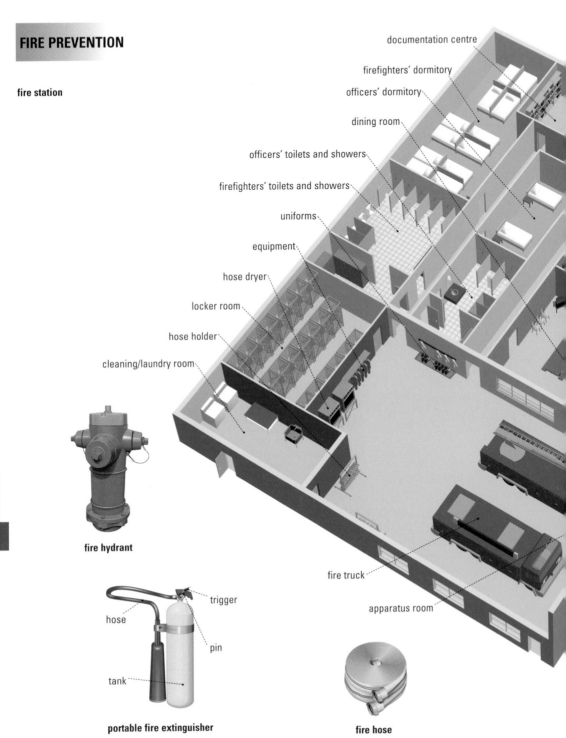

fire station

documentation centre

firefighters' dormitory

officers' dormitory

dining room

officers' toilets and showers

firefighters' toilets and showers

uniforms

equipment

hose dryer

locker room

hose holder

cleaning/laundry room

fire hydrant

fire truck

apparatus room

portable fire extinguisher

trigger

hose

pin

tank

fire hose

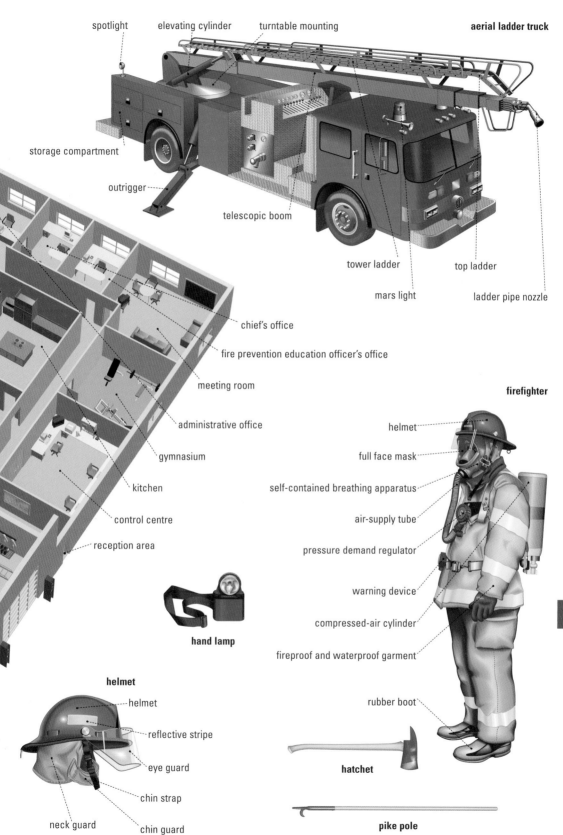

spotlight   elevating cylinder   turntable mounting   **aerial ladder truck**

storage compartment

outrigger

telescopic boom

tower ladder   top ladder

mars light   ladder pipe nozzle

chief's office

fire prevention education officer's office

meeting room

administrative office

gymnasium

kitchen

control centre

reception area

hand lamp

helmet

helmet

reflective stripe

eye guard

chin strap

neck guard   chin guard

firefighter

helmet

full face mask

self-contained breathing apparatus

air-supply tube

pressure demand regulator

warning device

compressed-air cylinder

fireproof and waterproof garment

rubber boot

hatchet

pike pole

CRIME PREVENTION

police station

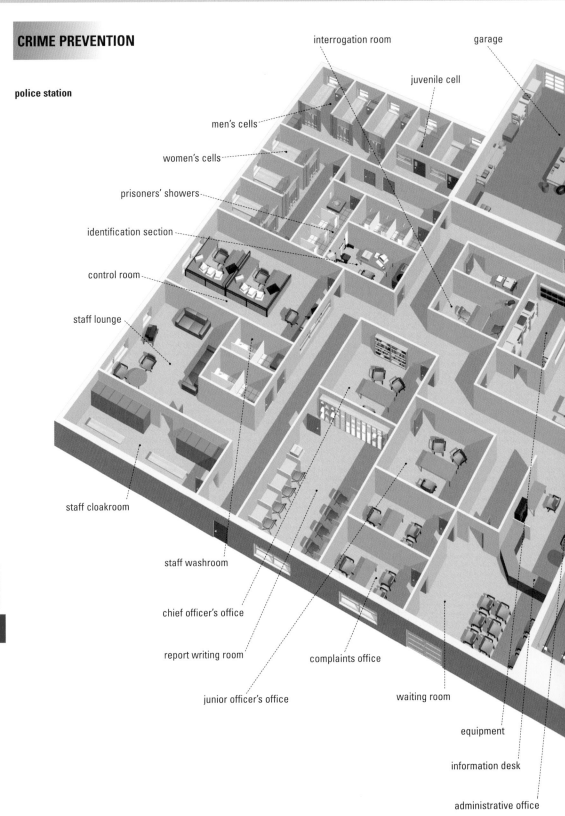

interrogation room

garage

juvenile cell

men's cells

women's cells

prisoners' showers

identification section

control room

staff lounge

staff cloakroom

staff washroom

chief officer's office

report writing room

complaints office

junior officer's office

waiting room

equipment

information desk

administrative office

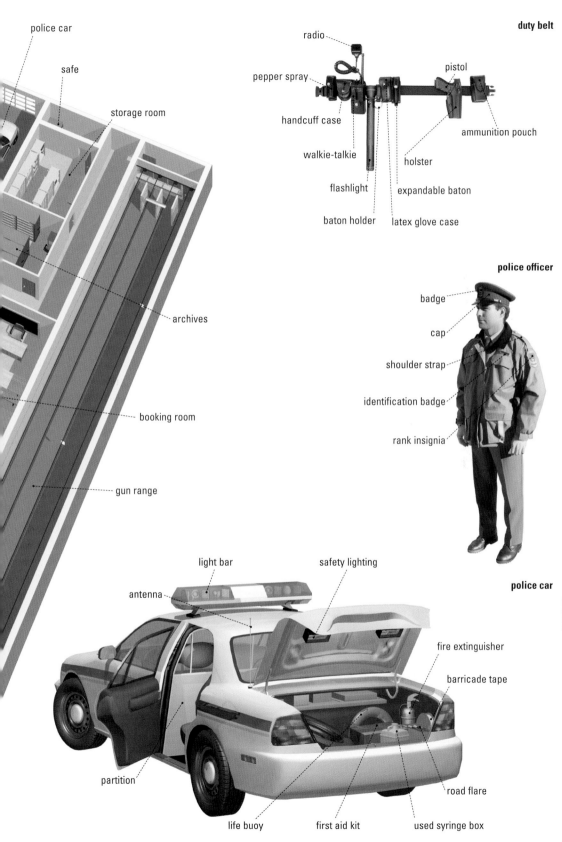

police car

safe

storage room

duty belt

radio

pistol

pepper spray

handcuff case

ammunition pouch

walkie-talkie

holster

flashlight

expandable baton

baton holder

latex glove case

archives

police officer

badge

cap

shoulder strap

identification badge

rank insignia

booking room

gun range

police car

light bar

safety lighting

antenna

fire extinguisher

barricade tape

partition

road flare

life buoy

first aid kit

used syringe box

HEALTH

Among the different establishments that provide health services to the public, hospitals are the most complete, and offer the widest range of care. In large cities, health institutions have become immense medical centres with staff specializing in every different field of medicine. Hospitals provide quality care to the sick and wounded, around the clock.

patient room

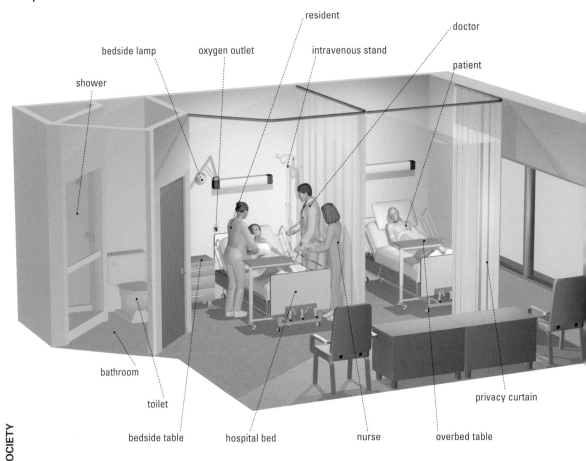

resident

doctor

bedside lamp   oxygen outlet   intravenous stand

patient

shower

bathroom

toilet

privacy curtain

bedside table   hospital bed   nurse   overbed table

wheelchair

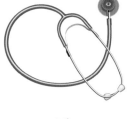

stethoscope

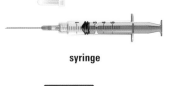

syringe

blood pressure monitor

ambulance

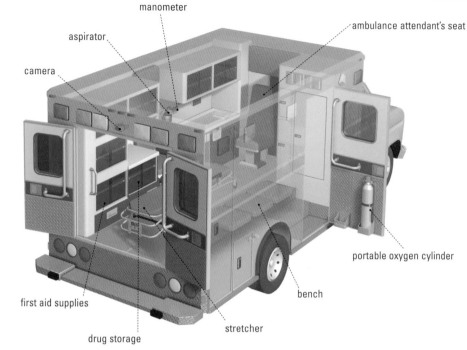

manometer

aspirator

camera

ambulance attendant's seat

portable oxygen cylinder

bench

first aid supplies

drug storage

stretcher

stretcher

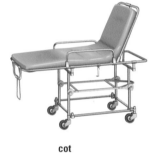

cot

first aid kit

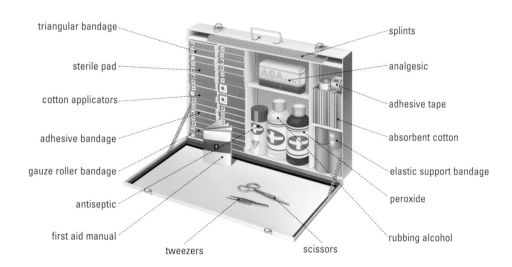

triangular bandage

sterile pad

cotton applicators

adhesive bandage

gauze roller bandage

antiseptic

first aid manual

tweezers

splints

analgesic

adhesive tape

absorbent cotton

elastic support bandage

peroxide

rubbing alcohol

scissors

EDUCATION

In most developed countries, school is obligatory up to a certain age. Primary education, which begins around the ages of four to seven, is generally offered at no cost. As school children improve their skills in reading, writing, and counting, they also develop their moral, intellectual, and physical abilities. Many children in developing countries, however, do not receive any formal education because of a lack of resources.

SCHOOL

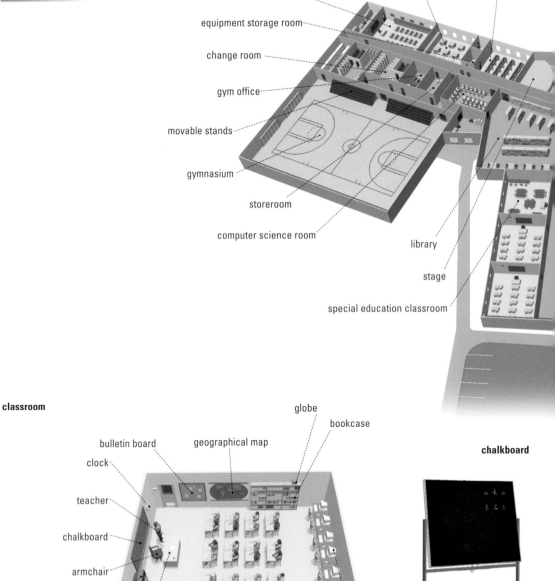

science room

art room

music room

equipment storage room

change room

gym office

movable stands

gymnasium

storeroom

computer science room

library

stage

special education classroom

classroom

globe

bookcase

bulletin board

geographical map

clock

teacher

chalkboard

armchair

television set

teacher's desk

student's desk

student

computer chair

computer

chalkboard

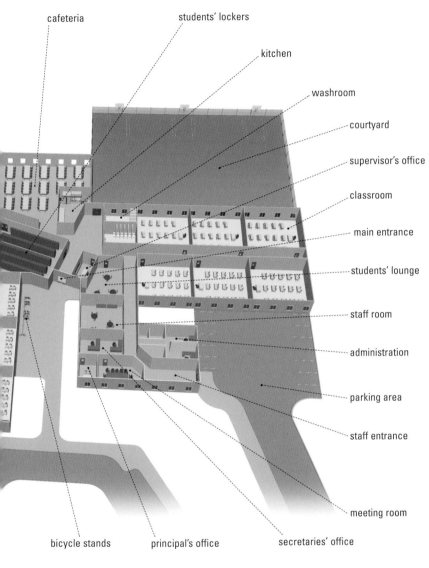

cafeteria

students' lockers

kitchen

washroom

courtyard

supervisor's office

classroom

main entrance

students' lounge

staff room

administration

parking area

staff entrance

meeting room

bicycle stands

principal's office

secretaries' office

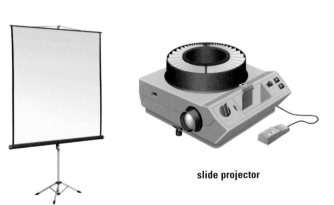

projection screen

slide projector

projection head

mirror

optical lens

optical stage

overhead projector

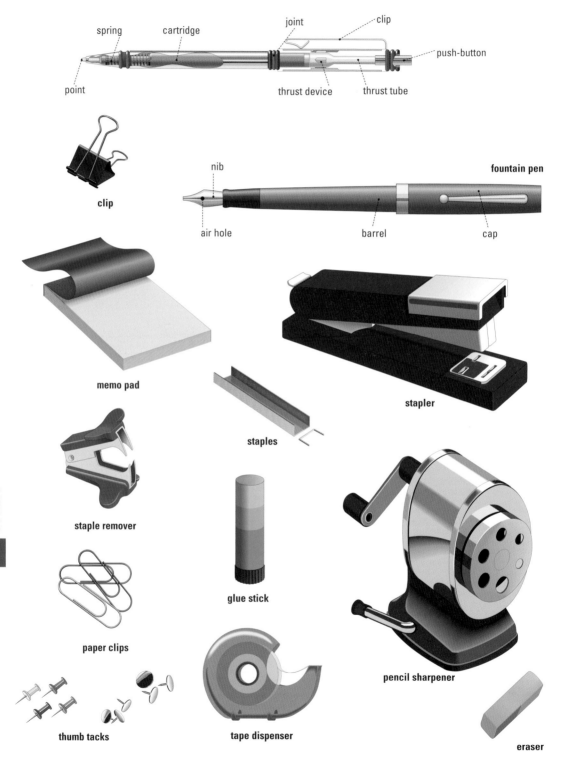

ballpoint pen

spring cartridge joint clip push-button

point thrust device thrust tube

clip

nib **fountain pen**

air hole barrel cap

memo pad

stapler

staples

staple remover

glue stick

paper clips

pencil sharpener

thumb tacks **tape dispenser**

eraser

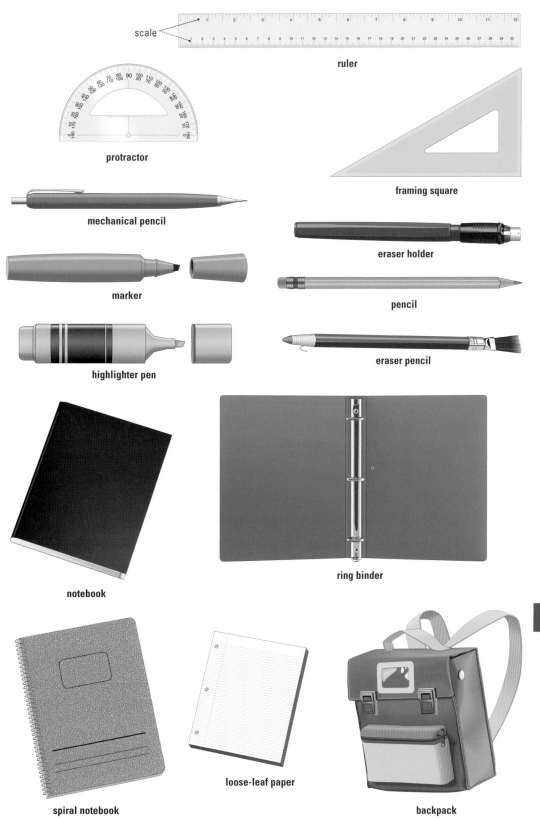

scale

ruler

protractor

framing square

mechanical pencil

eraser holder

marker

pencil

highlighter pen

eraser pencil

notebook

ring binder

spiral notebook

loose-leaf paper

backpack

Whether they work on a movie set where the scenes are shot or go to the movie theatre to see the finished product, movie fans are found all over the world. For many, the seventh art is much more than entertainment or a process of photographing and projecting moving images. Movies allow people to experience powerful emotions and live great adventures while sitting comfortably in their seats.

CINEMA

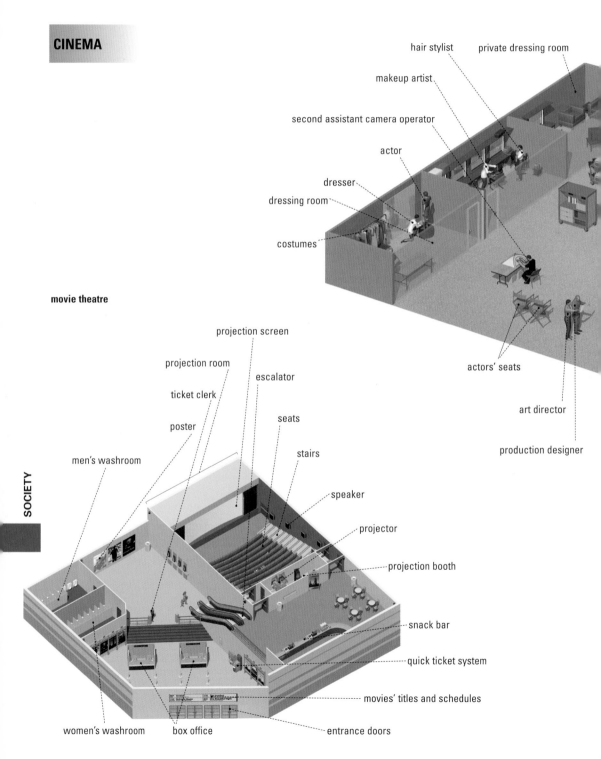

hair stylist

private dressing room

makeup artist

second assistant camera operator

actor

dresser

dressing room

costumes

movie theatre

projection screen

projection room

escalator

ticket clerk

seats

poster

stairs

men's washroom

speaker

projector

projection booth

actors' seats

art director

production designer

snack bar

quick ticket system

movies' titles and schedules

women's washroom   box office   entrance doors

movie set

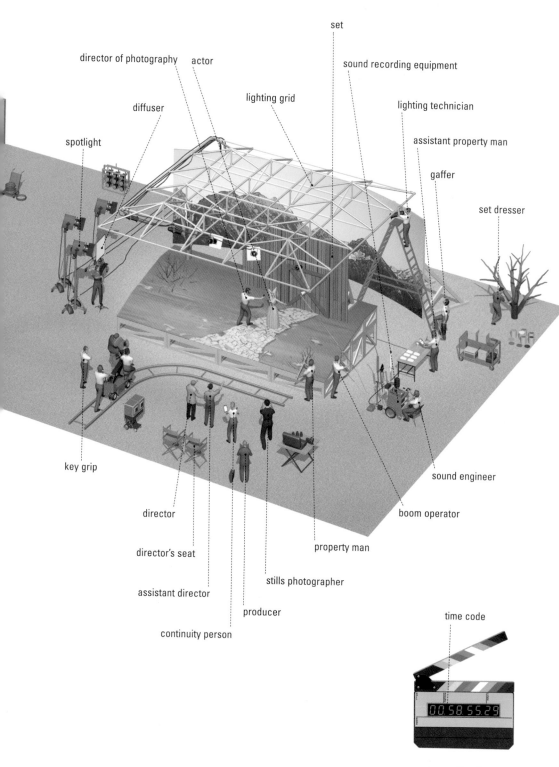

set

director of photography

actor

sound recording equipment

lighting grid

lighting technician

diffuser

assistant property man

spotlight

gaffer

set dresser

key grip

sound engineer

director

boom operator

director's seat

property man

assistant director

stills photographer

producer

continuity person

time code

clapper/the slate

GYMNASTICS

The goal in gymnastics is to perform movements as perfectly as possible. Artistic gymnastics require agility, strength, and flexibility. In rhythmic gymnastics, one must also have a good sense of choreography. Gymnasts who specialize in trampoline events perform complicated acrobatic figures in the air.

GYMNASTICS

event platform

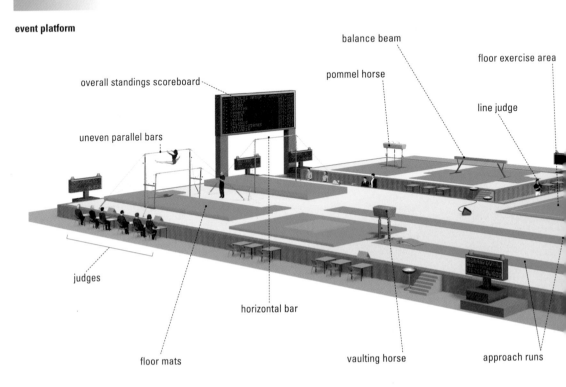

balance beam

floor exercise area

pommel horse

overall standings scoreboard

line judge

uneven parallel bars

judges

horizontal bar

floor mats

vaulting horse

approach runs

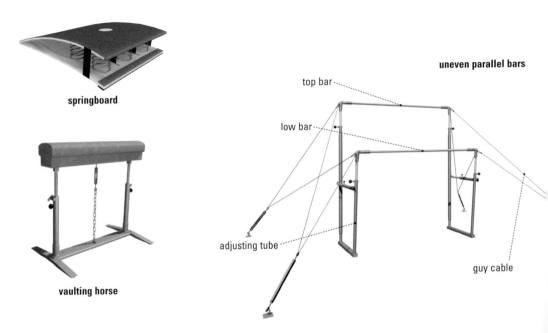

springboard

uneven parallel bars

top bar

low bar

adjusting tube

guy cable

vaulting horse

balance beam

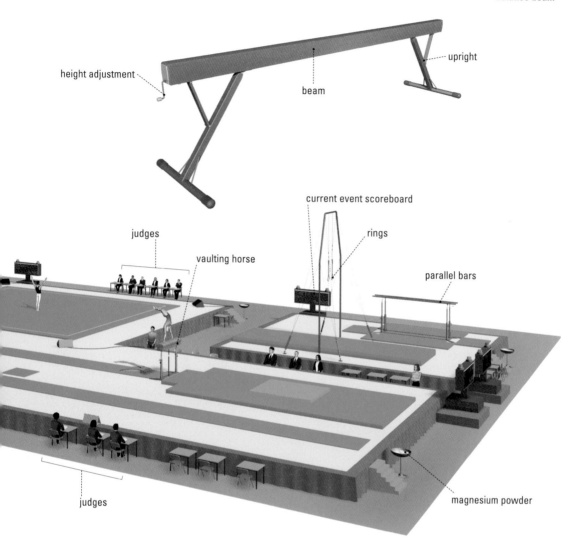

height adjustment

beam

upright

current event scoreboard

judges

rings

vaulting horse

parallel bars

judges

magnesium powder

TRAMPOLINE

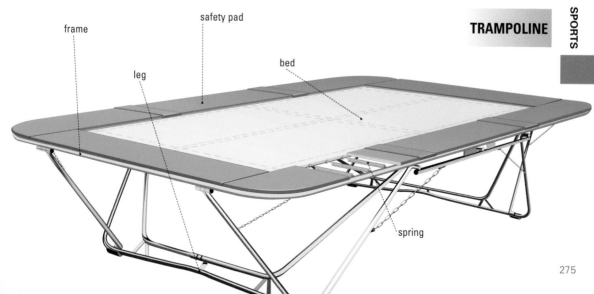

frame

safety pad

leg

bed

spring

SWIMMING

The goal of the swimmer is to glide through the water as quickly as possible with the least amount of effort. Swimmers must train constantly and intensively in order to perfect their technique. Athletes usually specialize in one of the four recognized styles of swimming: the front crawl, the butterfly stroke, the breaststroke, or the backstroke.

starting block

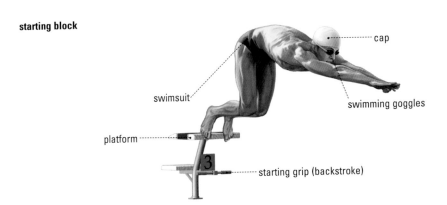

cap

swimsuit

swimming goggles

platform

starting grip (backstroke)

competitive course

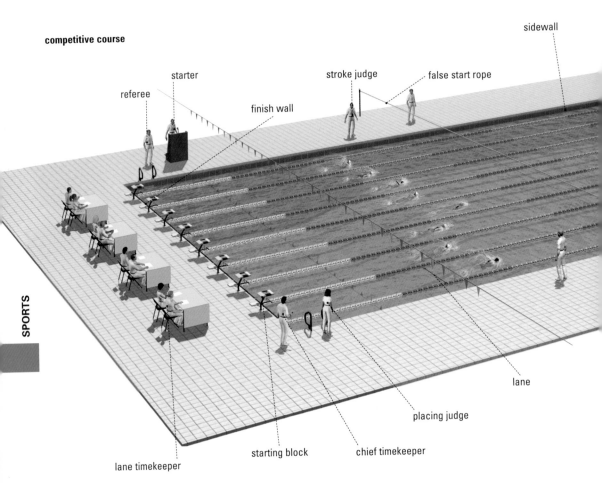

sidewall

starter

stroke judge

false start rope

referee

finish wall

lane

placing judge

starting block

chief timekeeper

lane timekeeper

butterfly stroke

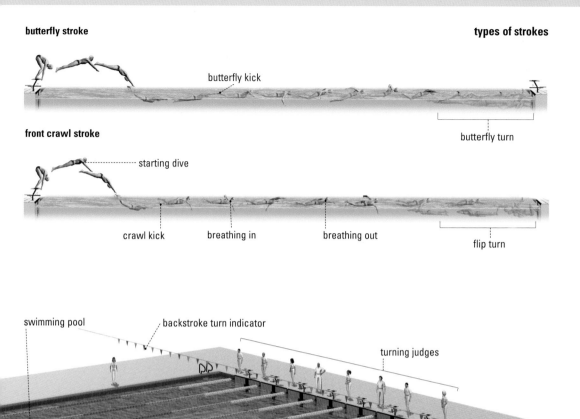

butterfly kick

butterfly turn

front crawl stroke

starting dive

crawl kick

breathing in

breathing out

flip turn

swimming pool

backstroke turn indicator

turning judges

turning wall

bottom line

lane rope

SPORTS

breaststroke

breaststroke kick

turning wall

breaststroke turn

backstroke

backstroke start

flip turn

Among the sports practised on water, some, like rowing, require the participation of a team. Several people must work together to synchronize their movements in order to cross the finish line. In other sports, like surfing, canoeing-kayaking, or windsurfing, athletes perform as individuals. In almost all of these sports in which speed is a factor, quick reflexes and an excellent sense of balance are also necessary.

WINDSURFER

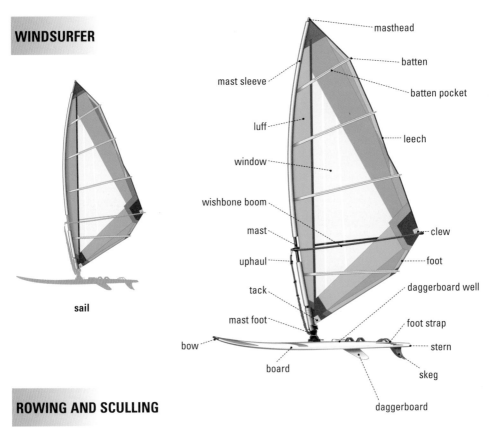

masthead
batten
batten pocket
mast sleeve
luff
leech
window
wishbone boom
mast
clew
uphaul
foot
tack
daggerboard well
mast foot
foot strap
bow
stern
board
skeg
daggerboard

sail

ROWING AND SCULLING

types of oars

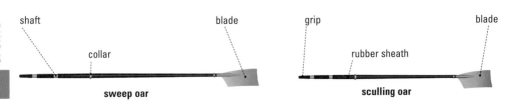

shaft
blade
collar
sweep oar

grip
blade
rubber sheath
sculling oar

parts of a rowboat

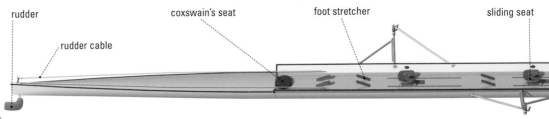

rudder
coxswain's seat
foot stretcher
sliding seat
rudder cable

CANOE-KAYAK

whitewater

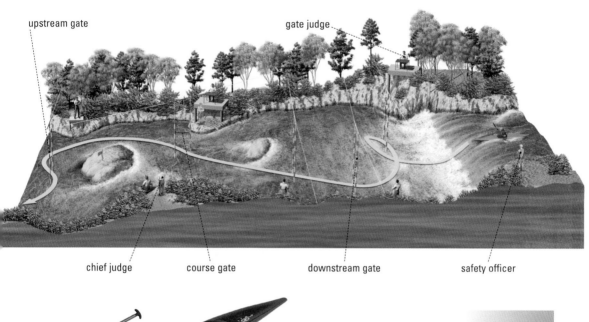

upstream gate

gate judge

chief judge

course gate

downstream gate

safety officer

SCUBA DIVING

scuba diver

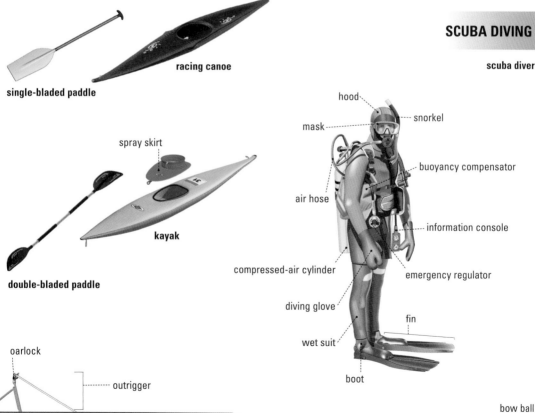

single-bladed paddle

racing canoe

spray skirt

kayak

double-bladed paddle

hood

mask

snorkel

buoyancy compensator

air hose

information console

compressed-air cylinder

emergency regulator

diving glove

fin

wet suit

boot

oarlock

outrigger

bow ball

SPORTS

EQUESTRIAN SPORTS

Horse racing, like all other equestrian sports, requires that both the rider and horse make a good team. The two of them must strive for perfection in their quest to reach the finish line. It is the jockey, however, who makes all the decisions during a race. Jockeys mainly use their legs and their hands to control and direct their horses.

HORSE RACING (TURF)

jockey

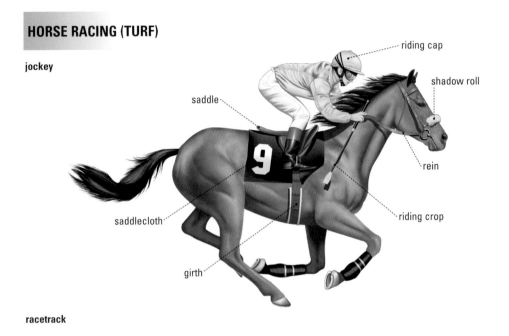

riding cap

shadow roll

saddle

rein

saddlecloth

riding crop

girth

racetrack

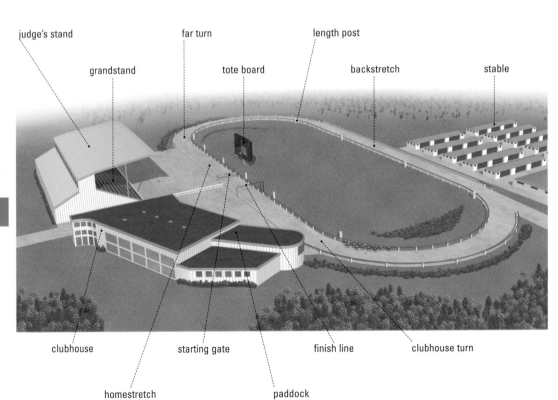

judge's stand

far turn

length post

grandstand

tote board

backstretch

stable

clubhouse

starting gate

finish line

clubhouse turn

homestretch

paddock

As the name suggests, precision and accuracy sports require a perfect mastery of one's movements as well as a high level of concentration. Whether the athlete is shooting an arrow, curling a stone across the ice, hurling a shot put, or hitting a small ball, every action must be performed with great precision to ensure the object being used arrives at its target, often located at a distance.

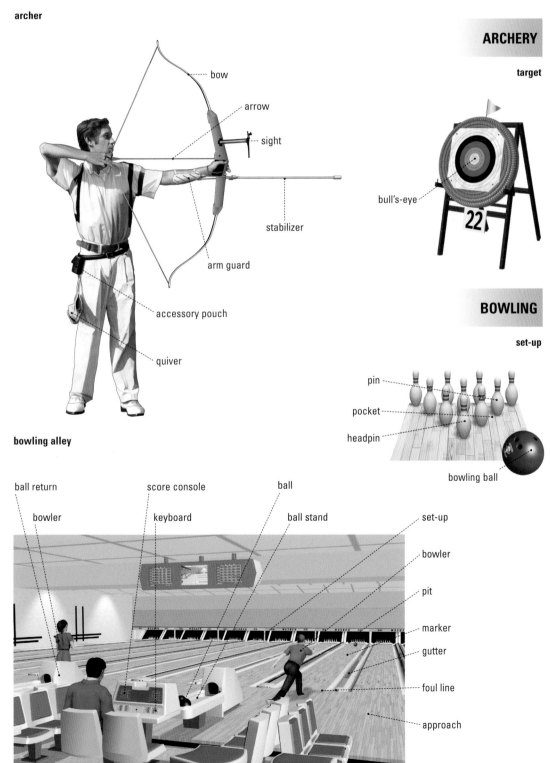

archer

bow

arrow

sight

stabilizer

arm guard

accessory pouch

quiver

ARCHERY

target

bull's-eye

22

BOWLING

set-up

pin

pocket

headpin

bowling ball

bowling alley

ball return

score console

ball

bowler

keyboard

ball stand

set-up

bowler

pit

marker

gutter

foul line

approach

GOLF

course

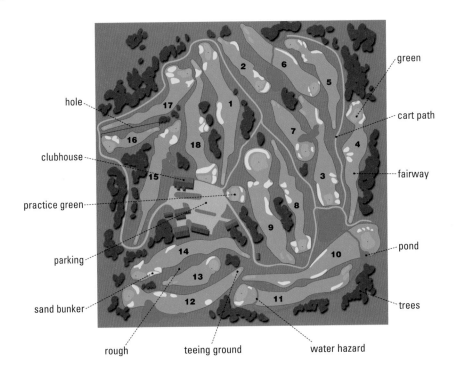

green

hole

cart path

clubhouse

fairway

practice green

parking

pond

sand bunker

trees

rough   teeing ground   water hazard

golf equipment and accessories

golf ball

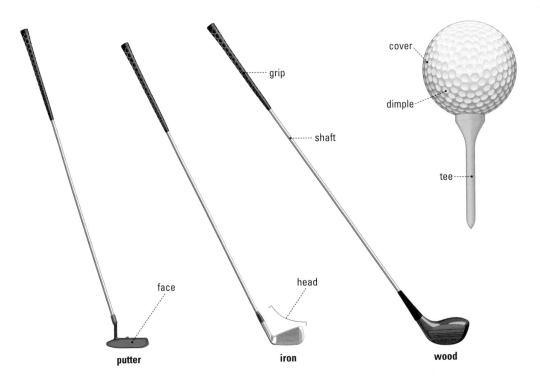

grip

cover

dimple

shaft

tee

face

head

putter   **iron**   **wood**

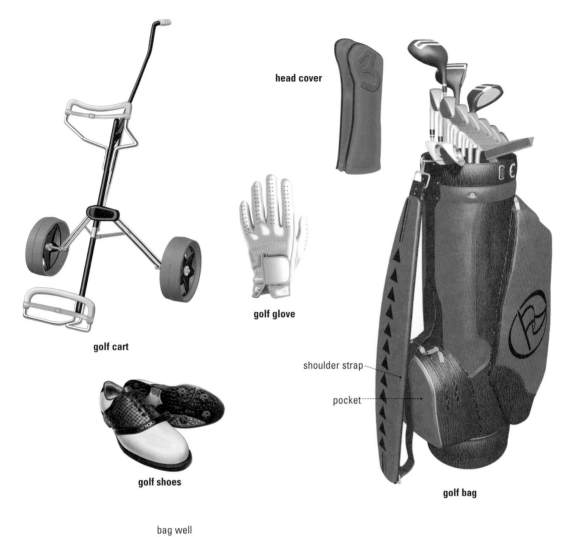

head cover

golf glove

golf cart

golf shoes

shoulder strap

pocket

golf bag

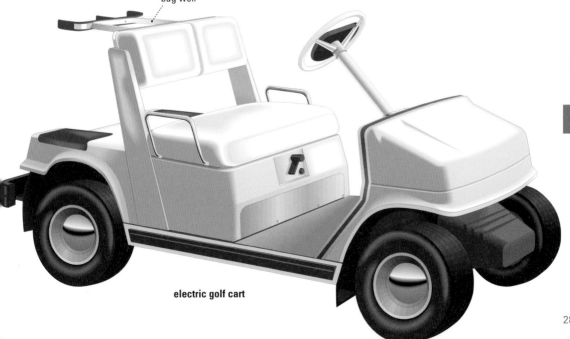

bag well

electric golf cart

Whether they take place on a skating rink, frozen track, or snow-covered slope, winter sports are among the fastest non-motorized sports in the world. Practised as a team or individually, as recreation or in competition, these sports require specific equipment such as skis, skates, snowshoes, or sleds.

ICE HOCKEY

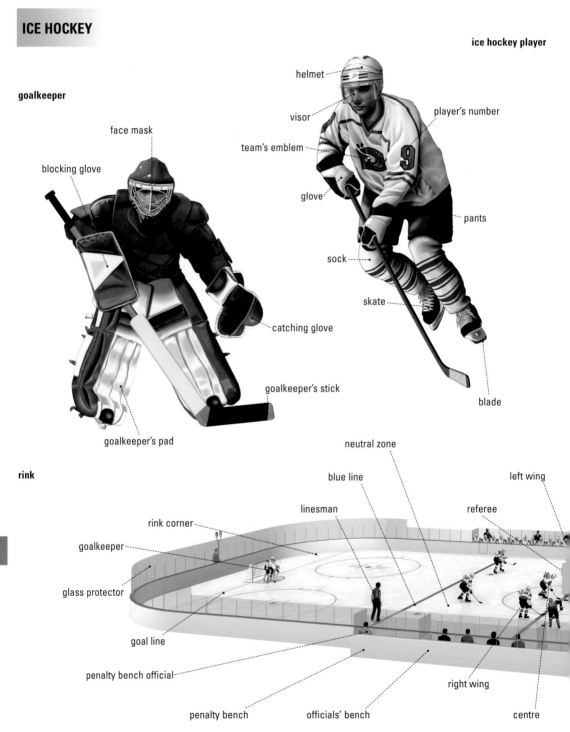

ice hockey player

helmet

visor

player's number

team's emblem

glove

pants

sock

skate

blade

goalkeeper

face mask

blocking glove

catching glove

goalkeeper's stick

goalkeeper's pad

rink

neutral zone

blue line

left wing

linesman

referee

rink corner

goalkeeper

glass protector

goal line

penalty bench official

penalty bench

officials' bench

right wing

centre

protective equipment

player's stick

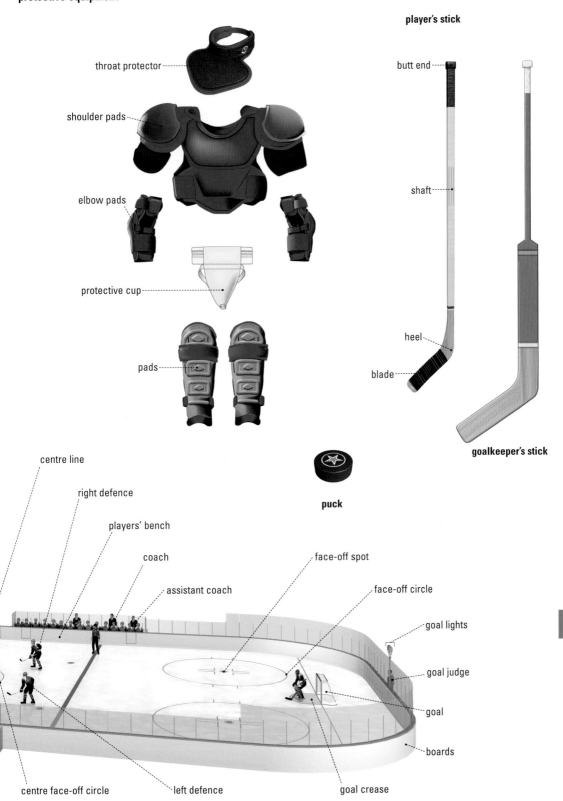

throat protector

shoulder pads

elbow pads

protective cup

pads

butt end

shaft

heel

blade

goalkeeper's stick

centre line

right defence

players' bench

coach

assistant coach

puck

face-off spot

face-off circle

goal lights

goal judge

goal

boards

centre face-off circle

left defence

goal crease

SKATING

hockey skate

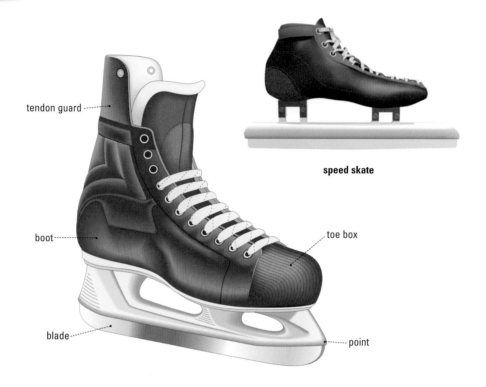

tendon guard

boot

toe box

blade

point

speed skate

figure skate

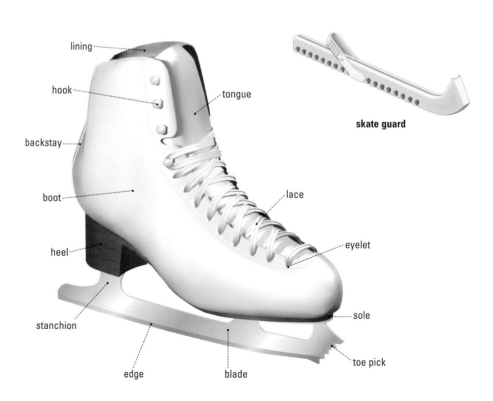

lining

hook

tongue

backstay

boot

lace

heel

eyelet

stanchion

sole

edge

blade

toe pick

skate guard

SNOWBOARDING

snowboarder

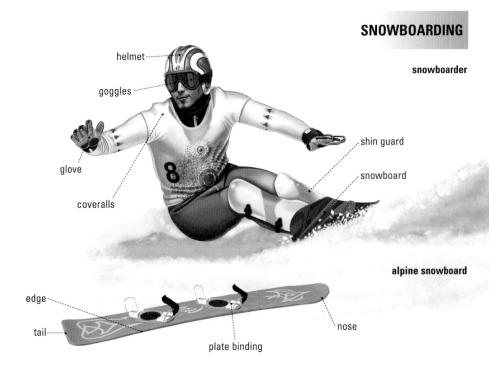

helmet

goggles

glove

coveralls

shin guard

snowboard

8

alpine snowboard

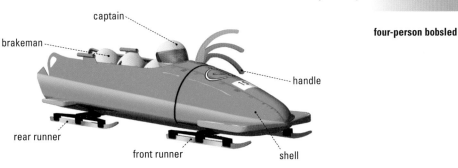

edge

tail

plate binding

nose

BOBSLED, LUGE, AND SKELETON

four-person bobsled

captain

brakeman

handle

rear runner

front runner

shell

luge racer

sled

one-piece suit

crash helmet

visor

glove

skeleton sledder

cleated shoes

crash helmet

skeleton

chin guard

SNOWSHOES

Michigan snowshoe

elliptical snowshoe

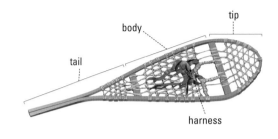

tip

body

tail

harness

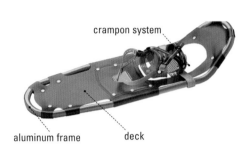

crampon system

aluminum frame

deck

CROSS-COUNTRY SKIING

ski

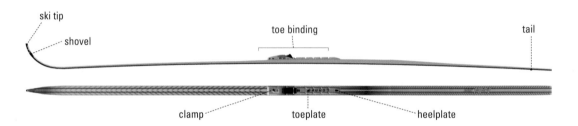

ski tip

shovel

toe binding

tail

clamp

toeplate

heelplate

cross-country skier

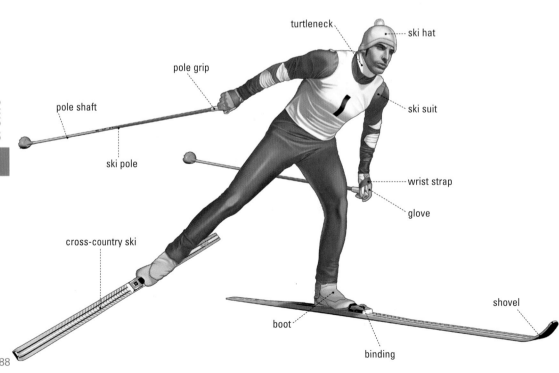

turtleneck

ski hat

pole grip

pole shaft

ski suit

ski pole

wrist strap

glove

cross-country ski

boot

binding

shovel

safety binding

ski boot

base plate

manual release

brake arm

brake pedal

anti-friction pad

heelpiece

toepiece

upper shell

tongue

upper strap

adjusting catch

buckle

hinge

lower shell

ski

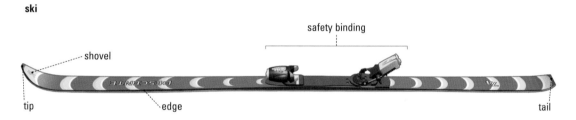

safety binding

shovel

tip

edge

tail

alpine skier

helmet

ski goggles

ski suit

ski glove

basket

ski pole

wrist strap

handle

ski boot

groove

bottom

ski

Ball sports are usually played in teams. Whether it is baseball, basketball, cricket, field hockey, football, or volleyball, players must follow the rules of the game while trying to outmaneuver their opponents' tactics and strategies. The object in these kinds of sports is usually to move the ball into a goal as often as possible.

BASEBALL

player positions

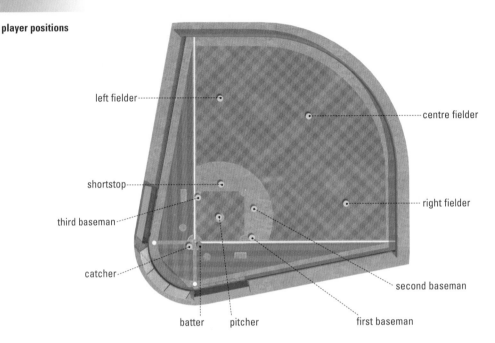

left fielder

centre fielder

shortstop

right fielder

third baseman

catcher

second baseman

batter   pitcher

first baseman

field

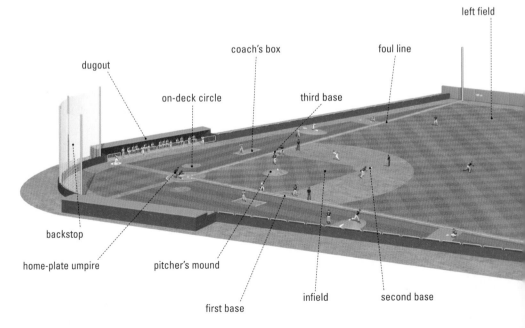

left field

coach's box

foul line

dugout

on-deck circle

third base

backstop

home-plate umpire   pitcher's mound

first base

infield   second base

SPORTS

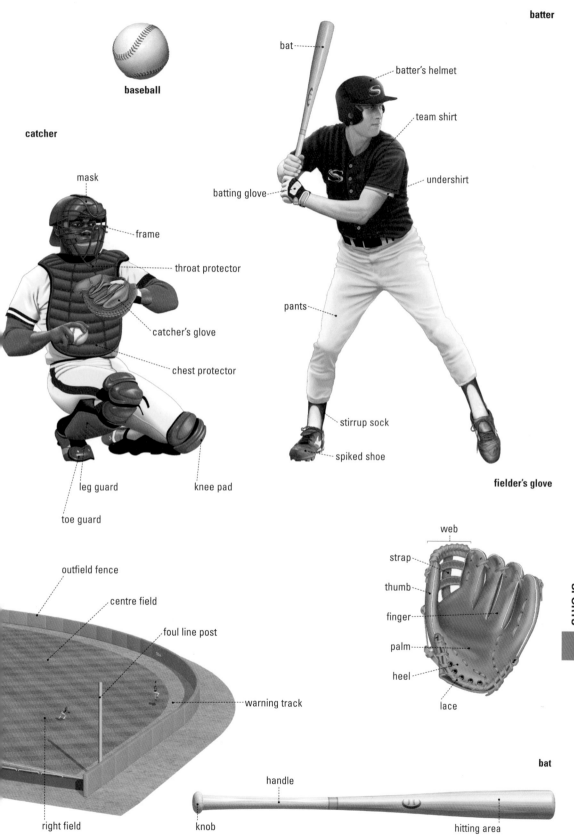

batter

bat

batter's helmet

team shirt

undershirt

batting glove

baseball

catcher

mask

frame

throat protector

catcher's glove

chest protector

pants

stirrup sock

spiked shoe

leg guard

knee pad

toe guard

fielder's glove

web

strap

thumb

finger

palm

heel

lace

outfield fence

centre field

foul line post

warning track

right field

bat

handle

knob

hitting area

CRICKET

cricket player (batsman)

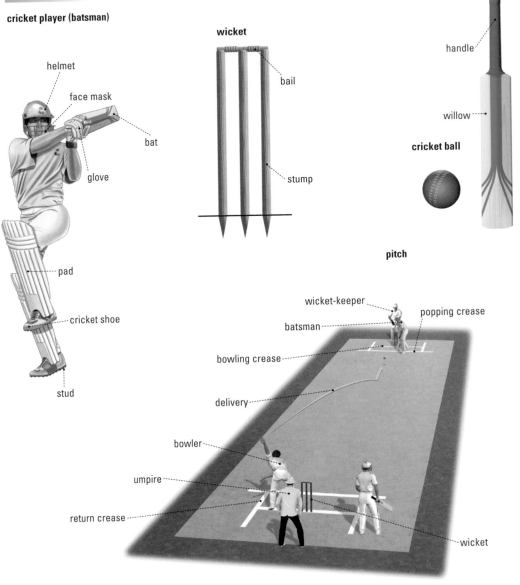

helmet

face mask

bat

glove

pad

cricket shoe

stud

wicket

bail

stump

bat

handle

willow

cricket ball

pitch

wicket-keeper

batsman

popping crease

bowling crease

delivery

bowler

umpire

return crease

wicket

field

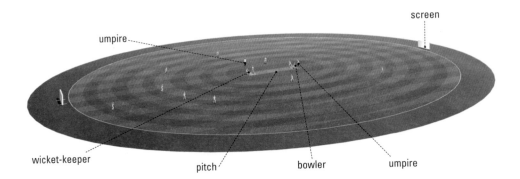

screen

umpire

wicket-keeper

pitch

bowler

umpire

FIELD HOCKEY

field player

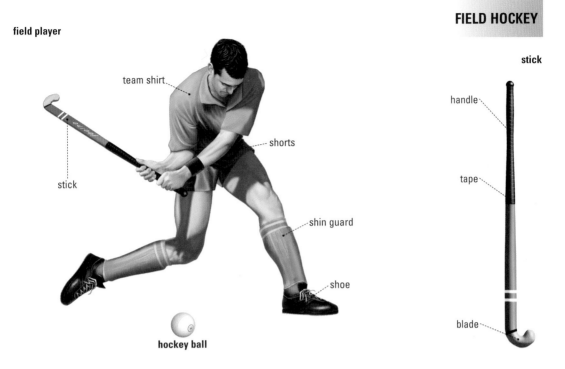

team shirt

stick

shorts

stick

shin guard

shoe

hockey ball

stick

handle

tape

blade

playing field

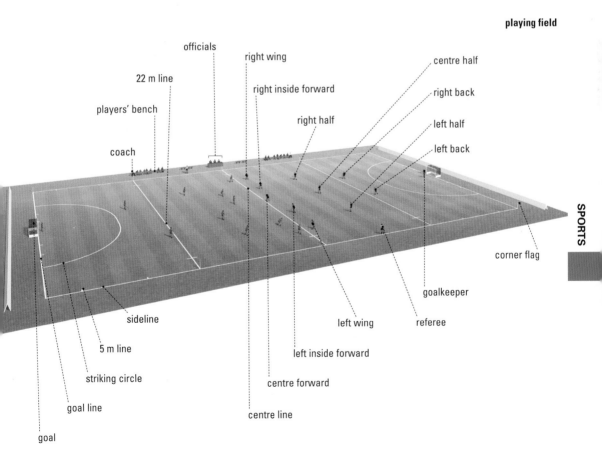

officials

right wing

centre half

22 m line

right inside forward

right back

players' bench

right half

left half

coach

left back

corner flag

goalkeeper

sideline

left wing

referee

5 m line

striking circle

left inside forward

goal line

centre forward

goal

centre line

BASKETBALL

player positions

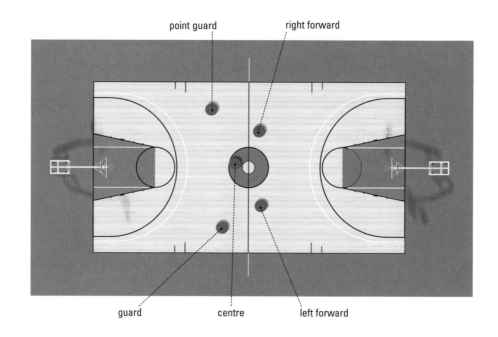

point guard

right forward

guard

centre

left forward

court

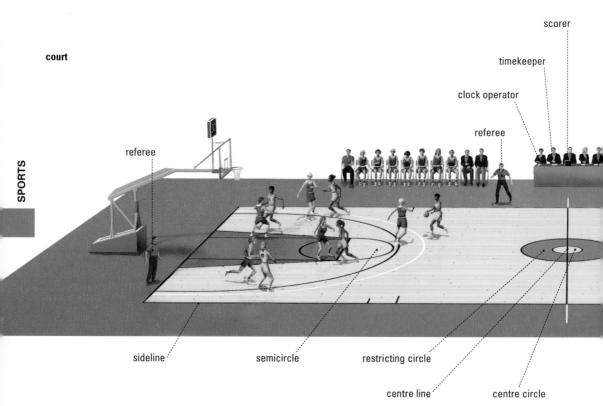

scorer

timekeeper

clock operator

referee

referee

sideline

semicircle

restricting circle

centre line

centre circle

basketball player

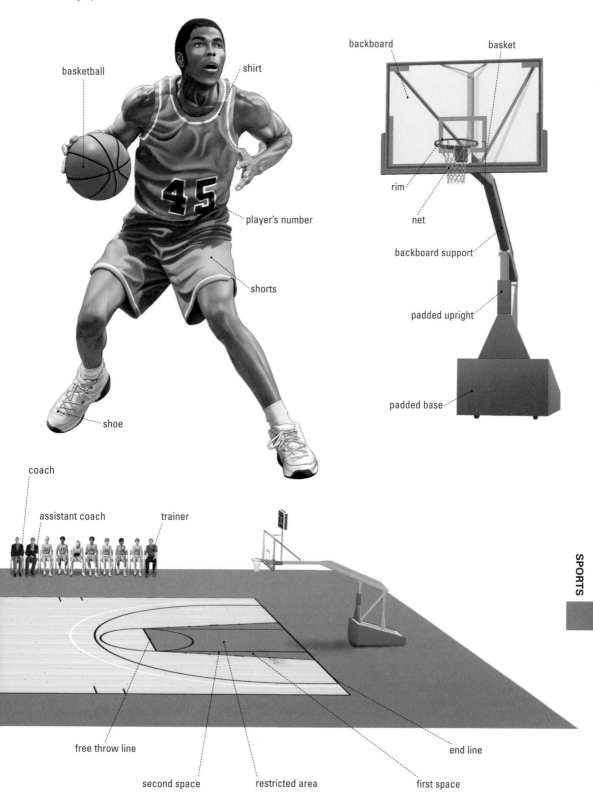

basketball

shirt

backboard

basket

player's number

rim

net

shorts

backboard support

padded upright

shoe

padded base

coach

assistant coach

trainer

free throw line

end line

second space

restricted area

first space

AMERICAN FOOTBALL

scrimmage (defence)

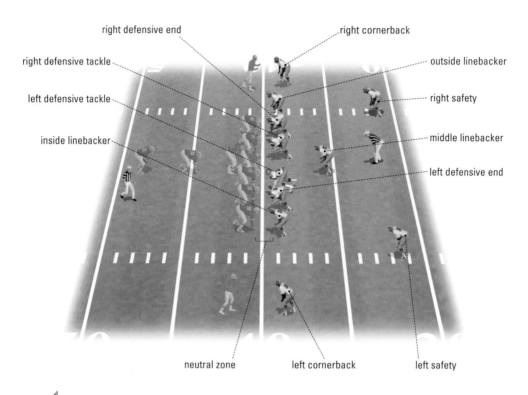

right defensive end

right cornerback

right defensive tackle

outside linebacker

left defensive tackle

right safety

inside linebacker

middle linebacker

left defensive end

neutral zone

left cornerback

left safety

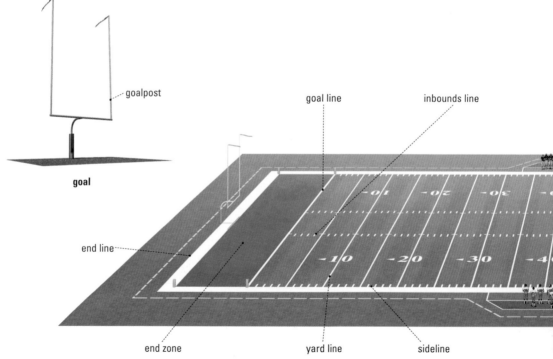

goalpost

goal

goal line

inbounds line

end line

end zone

yard line

sideline

scrimmage (offence)

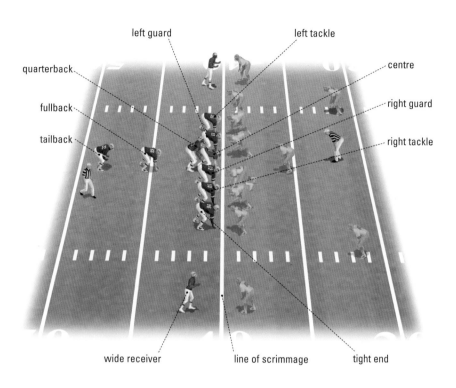

left guard

left tackle

quarterback

centre

fullback

right guard

tailback

right tackle

wide receiver

line of scrimmage

tight end

fifty-yard line

back judge

side judge

line judge

referee

playing field

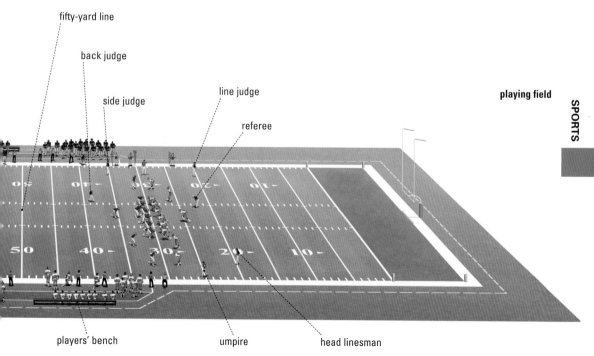

players' bench

umpire

head linesman

football player

protective equipment

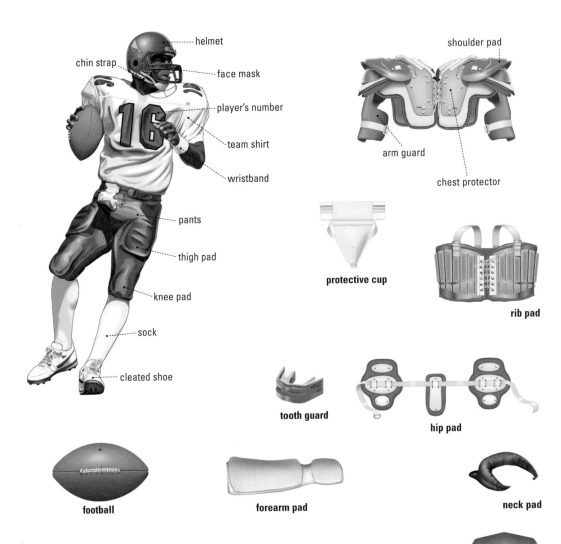

helmet

chin strap

face mask

player's number

team shirt

wristband

pants

thigh pad

knee pad

sock

cleated shoe

shoulder pad

arm guard

chest protector

protective cup

rib pad

tooth guard

hip pad

football

forearm pad

neck pad

elbow pad

CANADIAN FOOTBALL

playing field

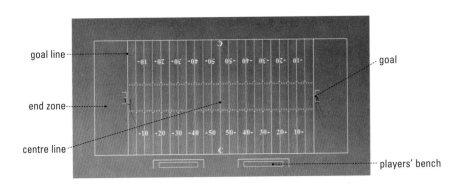

goal line

end zone

centre line

-10 -20 -30 -40 -50 50 40 30 20 10

goal

players' bench

VOLLEYBALL

court

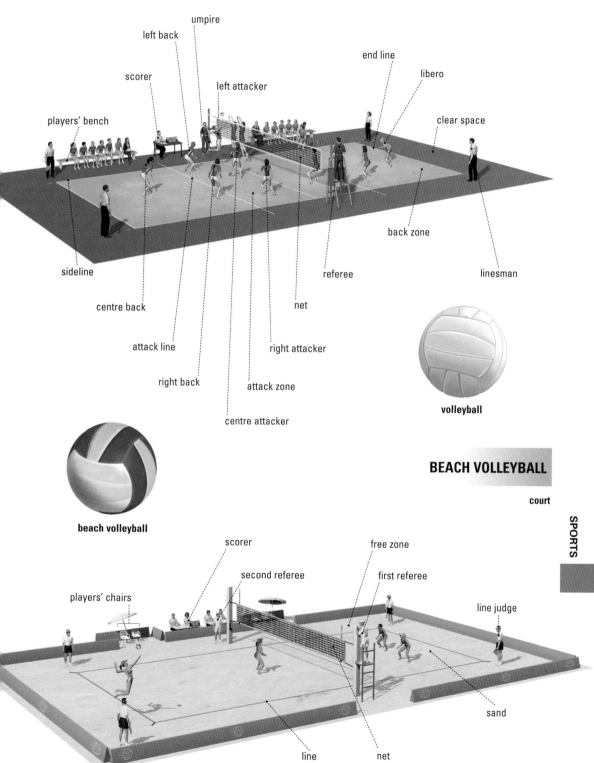

umpire

left back

scorer

left attacker

end line

libero

players' bench

clear space

back zone

sideline

linesman

centre back

net

referee

attack line

right attacker

right back

attack zone

centre attacker

volleyball

beach volleyball

BEACH VOLLEYBALL

court

scorer

free zone

second referee

first referee

players' chairs

line judge

sand

line

net

SOCCER

player positions

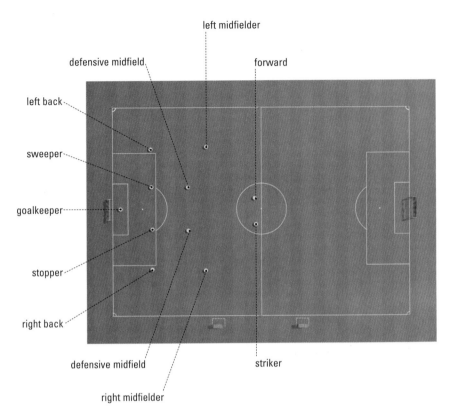

left midfielder

defensive midfield

forward

left back

sweeper

goalkeeper

stopper

right back

defensive midfield

right midfielder

striker

playing field

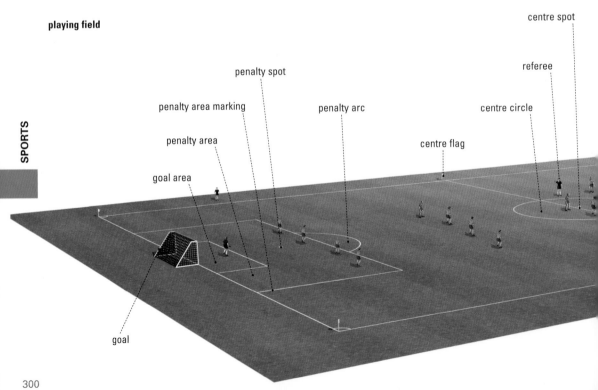

centre spot

penalty spot

referee

penalty area marking

penalty arc

centre circle

penalty area

centre flag

goal area

goal

soccer player

goalkeeper's gloves

team shirt

soccer shoe

shorts

shin guard

interchangeable studs

sock

soccer ball

corner flag

corner arc

touch line

halfway line

linesman

substitute's bench

Tennis is played in most countries. It is played by two people or in teams of two on a clay court, grass court, or artificial surface. Players hit the ball back and forth to each other over a net. The ball may travel more than 200 km/h (120 mph). Several large tournaments draw many spectators each year. The oldest and most famous of these is the Wimbledon tournament in England.

TENNIS

tennis racket

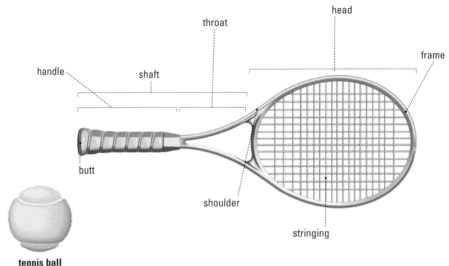

throat

head

frame

handle

shaft

butt

shoulder

stringing

tennis ball

court

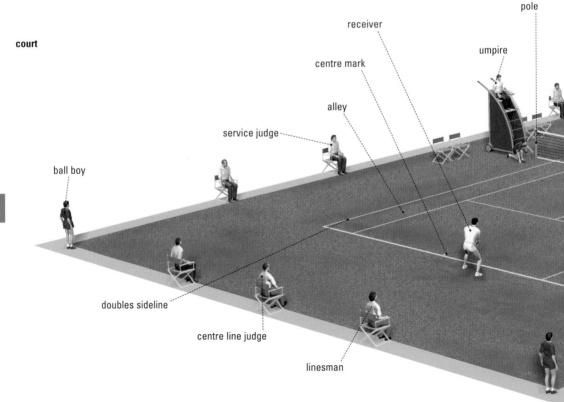

pole

receiver

umpire

centre mark

alley

service judge

ball boy

doubles sideline

centre line judge

linesman

tennis player

polo shirt

skirt

wristband

sock

foot fault judge

centre strap

tennis shoe

net band

server

right service court

left service court

service line

baseline

net judge

net

singles sideline

forecourt

centre service line

backcourt

COMBAT SPORTS

Karate, boxing, wrestling, and judo are combat sports in which two opponents of matching weight fight hand to hand. Top physical and mental conditioning is a requirement for the karateka, the athlete who practises karate, while the boxer needs dexterity and exceptional strength. To perform any martial art, combat or self-defence technique, athletes must have complete mastery of their own strength as well as their movements.

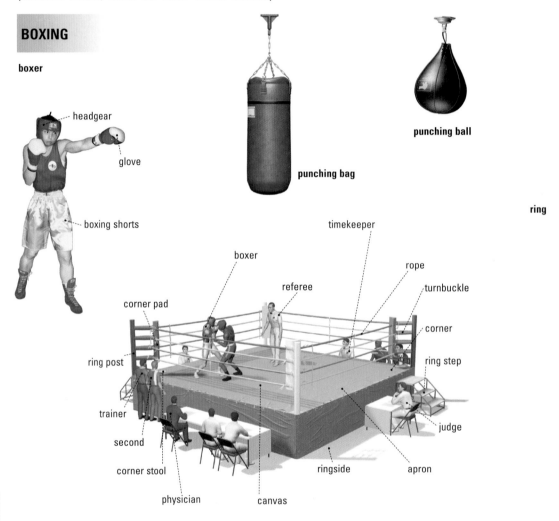

BOXING

boxer

headgear

glove

boxing shorts

punching bag

punching ball

ring

timekeeper

boxer

referee

rope

turnbuckle

corner pad

corner

ring post

ring step

trainer

judge

second

corner stool

ringside

apron

physician

canvas

WRESTLING

wrestling area

wrestler

protection area

passivity zone

judge

referee

central wrestling area

mat chairperson

competition area

karateka

corner judge

timekeeper

arbitration committee

scorekeeper

referee

karate-gi

obi

karateka

JUDO

judogi

jacket

belt

trousers

mat

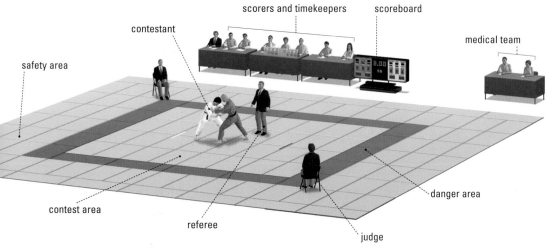

scorers and timekeepers

scoreboard

contestant

medical team

safety area

contest area

referee

judge

danger area

MOTOR SPORTS

Automobile racing takes place on different kinds of tracks where specially constructed high-speed vehicles race against one another. The drivers of these vehicles, as in other motor sports, require nerves of steel and extremely fast reflexes. They must be able to maintain complete control over their high-powered race cars at all times.

CAR RACING

Formula 1 car

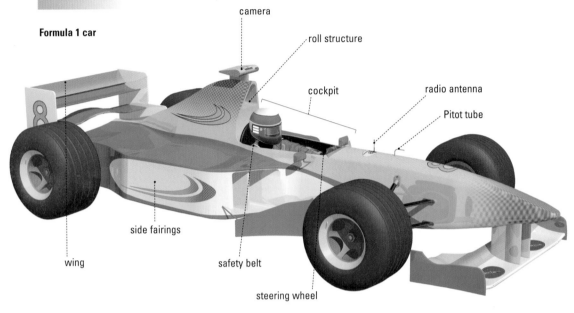

camera

roll structure

cockpit

radio antenna

Pitot tube

side fairings

wing

safety belt

steering wheel

MOTORCYCLING

motocross and supercross motorcycle

protective suit

helmet

glove

protective goggles

pants

hand protector

boot

number plate

nubby tire

fork

protective plate

Skateboarding and in-line skating are two sports that require excellent reflexes and coordination as well as a good sense of balance. Skateboarders use creativity and technical skill to perform acrobatic figures on a variety of specially designed surfaces. In-line skating can take the form of acrobatics, speed skating, or games such as hockey.

skateboarder

in-line skate

inner boot

upper shell

boot

adjusting buckle

axle

heel stop

wheel

truck

skateboard

grip tape

wheel

skater

helmet

elbow pad

wrist guard

knee pad

ramp

guardrail

platform

coping

vertical section

flat

SPORTS

307

CYCLING

Whether they practise on uneven terrain or on a track, cyclists must have a good sense of balance, excellent reflexes, and great endurance. Bicycles used in the different cycling sports are made for specific events. The racing bike, for example, is designed to reach high speeds, while the cross-country bike is made for jumping over obstacles and riding on difficult trails.

ROAD RACING

road-racing bicycle and cyclist

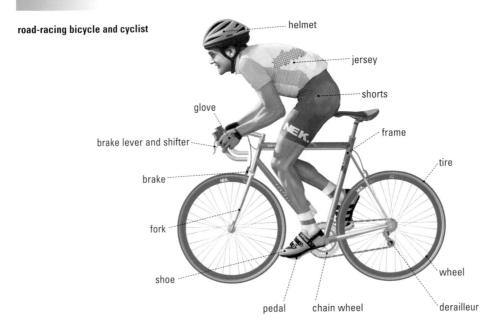

helmet

jersey

shorts

glove

brake lever and shifter

frame

brake

tire

fork

shoe

wheel

pedal

chain wheel

derailleur

BMX

BMX and cyclist

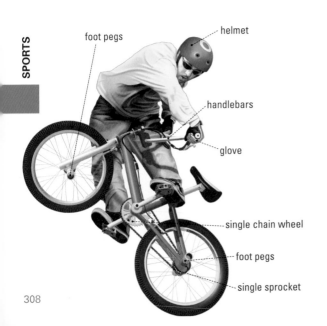

foot pegs

helmet

handlebars

glove

single chain wheel

foot pegs

single sprocket

MOUNTAIN BIKING

cross-country bicycle and cyclist

back suspension

goggles

front fork

clipless pedal

Camping is the ideal activity for travellers on a budget who want to enjoy the great outdoors. A sleeping bag and a few utensils are all one requires. A complete camping outfit would include a tent, mattress, and cooler to make the activity more comfortable. One of the many benefits of wilderness camping is that it is possible to explore regions that are inaccessible by road.

TENTS

family tent

frame

living space

bedroom

window canopy

guy line

screen window

elastic strainer

canvas divider

sewn-in floor

wall

stake loop

wall tent

two-person tent

one-person tent

wagon tent

pup tent

dome tent

pop-up tent

LEISURE ACTIVITIES AND GAMES

SLEEPING BAGS

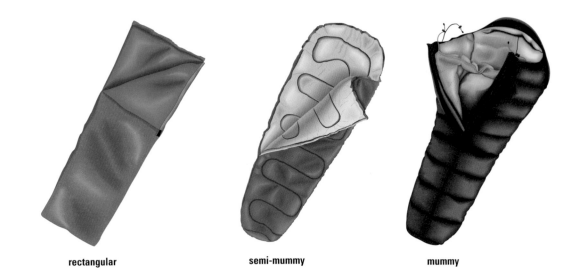

rectangular

semi-mummy

mummy

BED AND MATTRESS

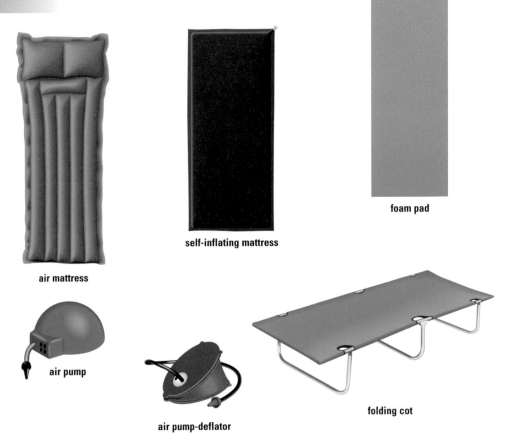

air mattress

self-inflating mattress

foam pad

air pump

air pump-deflator

folding cot

CAMPING EQUIPMENT

Swiss Army knife

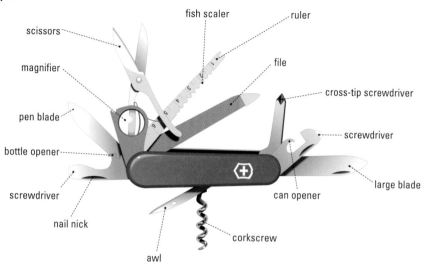

scissors
fish scaler
ruler
magnifier
file
pen blade
cross-tip screwdriver
bottle opener
screwdriver
screwdriver
large blade
nail nick
can opener
awl
corkscrew

bottle
cup
stopper

vacuum bottle

coffee pot

cup

cup

saucepan

plate

handle

frying pan

cooler

water carrier

hurricane lamp

canteen

backpack

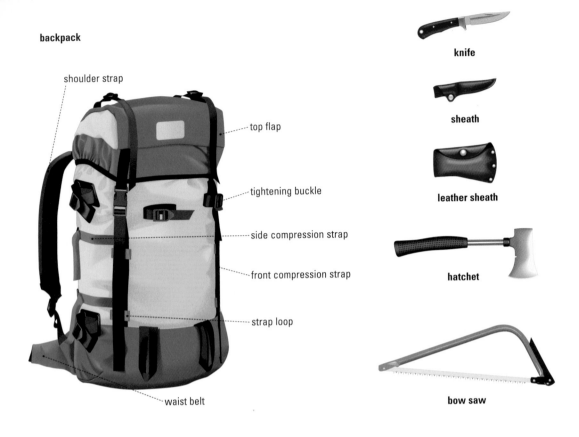

shoulder strap

top flap

tightening buckle

side compression strap

front compression strap

strap loop

waist belt

knife

sheath

leather sheath

hatchet

bow saw

magnetic compass

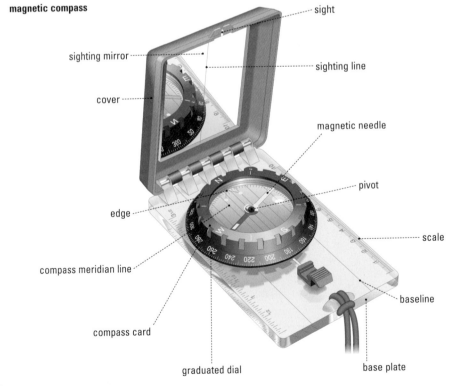

sight

sighting mirror

sighting line

cover

magnetic needle

pivot

edge

scale

compass meridian line

baseline

compass card

graduated dial

base plate

Table games have probably been around as long as people have enjoyed play. Dice were discovered in ancient Egyptian tombs and the game of chess dates back to the Dark Ages. Indoor games today are quite varied. They include dominoes, cards, backgammon, darts, and video games, to name a few. Whether individually or in a group, games are usually played for pleasure.

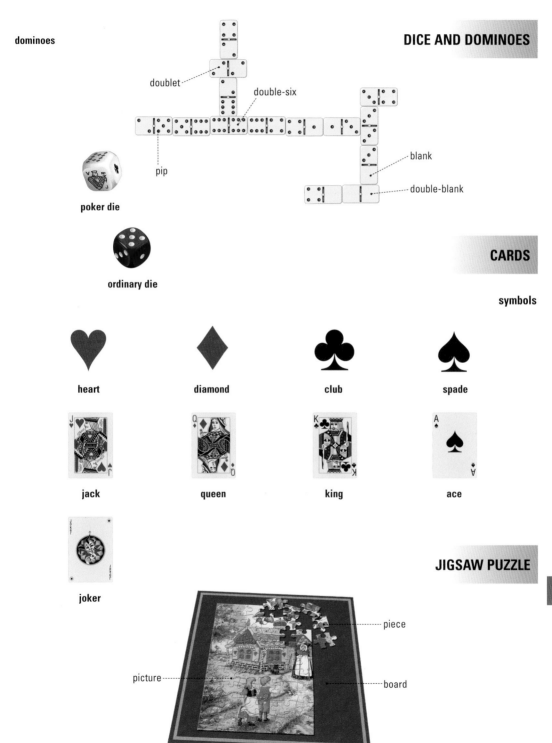

dominoes

DICE AND DOMINOES

doublet

double-six

pip

blank

double-blank

poker die

ordinary die

CARDS

symbols

heart

diamond

club

spade

jack

queen

king

ace

joker

JIGSAW PUZZLE

piece

picture

board

CHESS

chessboard

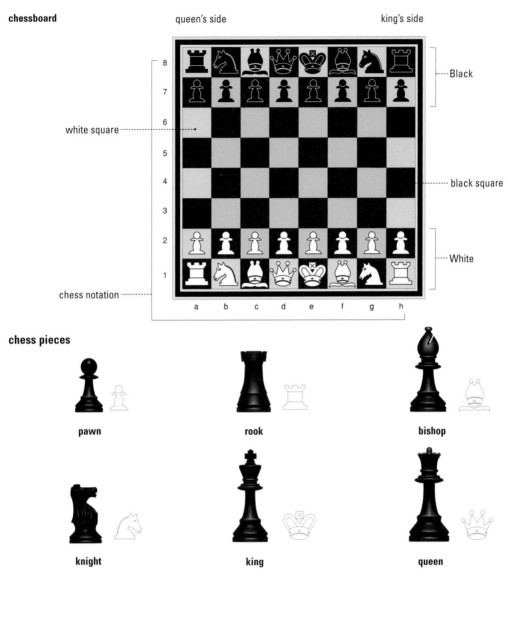

queen's side   king's side

Black

white square

black square

White

chess notation

chess pieces

pawn

rook

bishop

knight

king

queen

types of movements

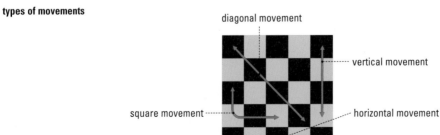

diagonal movement

vertical movement

square movement

horizontal movement

BACKGAMMON

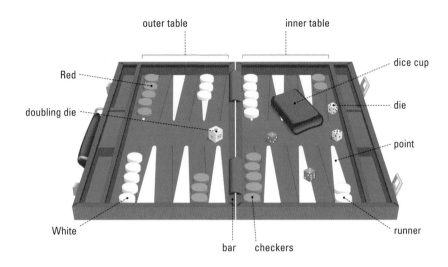

outer table

inner table

Red

dice cup

doubling die

die

point

White

runner

bar   checkers

CHECKERS

checker

checkerboard

GO

major motions

connection

capture

contact

board

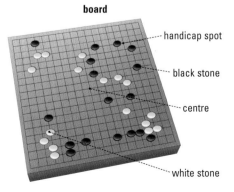

handicap spot

black stone

centre

white stone

DARTS

dartboard

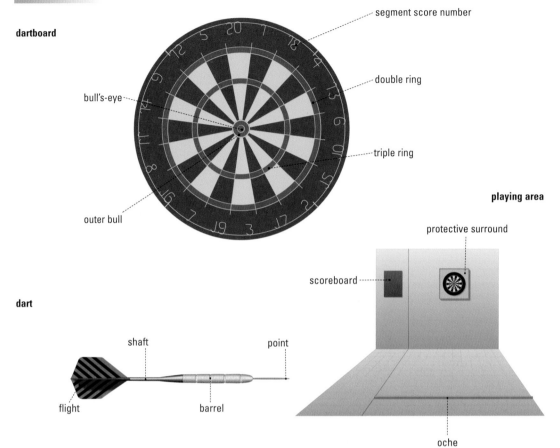

segment score number

double ring

bull's-eye

triple ring

outer bull

playing area

protective surround

scoreboard

dart

shaft

point

flight

barrel

oche

VIDEO GAME SYSTEM

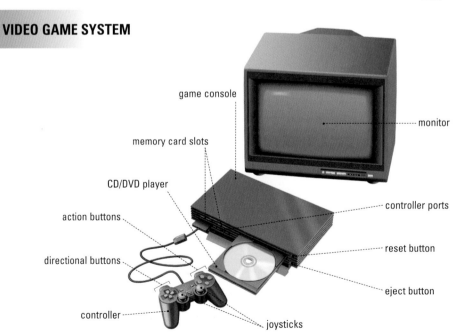

game console

monitor

memory card slots

CD/DVD player

controller ports

action buttons

reset button

directional buttons

eject button

controller

joysticks

Most major roads are marked with signs to guide drivers. Many of these signs are international, which means that no matter where drivers come from they can understand a road's particular code, such as the direction it is taking and where obligatory stops are located. Other road signs can be specific to a given region while taking their inspiration from international road signs.

MAJOR INTERNATIONAL ROAD SIGNS

stop at intersection

no entry

yield

signal ahead

direction to be followed

direction to be followed

direction to be followed

closed to pedestrians

falling rocks

deer crossing

closed to motorcycles

closed to trucks

school zone

pedestrian crossing

road works ahead

slippery road

MAJOR NORTH AMERICAN ROAD SIGNS

stop at intersection

no entry

yield

closed to motorcycles

closed to pedestrians

closed to bicycles

no U-turn

closed to trucks

direction to be followed

direction to be followed

direction to be followed

direction to be followed

school zone

pedestrian crossing

slippery road

signal ahead

falling rocks

road works ahead

Many different kinds of symbols surround us. Common symbols usually consist of simple pictures that provide a variety of information in the blink of an eye. These signs are easy to understand, and can even tell a person who cannot read where a hospital is located or where to find the closest information centre. The messages conveyed by these symbols are universal, and are not hampered by language barriers.

men's washroom

women's washroom

currency exchange

wheelchair access

camping (trailer and tent)

picnic area

coffee shop

camping (tent)

service station

fire extinguisher

camping (trailer)

hospital

telephone

restaurant

pharmacy

police

first aid

information

information

lost and found articles

no wheelchair access

picnics prohibited

camping prohibited

taxi transportation

SYMBOLS

SAFETY SYMBOLS

Safety symbols are essential. They alert people to possible dangers, label hazardous ingredients in products, and advise people to use certain protective equipment to avoid accidents. On a construction site, for example, a sign showing a head covered in a helmet reminds people to wear a safety helmet.

DANGEROUS MATERIALS

corrosive

electrical hazard

explosive

flammable

radioactive

poison

PROTECTION

eye protection

ear protection

head protection

hand protection

foot protection

respiratory system protection

A

C

D

double-six 313
doubles sideline 302
doublet 313
doubling die 315
doubly dentate 49
dousing water tank 177, 178
dousing water valve 177
downspout 134
downstream gate 279
downtown 250
draft tube 175
dragonfly 63
draw tube 167
drawbridge 220
drawer 141, 143, 153
drawing 211, 213
drawstring 127
drawstring bag 127
drawstring hood 121
dresser 141, 272
dressing room 272
drilling 180
drilling rig 180
drip bowl 153
drip molding 185
drive chain 194
drive shaft 203
driver's cab 196, 198
driveway 135
driving glove 123
drizzle 36
dromedary camel 87
drone 60
drone pipe 224
droop nose 208
drug storage 267
drum 232
drumlin 28
drums 232
drumstick 225
drupelet 109
dry cleaner 259
dry climates 34
dry dock 200
dry fruits 113
dry gallery 30
dryer 160
dual launch structure 16
dual seat 191
duck 75
duffle coat 117
dugout 290
dump body 210
dump truck 192, 210
dune 31
duodenum 96
dura mater 97
dust tail 10
dustpan 159
duty belt 265
duty-free shop 253
DVD 240
DVD player 240
dynamic brake 196

E

E 222
e-commerce 249
e-mail 249
e-mail software 248
eagle 74
ear 79, 82, 90, 140
ear drum 100
ear flap 124
ear protection 320
ear, structure 100
earbud 245
earphone 241
earphone jack 246
earphones 243
earpiece 128
Earth 6, 8, 9
Earth's atmosphere, profile 32
Earth's crust 24, 26
Earth's crust, cross-section 24
Earth's features 28
Earth's orbit 8, 9
Earth, structure 24
earthquake 26
East 23
East-Northeast 23
East-Southeast 23
Eastern hemisphere 20
Eastern meridian 20
eau de toilette 132
eccrine sweat gland 101
echinoderms 56
eclipses, types 8, 9
edge 214, 286, 287, 289, 312
edit search button 240
education 268
educational institution 249
eel 65
effusive volcano 27
egg 61, 72
egg beater 148
egg tray 152
eggplant 107
eggs 66, 114
eighth note 223
eighth rest 223
eject button 316
elastic 142
elastic strainer 309
elastic support bandage 267
elastic waistband 117
elastic webbing 116
elasticized leg opening 117
elbow 78, 82, 85, 91
elbow pad 298, 307
elbow pads 285
electric baseboard heater 158
electric can opener 150
electric circuit 175
electric drill 162
electric golf cart 283

electric guitar 228
electric knife 150
electric range 153
electric razor 131
electric wire 175
electrical hazard 320
electrical tools 162
electricity transmission 176, 178
electrode 156
electronic ballast 156
electronic drum pad 233
electronic flash 235
electronic instruments 233
electronic payment terminal 257
electronic piano 233
electronic scale 170
electronic viewfinder 240
electronics store 258
elements of a house 136
elephant 87
elevating cylinder 193, 263
elevation 138
elevation zones 40
elevator 207
elevon 15
elliptical snowshoe 288
embankment dam 174
emerald 129
emergency brake 199
emergency regulator 279
emergency station 182
emergency truck 182
emery boards 132
enamel 94
end aisle display 257
end button 227
end key 245
end line 295, 296, 299
end moraine 29
end zone 296, 298
endocarp 110, 111
endoplasmic reticulum 56
energy 173
energy integration to the
   transmission network 176
energy transmission at the
   generator voltage 176
energy-saving bulb 156
engaged Corinthian column 218
engaged Doric column 218
engaged Ionic column 218
engine 191
engine mounting pylon 207
engine room 201
English horn 231
English horns 234
enhanced greenhouse effect 43
entablature 217
entertainment 273
entire 49
entrance 61, 182
entrance doors 272
entrance hall 138
entrance slide 61

entrance to the pyramid 217
entrance turnstile 254
environment 40
epicalyx 109
epicentre 26
epidermis 101
epiglottis 97
Equator 20
equestrian sports 280
equipment 262, 264
equipment storage room 268
eraser 270
eraser holder 271
Erlenmeyer flask 166
escalator 254, 272
escape wheel 169
escarole 106
escutcheon 136
esophagus 96, 97
espadrille 125
Eurasia 18
Europa 6
Europe 19
European experiment module 14
European outlet 155
European plug 155
Eustachian tube 100
evacuation route 182
evaporation 42
evening glove 123
event platform 274
examples of airplanes 208
examples of amphibians 66
examples of angles 171
examples of arachnids 59
examples of bats 82
examples of bicycles 195
examples of bills 73
examples of broad-leaved trees 54
examples of carnivorous mammals
   80
examples of conifers 55
examples of dams 174
examples of doors 136
examples of feet 73
examples of flowers 50
examples of freight cars 196
examples of helicopters 203
examples of hoofs 85
examples of insectivorous
   mammals 76
examples of insects 63
examples of marine mammals 88
examples of marsupials 76
examples of molluscs 57
examples of motorcycles 191
examples of primates 83
examples of reptiles 68
examples of rodents 77
examples of shorelines 31
examples of space launchers 16
examples of tail shapes 207
examples of tools 213
examples of trucks 192

F

INDEX

M

INDEX

X

Y

Z